The Basketball Book

JOHN W. SCOTT
Sport America

D1254220

Allyn and Bacon

Boston   London   Toronto   Sydney   Tokyo   Singapore

Publisher: Joseph E. Burns
Editorial Assistant: Annemarie Kennedy
Senior Marketing Manager: Brad Perkins
Production Editor: Christopher H. Rawlings
Editorial-Production Service: Omegatype Typography, Inc.
Composition and Prepress Buyer: Linda Cox
Manufacturing Buyer: Julie McNeill
Cover Administrator: Linda Knowles
Electronic Composition: Omegatype Typography, Inc.

Copyright © 2001 by Allyn & Bacon
A Pearson Education Company
160 Gould Street
Needham Heights, MA 02494

Internet: www.ablongman.com

Library of Congress Cataloging-in-Publication Data

Scott, John W. (John William)
    The basketball book / John W. Scott.
      p. cm.
    Includes index.
    ISBN 0-205-31937-8 (alk. paper)
     1. Basketball. I. Title.
  GV885 .S378 2001
  796.323—dc21

                      00-059409

Printed in the United States of America

10 9 8 7 6 5 4 3   05 04 03

Contents

Preface

The purpose of this book is to make available drills, information, concepts, techniques, moves, and fundamentals to basketball players and coaches who want to develop and improve their basketball knowledge and skills as well as raise their level of play. This book will also benefit coaches who want to improve their ability to teach fundamental skills, moves, drills, and techniques. This book is not designed to be a coaches' manual for X's and O's. As a coach, you will learn, however, practice drills that are designed to simulate and prepare for game situations.

This book includes chapters on every facet of basketball fundamentals, from shooting and fast-break fundamentals to scoring and how to practice and play the game. In each chapter you will find numerous training tips addressing concepts of the game and how to play it. Throughout the book are new ideas, techniques, and principles. Each chapter also contains a coaches' chalk talk, discussing how to use or implement skill drills in team settings. You will discover history, information, and new insights into the game. An entire chapter is devoted just to backyard basketball games—games that have been going on for over a century at the local gym, in the driveway, and at the schoolyard that promote fun, competition, and practice. Last but not least, this book also provides a basketball dictionary containing the most in-depth definitions and explanations of the game available.

The objective of this book is to simply and *completely* explain the many skill areas of the game, while providing drills for their development in a format that is easy to understand. No matter your level of skill or competition, this book will benefit you and challenge you to excel. This is the purpose of *The Basketball Book.*

You can also improve your game by internalizing information about it. Simply read one chapter a day, and you will gain greater insights into basketball, its fundamentals, and how to use them in game situations. No matter what your age or skill level, this book can help you become a better basketball player and coach.

A VERY SPECIAL AGONY

It starts as a childhood dream: the fame, the glitter, the pride. It's all a hope, a prayer, a quest, a sleeper's reality.

The trial is hard and long; the vehicle—yourself, the fuel—desire. Time passes slowly, yet too quickly. You do not reach all your goals and it seems that with more time you would, but that is part of this grueling process.

You are disappointed often, and at first, success is slow and almost seems forever in coming, but that sparkle, that desire within, that belief in yourself, and that disbelief others have in you keep you going, striving, pushing, and straining every fiber of your body.

Many obstacles stand in the way. Each seems bigger than the last, but you still go on, sometimes feeling nothing can stop you, and other times feeling you'll never make it. As time passes on, these trials become stepping-stones on the stairway to your goal.

Time, pain, failure, sweat, and more pain. Work, desire, hustle, success, and more sweat. You fail, get up, and fail again. You stand, you trip, you rise again.

Why? Because it is simple. It's all part of the struggle to be the best, part of the trial you must endure; it's all part of something only you can understand.

It's a very special agony.

ACKNOWLEDGMENTS

For God and my family, who brought me into this world and brought me up in it, my wish is that I will always make you proud and live my life as you have taught me. Without your belief and support, I would never have had the courage to try. My wife Deborah made it possible for me to still be a boy at heart and play a part in the game of basketball as an adult. All my friends and coaches of past and present have encouraged, loved, and supported me, and helped me to learn to respect myself, especially coaches George Gracie, Jon Sidorvich, Arthur Podaras, Ed James, and Lee Smelser. A special thanks to my former professional coach, Gerald Oliver. A heartfelt tribute to my Norwegian grandpa and grandma who toiled for twenty years to achieve their dream of coming to America so that one day I, too, could have the freedom to live mine.

Enormous gratitude to Stephanie Rasmussen and Chris Miller. Stephanie spent numerous hours sketching models and photos to illustrate this book in a professional manner. Chris, from Sport America, was the artist behind the graphic layout and design. Heartfelt appreciation to the people at Allyn & Bacon for their belief in this project and the foresight to see into the future. I am grateful for the comments of the following reviewers: Bob Hurley, St. Anthony's Catholic High School; Carolyn Lehr, University of Georgia; Michael Mondello, University of Florida; and Michael Scarano, University College Riverside.

Finally, thank you to the thousands of players and coaches I have coached and worked with over the years to polish and perfect the concepts, skills, and fundamentals presented in this book. This book is dedicated to them and all of those players and coaches in the future who will use this to participate in and play the game of basketball.

About the Author

As a player John Scott is a veteran of more than twenty years of competition in the high school, college, and professional ranks, having played and coached at every level of the game. Coach Scott has served as the National Basketball Clinic Director for Converse since 1992. He has conducted camps, clinics, and lectures for companies and organizations such as Foot Locker, Nike, Kraft General Foods, Rawlings, Special Olympics, Sport Court, Spalding, and thousands of high schools, colleges, and basketball associations worldwide.

Coach Scott is also the founder and president of Sport America Inc., the largest sports education and motivation company of its kind. He travels the globe, working with organizations and teams to enhance their sports performance, systems, organizations, and productivity. As a motivational speaker, he has addressed hundreds of groups, athletic programs, businesses, and associations throughout the country.

In the past fifteen years of working with players, he has helped to develop and send more than 200 players into the college ranks and more than a dozen players into the professional ranks.

Coach Scott has published four other sports books as well as producing over fifty basketball videos (available at sportamerica.com), more than any other coach in the history of the game. Dozens of NBA and college programs have used Coach Scott's instructional materials, making them among the most highly endorsed and sought after basketball products on the market today. His videos and books have been translated into many languages and used in Australia, Germany, Greece, Italy, Korea, Spain, Taiwan, the United Kingdom, and many other countries. Coach Scott is considered one of the top coaching authorities on basketball fundamentals in the world today.

The Game of Basketball

HISTORY AND GENERAL INFORMATION

IN THIS CHAPTER YOU WILL LEARN:
- Origins of the game—how it all started
- History of the game with chronological developments
- Court dimensions and equipment needed to play the game
- Officials' signals and a general overview of the rules of the game

▌ PLAYING THE GAME OF BASKETBALL

No other sport encompasses as much grace and athleticism as the game of basketball. Speed, quickness, jumping ability, coordination, strength, agility, intelligence, and a high degree of sports skill are all necessary for success in the game.

A basketball team consists of five players. They are restricted to a court area that has a standard size of 94 feet in length by 50 feet in width. A basket is located at each end of the court, standing at a height of 10 feet from the floor to the rim (see Figure 1.1). The circular rim is wide enough to accomodate two balls at one time. A rectangular or rounded backboard situated behind the rim keeps missed shots from going out of bounds so that they can be rebounded and kept in play (Figure 1.2).

All ten players (five on each team) must be able to play both offense and defense. They can move the ball by passing it to a teammate or by dribbling (bouncing) it by hand. Although individual playing skills are essential, teamwork and team strategy are also key elements in playing the game. When teams are on the offense, they run offensive plays to create open shots for players, and when teams are on the defense, they will run a man-to-man, zone, or pressing defense to confuse an offensive team, breaking up its rhythm or pattern of plays. In a man-to-man defense, each player is assigned to, or guards, a specific player or opponent on the other team. In a zone defense, a defensive player typically protects a particular area of the court. In a press defense, two defensive players usually trap an offensive player with the ball in certain areas of the court. A press defense forces an offensive team into making a turnover or throwing a bad pass that the defensive team can steal to make an easy layup or shot.

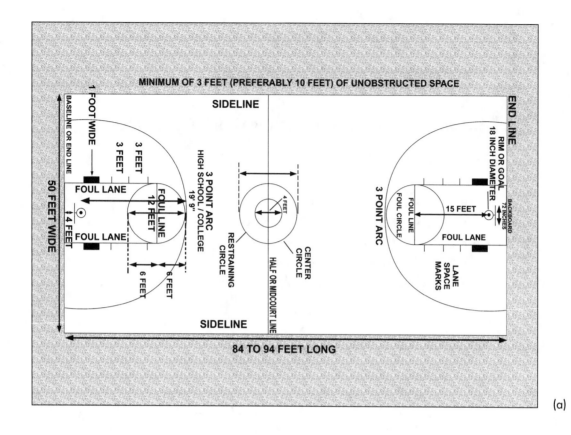

MINIMUM OF 3 FEET (PREFERABLY 10 FEET) OF UNOBSTRUCTED SPACE

SIDELINE

1 FOOT WIDE

BASELINE OR END LINE

50 FEET WIDE

3 FEET

3 FEET

FOUL LANE

4 FEET

FOUL LANE

3 POINT ARC
HIGH SCHOOL / COLLEGE
19' 9"

FOUL LINE
12 FEET

6 FEET

6 FEET

RESTRAINING CIRCLE

4 FEET

CENTER CIRCLE

HALF OR MIDCOURT LINE

SIDELINE

END LINE

RIM OR GOAL
18 INCH DIAMETER

3 POINT ARC

FOUL LINE

FOUL CIRCLE

15 FEET

BACKBOARD
72 INCHES

FOUL LANE

LANE SPACE MARKS

84 TO 94 FEET LONG

(a)

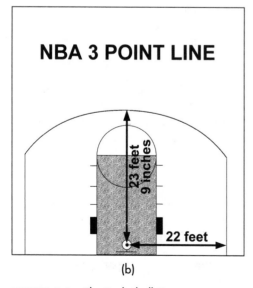

NBA 3 POINT LINE

23 feet 9 inches

22 feet

(b)

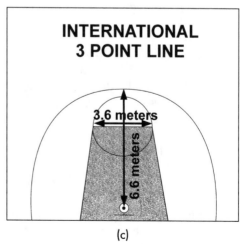

INTERNATIONAL 3 POINT LINE

3.6 meters

6.6 meters

(c)

FIGURE 1.1   The Basketball Court

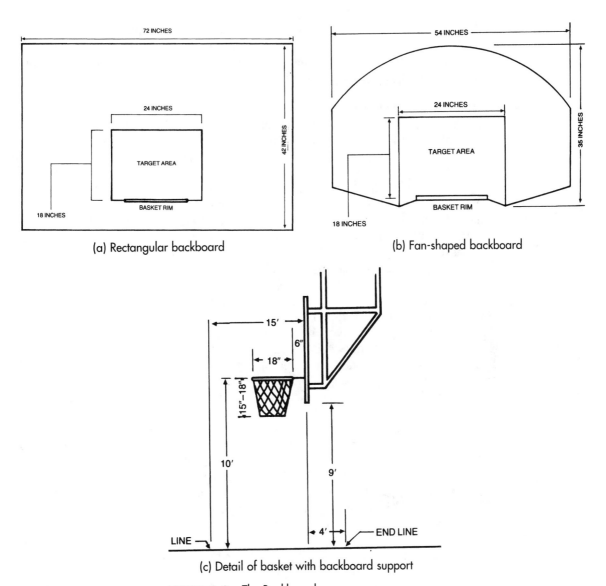

(a) Rectangular backboard   (b) Fan-shaped backboard

(c) Detail of basket with backboard support

FIGURE 1.2   The Backboard

Two types of shots can score points: a field goal and a foul shot or free throw. A field goal can be worth two points or three points, depending on the spot from which the shot is taken (Figure 1.1). A successful shot made from 19 feet, 9 inches (in college) or farther from the basket is worth three points. A shot scored from less than 19 feet, 9 inches to the basket is worth two points. This is because it is easier to score the closer to the basket you shoot, and therefore, longer shots are rewarded with three points because the degree of difficulty is much higher. A foul shot, or free throw, is awarded to a team or player when a foul has been committed by the opposing team (usually when that team is on the defensive). The foul shot or free throw awarded is free and cannot be contested by the defense. A foul shot is taken at the foul line, which is 15 feet away from the back of the rim (Figure 1.1). The foul shot is a penalty against the opposing team and is designed to keep the game from becoming injurious.

Each player is allowed five fouls before being disqualified from the game. (NBA rules allow six fouls because the games are longer.) Limiting the number of fouls allowed within the game promotes finesse, flow, and skill and makes the game more enjoyable to watch as well as play.

In this game of skill, shooting probably plays the most critical role. Shooting the ball is the only way to score points. The ball itself is lightweight and easy to handle (see Figure 1.3). The objective of the game is for one team to score more points than the opposing team before the time allotted for the competition expires. A basketball game can be played using four 8- to 12-minute quarters or two 20-minute halves, and all games have a long (15 to 20 minutes) halftime break in which the teams meet to reevaluate strategy. When time is up, the team with the most points wins. If the score is tied, one or more 5-minute overtime periods are played until a winner is determined.

The key skills involved in basketball are shooting, passing, dribbling, rebounding, defense, and solid execution of offensive and defensive plays. (These skills are discussed in detail in later chapters.) Although basketball is well suited to tall athletes, many short athletes have succeeded because they developed exceptional shooting, dribbling, and passing skills to offset their lack of height.

The game is fun to watch and play. Scoring is frequent and fast paced, providing continual excitement. The ball can change possession quickly from team to team, sometimes within seconds. Change of possession can occur when there is a turnover or rule violation, a rebound of a missed shot, a scored basket, or even a steal by the opposing team. All of this makes for a wide-open, nonstop, action-filled, high-scoring, explosive game that is fun for players and fans alike.

Basketball is also the fastest growing game in the world today. One reason for basketball's success is that many of its skills can be practiced alone. All you need is a ball and a basket. Both are relatively inexpensive and can be set up in a yard or a driveway or beside a street. Basketball can be played almost anywhere, indoors

A leather basketball may be used indoors. A rubber or plastic basketball is suitable for indoor or outdoor play.

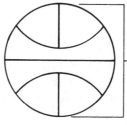

The circumference of a standard basketball is 29½ to 30 inches.

The women's ball is 28½ to 29 inches. 1 inch smaller in circumference. The women's ball is 2½ ounces lighter than the men's ball. But in international women's competition, standard size ball is used.

FIGURE 1.3   The Basketball

or outdoors, at any time of year. Another reason that people love the game is that it is fun to practice. The rewards are instantaneous—you feel good every time you make a successful shot and score a basket, even when you are practicing alone. No other game or sport can offer the same enjoyment and benefits. Now let's learn more about how the game started and how to play the game even better.

ORIGINS OF THE GAME—HOW IT ALL STARTED

Basketball was invented by Dr. James A. Naismith in December 1891 in Springfield, Massachusetts. Naismith was a physical education instructor at the YMCA International Training School (now Springfield College). In the fall of 1891 he was asked by the head of the school's physical education department, Luther H. Gulick, to develop a team game that students could play in the gym during the cold winter months.

Dr. Naismith obtained a soccer ball and two wooden peach baskets. He hung the baskets on the balcony railings 10 feet above the floor at opposite ends of the gymnasium. Today the height of the baskets is still 10 feet above the court. The object of the game was to toss the soccer ball into the peach basket defended by the opposing team. The first basketball game was played by Dr. Naismith's physical education students in December 1891. There were nine players on each team.

In the January 15, 1892, issue of the *Triangle*, the YMCA Training School's paper, Naismith published the first set of rules for the new game. The popularity of the game spread quickly. Schools and the YMCA soon adopted the sport and organized teams and leagues throughout the United States. Today basketball is considered one of the most popular sports in the world. It is widely played and watched, extending to more than 170 countries around the globe.

The James A. Naismith Memorial Basketball Hall of Fame was established in Springfield in 1941, the game's fiftieth anniversary. The Hall of Fame houses inductees, historical exhibits, and basketball memorabilia. It is open to the general public year-round. The Women's Basketball Hall of Fame has also been established in recent years in Knoxville, Tennessee. Both sites offer wonderful information about the game and preserve the major events, history, pioneers, and other contributors and people that have made basketball a popular sport. Contact the Hall of Fame for more details and to arrange visits to the sites.

PHOTO 1.1
Dr. James Naismith showing a youngster some of the fundamentals of basketball.
Reprinted by permission of the Basketball Hall of Fame.

PHOTO 1.2
The first basketball team, December 1891.
Reprinted by permission of the Basketball Hall of Fame.

Basketball Hall of Fame
1150 West Columbus Avenue
Springfield, MA 01105
www.hoophall.com
(413) 781-6500

Women's Basketball Hall of Fame
700 Hall of Fame Drive
Knoxville, TN 37915
www.wbhof.com
(423) 633-9000

    In addition to growing faster in participation and popularity than any other sport in modern times, basketball itself has changed and evolved. Additions such as the three-point shot, the shot clock, three-second lane area, slam dunks, and fast-paced skills have made the game even more interesting. Many key developments in the game are listed in the following historical chronology.

HISTORICAL CHRONOLOGY OF THE GAME

1891   December: James A. Naismith invents the game of basketball at the YMCA International Training School in Springfield, Massachusetts; the first game is played there in a physical education class.

1892   January 15: Dr. Naismith publishes the first set of rules for the game (thirteen of them).

1893   Metal hoops or rings with net bags replace the wooden peach baskets.

1896   January 16: The first college game is played, in Iowa City, Iowa; the University of Chicago defeats the University of Iowa, 15–12.

PHOTO 1.3

Game and equipment as used in 1892 (from lecture material of Amos Alonzo Stagg).

Reprinted by permission of the Basketball Hall of Fame.

1896   The first women's college game is played between Stanford and the University of California.

1897   Teams are reduced to five players on the court at one time.

1898   The first professional league, the National League, is formed with six teams.

1899   First official rules are adopted for women, in Springfield, Massachusetts.

1901   First basketball rules committee is formed by the Amateur Athletic Union (AAU); the Ivy League Basketball Conference is established.

1904   Basketball is demonstrated at the Olympic Games in St. Louis.

1905   April: Colleges organize their own rules committee.

1907   Five-minute overtime period is adopted to break ties.

1908   Personal foul limit is introduced—five fouls disqualify a player.

1913   National AAU championships are established; baskets with bottomless nets are put into use.

1918   The original Celtics of New York City are founded; the team won 111 straight games and had an overall record of 720–75.

1922   Chuck Taylor, of Converse fame, does what becomes known as the "first basketball clinic" at North Carolina State. Converse goes on to name a shoe after Chuck, who is later inducted into the Basketball Hall of Fame and crowned the "First Ambassador for Basketball."

1925   The American Basketball League is formed; folds in 1931.

PHOTO 1.4

Miss Senda Berenson, in long dress, with Smith College students in Northampton, Massachusetts, where women played the first public basketball game March 22, 1893.

Reprinted by permission of the Basketball Hall of Fame.

1930   Harlem Globetrotters are organized; Abe Saperstein helps make them famous.

1932   Clair Bee, coach of Long Island University, introduces the foul lane area with the rule of three seconds in the lane.

1934   The first basketball doubleheaders, organized by Ned Irish, are played at Madison Square Garden in New York City.

1936   In a game at Madison Square Garden, Hank Luisetti of Stanford shoots with one hand while hanging in midair—the accidental introduction of the one-hand shot.

1936   Basketball becomes a regular Olympic event; the United States wins the gold medal.

1937   Jump ball after each basket is abolished.

1938   First National Invitational Tournament (NIT) is held; it is won by Temple University.

1939   First NCAA tournament is won by the University of Oregon. The original tournament fielded only sixteen teams.

1941   Naismith Memorial Basketball Hall of Fame is founded on the campus of Springfield College on the fiftieth anniversary of the invention of the game.

1944   Joe Fulks of the Philadelphia Warriors becomes known as the inventor of the jump shot.

1946   Basketball Association of America (BAA), a professional league, is established.

1949   The BAA merges with the new National Basketball League to form the National Basketball Association (NBA).

1950   City College of New York wins both the NIT and the NCAA tournaments, the only team ever to do this.

1950   The Boston Celtics become the first team to draft an African American player, Chuck Cooper, into the NBA.

1950   NBA adds "rebounding" as a statistical category.

1952   First version of the one-and-one free-throw rule is used in college.

1954   NBA adopts the 24-second shot clock to make the game faster and more exciting. The shot clock is invented by Danny Biascone, owner of the NBA Syracuse Nationals.

1955   Foul lane area is widened from 6 to 12 feet. The change largely considered a response to the skill of George Mikan of the Minneapolis Lakers.

1957   The three-second rule in foul lane on offensive team is officially added as part of the game.

1961   Abe Saperstein, founder of the Harlem Globetrotters, invents the three-point line and shot at a distance of 23 feet, 9 inches (currently used by the NBA). The shot was a gimmick to accompany his new league, the American Basketball League (ABL), which tried to compete with the NBA but lasted only a year and a half.

1964   NBA foul lane is widened from 12 to 16 feet. The change is primarily credited to the dominance of Wilt Chamberlain of the Philadelphia 76ers.

1966   The Boston Celtics become the first NBA team to start a game with five African American players.

1966   Texas Western (now UTEP) is the first NCAA team to start five African American players in an NCAA championship final game. Score: Texas Western 72, Kentucky 65.

1967   Bill Russell of the Boston Celtics become the first African American head coach in the NBA.

1967   American Basketball Association (ABA), a professional league, is established: promotes the three-point shot and a red, white, and blue basketball.

1972   June 23: Title IX is passed into law entitling women's basketball to receive equal rights and funding in all athletic programs.

1973   NBA adds "steals" and "blocked shots" as statistical categories (after the dominating shot-blocking career of Bill Russell of the Boston Celtics, with eleven NBA championships).

1975   The first ever women's Kodak All American team is announced.

1975   The first women's college game played in Madison Square Garden occurs (Queens vs. Immaculata).

1976   NBA and ABA merge into a professional league of twenty-two teams after nine years of bitter competition for players.

1976	Ann Cape wins lawsuit versus the High School Athletic Association of Tennessee. This suit leads to boys' rules (five players on a team and full-court play) being instituted in girls' basketball.
1981	NBA adopts the three-point field goal with sideline distance of 22 feet and top of the key distance of 23 feet, 9 inches.
1983	Idaho is the first state to use the three-point shot on an experimental basis; distance is 19 feet, 9 inches.
1984	June 23: the Federation of International Basketball Associations (FIBA) and the World Basketball Congress approve of the international three-point line for competition at a distance of 21 feet, 6 inches or 6.6 meters. The three-point line will not be used in the Olympics until 1988.
1984	NCAA adopts a smaller basketball for women's basketball. It is 1 inch smaller in circumference, and 2½ ounces lighter. (Women's international competition still uses a regular ball.)
1984	The ACC is the first conference in the NCAA to experiment with the three-point line on a trial basis.
1985	NCAA officially adopts the shot clock and the three-point line at a distance of 19 feet, 9 inches.
1987	National Federation of High Schools officially adopts the three-point line, distance 19 feet, 9 inches.
1988	NBA increases number of referees from two to three.
1992	NBA players are allowed to participate in the Olympics for the first time. The United States easily wins the gold medal.
1996	April 24: The NBA forms and financially backs the WNBA women's professional league in the United States.
1997	June: the WNBA women's pro league begins play. Backed by the NBA, it competes against another women's league, the American Basketball League (ABL).
1999	The ABL women's pro league folds; ABL players are drafted into the WNBA.

BASKETBALL DIAGRAMS

In this book, diagrams are used to show patterns of play, practice, and movement of players to help you better understand what is happening or what should happen. The standard symbols given in Figure 1.4 are used to describe basketball patterns, players, ball movements, plays, and drills. Whether you are a player, coach, parent, fan, or student of the game, it will be beneficial to know these universal keys.

Basketball officials use various signals to indicate fouls and violations during a game. Any official on the court can call a foul or violation. The most common signals used at all levels of basketball competition (amateur to professional) are shown in Figure 1.5.

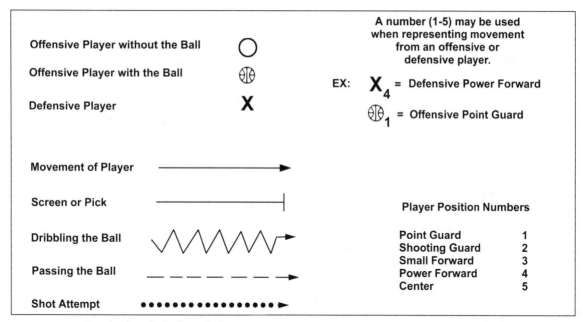

FIGURE 1.4 Standard Basketball Symbols

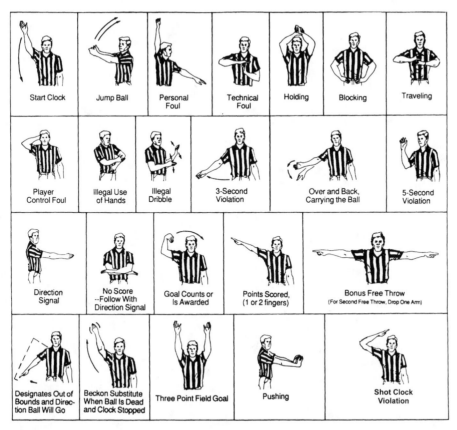

FIGURE 1.5 Signals Used by Basketball Officials (for definitions of rules, see the Basketball Dictionary on page 295)

CHAPTER QUESTIONS_____

1. What two types of shots can score points?

2. Explain how the game of basketball was invented and why.

3. How did the basket height of 10 feet come about?

4. List three things from the chronological history of the game that you find the most interesting. What is significant about them?

5. Why is a foul shot also called a free throw?

6. How many fouls is a player allowed in a game? What happens when the limit is passed?

7. List five important skills that athletes need to master to be a good basketball player.

8. Give two reasons why basketball has become the most popular sport in the world.

9. Diagram, with a correct key, the following game situations:
   a. a point guard dribbling the ball
   b. a power forward on defense
   c. a shooting guard with the ball, taking a shot attempt
   d. a center setting a screen for a small forward
   e. a point guard passing the ball to a power forward

Shooting Fundamentals and the Sure-Shot Shooting System

IN THIS CHAPTER YOU WILL LEARN:

- Mechanics for the most important basketball skill—shooting
- Fundamental skills for beginners as well as techniques for future stars
- How to develop confidence in your shooting skills
- That your ability to shoot a basketball is in direct proportion to your practice habits
- How to make both left- and right-handed layups
- Numerous drills and concepts to help build shooting mastery
- Target sight—what to aim for when shooting and where to focus
- Five practice rules for achieving greater success

Very few players—even professionals—are great shooters or have perfect shooting form. That is where the concept of a "role player" comes in. If you cannot shoot well, you had better be able to do something else really well, such as pass, dribble, defend, or rebound. You need to be a role player. But the truth is, *anyone* can be a good shooter. Shooting a basketball correctly is easy to learn, but improving and perfecting your shooting takes a great deal of practice. Anyone can learn to shoot well, but everyone must start from the beginning and learn to perform the skill correctly.

This chapter is for new players who want to learn how to shoot correctly, advanced players who want to improve their shooting skills, and coaches who seek an easier way to teach shooting. You will find various shooting drills to improve your game. No matter what your current skill level is, you will gain valuable insights, tips, and techniques for shooting.

FOUR SHOOTING FUNDAMENTALS FOR EASY LEARNING

All players can and should benefit from learning the correct mechanics and choreography for shooting the ball and making layups. The Sure-Shot Shooting System will enable every player, parent, or coach to easily learn, teach, and develop great shooting skills. We will study each element of shooting, from ball and hand position to follow-through and mental training, as well as advanced shooting principles for practice and shooting drills that have proved valuable at all levels of play, from youth league through professional basketball.

Fundamental 1: Arm Position (The L Form)

The L position is the first essential element of shooting the basketball correctly, and it is easy to learn and teach. Use this letter of the alphabet to paint a mental picture of how your arm should look and feel when shooting.

Here are the steps for the L position.

FUNDAMENTAL 1: ARM POSITION (THE L FORM)

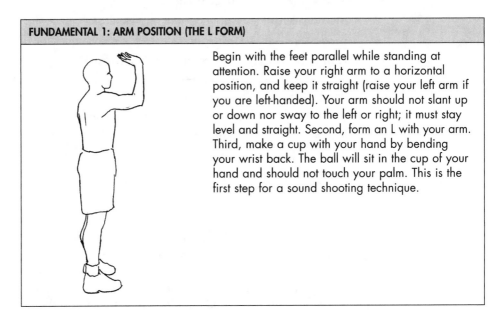

Begin with the feet parallel while standing at attention. Raise your right arm to a horizontal position, and keep it straight (raise your left arm if you are left-handed). Your arm should not slant up or down nor sway to the left or right; it must stay level and straight. Second, form an L with your arm. Third, make a cup with your hand by bending your wrist back. The ball will sit in the cup of your hand and should not touch your palm. This is the first step for a sound shooting technique.

▌ TRAINING TIP _____

For best results, practice these three steps to get used to holding the ball correctly:

1. Raise your arm to a horizontal position.
2. Form an L with your shooting arm.
3. Form a cup with your hand.

Do not shoot the ball. This is just a mechanical drill to help you prepare to shoot the ball.

DRILL PRACTICE LENGTH: 10–25 repetitions.

Fundamental 2: Hand-to-Hand Position

The next letter of the alphabet we use is *T.* Use the letter T to represent correct hand positions on the ball. The T position works as follows.

FUNDAMENTAL 2: HAND-TO-HAND POSITION

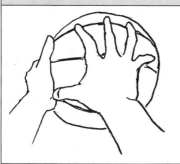

Position your left arm so that the thumb of your shooting hand touches the palm of your guide hand (or nonshooting hand). You will notice that this position forms a T between your right thumb and your left palm. For players with smaller hands, this position may require forming the T with both thumbs touching.

DRILL PRACTICE LENGTH: 10–25 repetitions.

▌ TRAINING TIP

Do not allow a player to practice shooting with the guide hand on top of the ball *or* in front of the ball. Both of these mistakes will cause the shooter to "pull" on the ball, often misdirecting the shot. This is one of the most common mistakes made by players with poor shooting mechanics.

Fundamental 3: Hand-to-Ball Position

During shooting, passing, or dribbling, the basketball should never touch the palm of the hand directly. The ball should always be touching the finger pads. This allows a much better "feel" of the ball, which in turn promotes better control. (See Figure 2.1).

Fundamental 4: Ball-to-Body Position (Alignment)

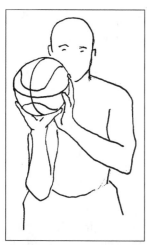

FIGURE 2.1   The Shooting Pocket

The next step in shooting a basketball is to develop the habit of holding and shooting the ball from the "shooting pocket," or shoulder pad area (see Figure 2.1). This fundamental is universally applicable, used when shooting and facing the basket on offense. Your shooting pocket is above your shoulder, to the side of your right ear if you are right-handed. (If you are left-handed, your shooting pocket is on the left side.) When on offense, always try to hold the ball and shoot the ball from the shooting pocket in a good triple-threat position (see Figure 2.2). Using the triple-threat position means that from one position, you can shoot the ball, pass the ball, or drive to the basket. (Study Chapter 6 to learn more about the triple-threat position, scoring moves, and options.)

There are only two exceptions to this rule for not maintaining this ball-to-body position. The first is when a defender comes within one arm's length to you or closer; then you must either pass or break the defender down by driving to the basket. The second is when an offensive player is playing in the low-post area with his or her back to the basket. The low-post area includes any spot 10–12 feet from the rim or closer.

FIGURE 2.2   The Triple-Threat Position

The reason for developing the habit of shooting the ball from your shooting pocket is that it will make you a faster player. How? If you hold the ball above your head, you will have to bring the ball down to your shooting pocket or your shoulder pad in order to shoot. Also, by holding the ball above your head, you are telling the defense you are prepared to use only one option out of the triple threat: to pass the ball. It will also take you one full second to bring the ball down to your shooting pocket to "reload" and shoot the ball. That is enough time for a defender to contest your shot. A good defender will take note of your bad habit and give you problems.

If you hold the ball below your shoulders in the waist area, you must also take one full second to bring it up to a shooting position in your shooting pocket. From this waist position, you also are prepared to execute only one option of the triple-threat position: to drive to the basket. Thus, both alternatives to the shooting pocket give you only one-third of the options available to you, making you only one-third of the offensive player you can be. The habit of holding and shooting the ball from the shoulder pad will make you one second quicker as a player. You will also be more effective offensively.

In fairness, many coaches and players have been taught that the triple-threat position is different from the one just described. You may not at first agree with the location of the ball in the triple-threat position just suggested, but you should try it and test it before you decide it is not the best. You will be pleasantly surprised.

▌▌ TRAINING TIP _____

As you complete your shot, you will shoot better if your shooting arm finishes over and *above* your head, not forward toward the basket. Finishing your shot this way will make your shot harder to block. You will be shooting over, not toward, your defender. This position will also provide better arc on your shot and increase your shooting success (see Figure 2.3).

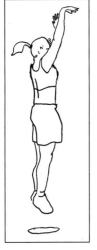

FIGURE 2.3
Position for
Finishing a Shot

SHOOTING LINES, LANES, AND ANGLES

Proper body balance, alignment, and shooting mechanics are critical to performing well on the court. Shooting lines, lanes, and angles must be correct in order to yield greatest results. Practicing correct shooting lines, lanes, and angles is no more difficult than practicing regular shooting. The difference will be in *what* you practice and in *how* you practice.

Shooting Lines

Your shooting line is simply a straight line to the basket that you form with your toe, knee, elbow, and ball. If your line is straight, then your shot will go straight. If your line is crooked and your elbow is positioned too far in or out, then your shot will more often than not miss to the left or right side of the rim. You can correct up to 20 percent of your misses by shooting the ball straight (see Figure 2.4).

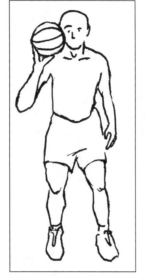 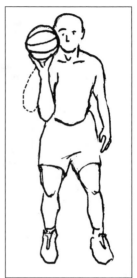

(a) Correct shooting line   (b) Incorrect shooting line

FIGURE 2.4   Shooting Lines

Shooting Lanes

Your Shooting Lane consists of the alignment of your body when facing the rim from the perimeter areas of the court. Make sure that your feet are lined up correctly in the Shooting Lane. Look at Figure 2.5 to see the difference between a correct Shooting Lane and an incorrect one. An incorrect Shooting Lane will increase the shot's degree of difficulty because your body will not be aligned to your target—the rim.

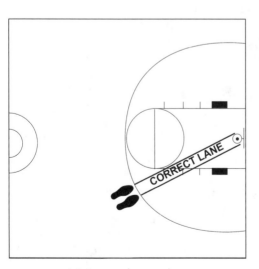 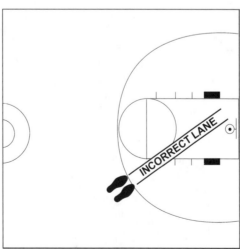

(a) Correct shooting lane   (b) Incorrect shooting lane

FIGURE 2.5   Shooting Lanes

Shooting Angles

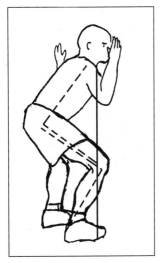

FIGURE 2.6   Correct Sports Position

Your shooting angles are two 45-degree body angles that put you into a correct Sports Position for shooting the ball. In a correct Sports Position, the knees are directly above the toes and the shoulders are directly above the knees in a vertical line. In this position an athlete achieves perfect body balance, with the feet placed shoulders' width apart. This balance helps an athlete move, react, and respond much more quickly. Because this fundamental body position is important in many sports (for a batter in baseball, a goalkeeper in soccer, and so on), its name is not associated with a particular sport.

A side shot of a player in a perfect Sports Position shows that the body forms two 45-degree angles, which provide perfect body balance (see Figure 2.6). The first angle extends from the shoulder to the hip to the knee. The second angle extends from the hip to the back of the knee to the back of the ankle. If these angles are not maintained, a shot will be less likely to reach its goal. With the correct angles, the ball will find the basket more consistently. The same mechanical principles apply to the triple-threat position. Your body should form two 45-degree angles with the ball in the shooting pocket, ready to shoot, pass, or drive.

▰▰ LAYUPS

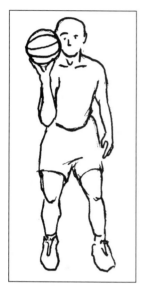

FIGURE 2.7   The Triple-Threat Position

A layup is the highest percentage shot you can take in basketball. Just as in shooting, you must use proper mechanics and footwork in order to make layups. When aiming a layup shot, the target will usually be a little different from normal shots because you often will use the backboard to aim and shoot the ball into the hoop (unless you are attempting a layup from the side of the rim or down the middle of the lane area). The backboard is a higher percentage shot. Try to shoot the ball off the top of the inside of the small square on the backboard when you approach the basket from the side. This will improve the chances that the ball will go in (see Figure 2.8). Don't just shoot the ball and hope it will go in! You must maintain eye contact with the target until the shot is released and goes in.

To learn how to make layups properly, start practicing close to the basket, then move farther away as your fundamentals improve. This stepping-stone process will eventually build skill in making layups in game situations. Whether you are a beginning or an advanced player, practicing and using the layup techniques shown here will allow you to create more three-point play opportunities because you'll be making a stronger approach to the basket. There are four different drills to use for the development of layups. These four drills should be practiced from both sides of the floor, shooting with the left hand on the left side and the right hand on the right side of the basket.

FIGURE 2.8   Approaching the Basket for a Layup

▰▰ TRAINING TIP

Players should learn to shoot layups with the ball in the shooting pocket or on the shoulder pad area for several reasons:

1. It is a stronger and a more controllable shot.
2. It provides a better chance of making the basket when challenged or fouled by a defender.
3. When a shooter lays the ball up from the shoulder pad or shooting pocket, it forces a defender to encounter the shooter's entire body in trying to block the shot. When a shooter attempts an underhanded layup, it is easier for a defender to block the ball (see Figure 2.9).

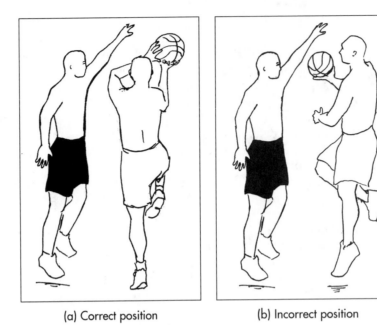

(a) Correct position   (b) Incorrect position

FIGURE 2.9   Arm Position for Shooting Layups

▚ **TRAINING TIP** _____

Always begin practicing a new drill or skill at half speed until you learn the proper movements and mechanics. Complete 25–50 repetitions perfectly before trying to move at a
faster pace or progress to the three-step layup. Remember, practice does *not* make perfect. *Perfect practice makes perfect.* However, practice does make permanent, so if you
practice drills perfectly, then you will play perfectly permanently.

Right-Handed One-Step Layup

The one-step layup should be practiced from both sides of the basket. This simple drill teaches a player to go up strong with the ball in a game situation as well as use correct footwork and mechanics for shooting layups. Use the verbal commands and instructions as follows:

RIGHT-HANDED ONE-STEP LAYUP

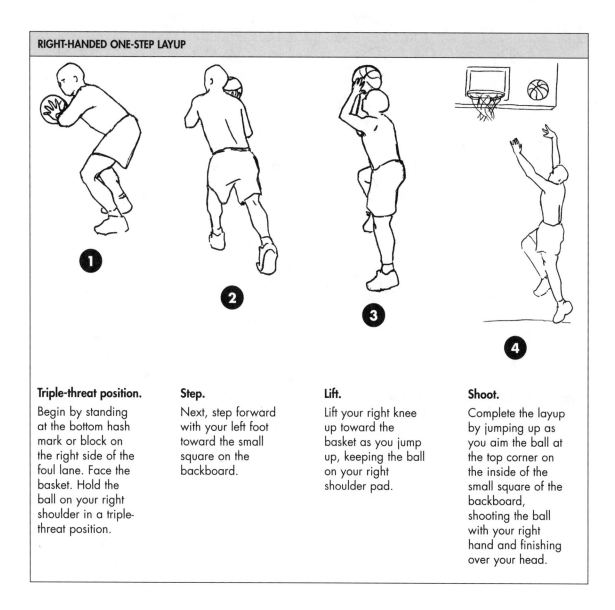

Triple-threat position.

Begin by standing at the bottom hash mark or block on the right side of the foul lane. Face the basket. Hold the ball on your right shoulder in a triple-threat position.

Step.

Next, step forward with your left foot toward the small square on the backboard.

Lift.

Lift your right knee up toward the basket as you jump up, keeping the ball on your right shoulder pad.

Shoot.

Complete the layup by jumping up as you aim the ball at the top corner on the inside of the small square of the backboard, shooting the ball with your right hand and finishing over your head.

Left-Handed One-Step Layup

The process for making a left-handed layup is the same as for the right-handed layup except that a player will begin on the left side of the basket, with the ball on the left shoulder pad. This time the player will step forward with the right foot and shoot with the left hand, as follows:

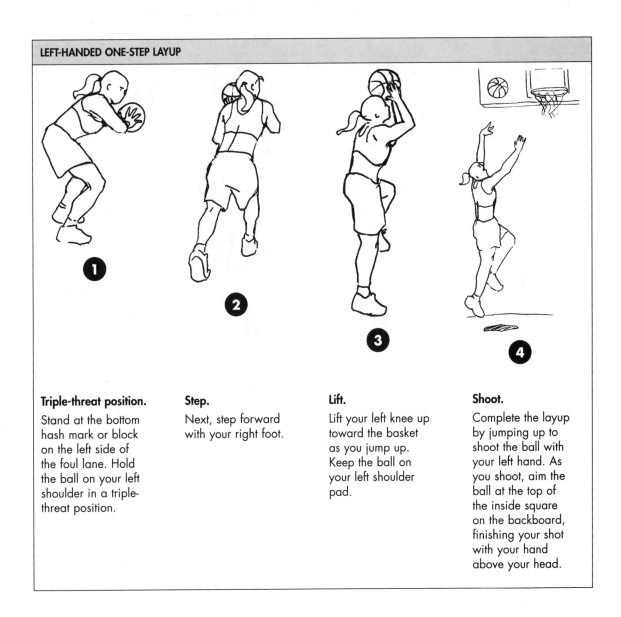

LEFT-HANDED ONE-STEP LAYUP

Triple-threat position.

Stand at the bottom hash mark or block on the left side of the foul lane. Hold the ball on your left shoulder in a triple-threat position.

Step.

Next, step forward with your right foot.

Lift.

Lift your left knee up toward the basket as you jump up. Keep the ball on your left shoulder pad.

Shoot.

Complete the layup by jumping up to shoot the ball with your left hand. As you shoot, aim the ball at the top of the inside square on the backboard, finishing your shot with your hand above your head.

THE FUNDAMENTALS NEVER CHANGE,

JUST THE NAMES OF THE PLAYERS WHO USE THEM.

SCOTISM

Right-Handed Three-Step Layup

Begin with your feet parallel, and hold the ball on your right shoulder pad in a triple-threat position. Start on the fourth hash mark closest to the foul line on the right side of the foul lane. The verbal commands and movements for a right-handed three-step layup are as follows:

RIGHT-HANDED THREE-STEP LAYUP

① Triple-threat position.

Begin by standing on the right side of the foul lane, just above the fourth hash mark (closest to the foul line). Hold the ball in a triple-threat position on your right shoulder pad.

② Left foot dribble.

Step forward, with your left foot stepping on the third hash mark and taking a dribble with your right hand. Note: The dribble and the step should make one sound, *not* two sounds.

③ Right foot, shoulder pad.

Next, step with your right foot to the second hash mark or block, while bringing the ball into your shooting pocket or shoulder pad.

④ Left foot, layup with the right hand.

Now step forward toward the basket with your left foot, lifting your right knee up toward the basket and shooting the ball with your right hand.

▮▮ TRAINING TIP _____

Say the commands out loud as you practice the steps—*"Left foot dribble; right foot, shoulder pad; left foot, layup with the right hand."* It will make learning easier and faster.

Left-Handed Three-Step Layup

Begin with the feet parallel, and hold the ball on your left shoulder pad in a triple-threat position. Start on the fourth hash mark closest to the foul line on the left side of the foul lane. Verbal commands and movements for a left-handed three-step layup are as follows:

LEFT-HANDED THREE-STEP LAYUP

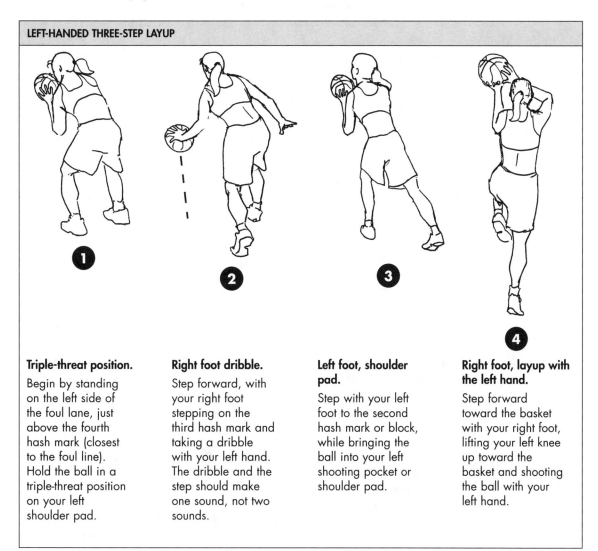

Triple-threat position.

Begin by standing on the left side of the foul lane, just above the fourth hash mark (closest to the foul line). Hold the ball in a triple-threat position on your left shoulder pad.

Right foot dribble.

Step forward, with your right foot stepping on the third hash mark and taking a dribble with your left hand. The dribble and the step should make one sound, not two sounds.

Left foot, shoulder pad.

Step with your left foot to the second hash mark or block, while bringing the ball into your left shooting pocket or shoulder pad.

Right foot, layup with the left hand.

Step forward toward the basket with your right foot, lifting your left knee up toward the basket and shooting the ball with your left hand.

▮▮I TRAINING TIP _____

If as a coach you are having a difficult time helping players master the correct footwork, buy some erasable chalk, go out to the schoolyard or driveway, and draw the footsteps on the ground. Players can follow these until they have done enough repetitions to achieve mastery. This is guaranteed to yield results! See Figure 2.10.

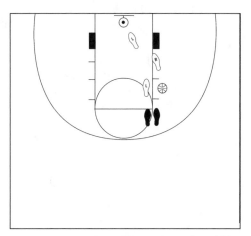

FIGURE 2.10   Three-Step Layup with Dribble

Left-Handed/Right-Handed Three-Step Layup Drill.   This drill will help a player to practice both left-handed and right-handed layups under game conditions and with game speed.

1. Begin by standing with both feet above the foul line at the left side of the foul lane.
2. Take a dribble with the left hand as you step forward with the right foot, completing the left-handed three-step layup.
3. Quickly rebound the ball, and dribble with your left hand toward the right side of the foul lane.
4. Keep your dribble as you cross the foul line with both feet, and quickly pivot 180 degrees, turning to your right side so that you are again facing the rim and dribbling the ball with your right hand.
5. Now step forward with your left foot as you take a last dribble with your right hand and complete the right-handed three-step layup. Repeat this procedure, this time going back to the left corner of the foul line. Do this drill for sixty seconds. Practice it once daily, and try to beat your score each day. See Figure 2.11 for the exact footwork.

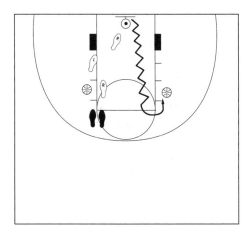
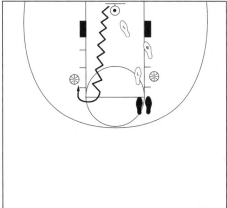

FIGURE 2.11   The Three-Step Layup Drill

Half-Court Layups

Once players have mastered the skill of making three-step layups with both hands, they are ready to move back to half court and practice at a farther distance. A half-court layup simulates a fast-break layup and is common in game situations. To practice half-court layups, begin by dribbling in from the half-court line (see Figure 2.12). Dribble full speed toward the basket. On reaching the foul line area, slow down to two-thirds or one-half speed, making a transition into the three-step layup to finish.

The following steps should be repeated when practicing from both the right and left side of the court.

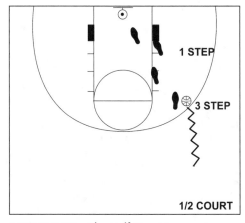

FIGURE 2.12   The Half-Court Layup

Layup Rules

1. *Eyes up.* As you dribble the ball, always keep your eyes focused on the backboard. This will allow you to see the defense, the entire court, and perhaps open teammates to whom you can pass the ball to make easy baskets. Keeping your eyes up will also help you focus on your target as you shoot the ball.
2. *Correct dribbling hand.* When practicing right-handed half-court layups, always dribble the ball on your right side. This will shield the ball from defenders who normally retreat back on defense in the middle of the court. When dribbling on the left side of the court, always dribble with the left hand.
3. *Three-step layup.* Once the dribbler reaches the foul line area, simply slow down to two-thirds or one-half your speed for greater control. Finish by using the three-step layup that you practiced previously.

The Two-Footed, or Power, Layup

The two-footed layup (or power layup) is an invaluable tool to develop and teach in preparation for game situations. It will benefit both beginning and advanced players. For younger or beginning players who have physical difficulty and control problems, it provides help in shooting the ball with more strength off both feet. For advanced players, the power layup gives an opportunity to push through defensive traffic and absorb a foul with a better chance of making the basket and getting free throws. Also, when a player is moving too quickly in a fast-break situation and does not have time to slow down for a one-step layup, the power layup literally puts on two brakes (both legs) and gives the player time to put up a strong on-balance shot.

Right-Handed Two-Footed Power Layup.   Follow these steps to practice and make a successful right-handed two-footed power layup.

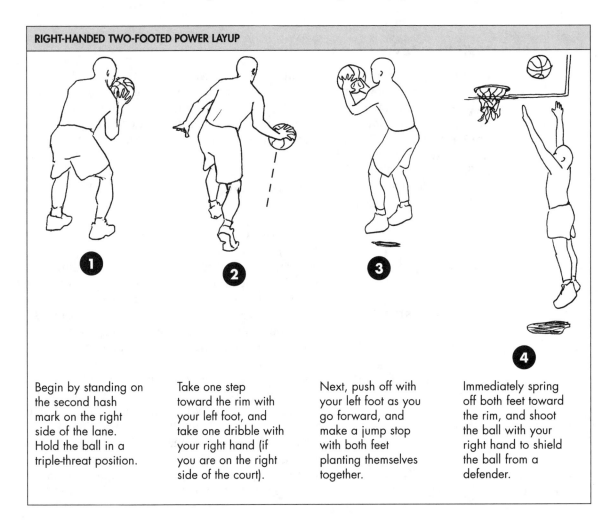

RIGHT-HANDED TWO-FOOTED POWER LAYUP

1. Begin by standing on the second hash mark on the right side of the lane. Hold the ball in a triple-threat position.

2. Take one step toward the rim with your left foot, and take one dribble with your right hand (if you are on the right side of the court).

3. Next, push off with your left foot as you go forward, and make a jump stop with both feet planting themselves together.

4. Immediately spring off both feet toward the rim, and shoot the ball with your right hand to shield the ball from a defender.

FIGURE 2.13
The Jump Stop

> ### ▌ TRAINING TIP _____
>
> ## What Is a Jump Stop?
>
> A jump stop is common in basketball. It is a two-footed stop in which both feet land on the floor at the same time to stop your progress. It is much more effective than using one foot at a time, or a "one, two" stop. A jump stop is an essential part of basketball, used in catching passes, rebounding, and defensive footwork. It also lets you establish either foot as a pivot on offense when you first catch the ball. See Figure 2.13.

Left-Handed Two-Footed Power Layup. Follow these steps to practice and make a successful left-handed two-footed power layup.

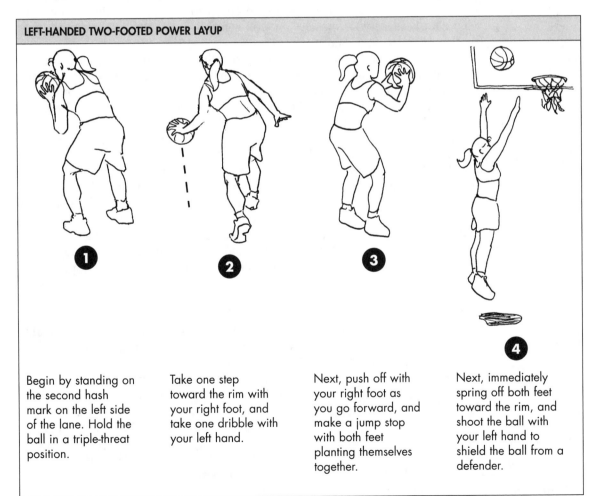

LEFT-HANDED TWO-FOOTED POWER LAYUP

① Begin by standing on the second hash mark on the left side of the lane. Hold the ball in a triple-threat position.

② Take one step toward the rim with your right foot, and take one dribble with your left hand.

③ Next, push off with your right foot as you go forward, and make a jump stop with both feet planting themselves together.

④ Next, immediately spring off both feet toward the rim, and shoot the ball with your left hand to shield the ball from a defender.

▓▌ TRAINING TIP _____

The power layup is an excellent drill to use to gather yourself and gain control in these offensive situations:

1. A fast break.
2. A backdoor cut to the basket.
3. Receiving the pass too close to the basket when you don't have room to lay the ball up normally.

▓▓▓▌ THE FIVE-SPOT WARM-UP DRILL

Always begin your daily shooting practice by taking a few minutes to warm up properly. By doing this, you allow your entire body—arms, ligaments, joints, muscles, tendons, tissues, and so on—to loosen up so you don't strain them or push your shot because your muscles are still contracted and tight. To warm up properly, use the Five-Spot Warm-Up Drill.

Most players begin practice or play by shooting long shots and three-point shots before properly warming up. This is a terrible habit. Your muscles are usually constricted and tight from not being used and you will push the ball instead of shooting it. Even worse, your shooting mechanics and habits may get thrown off. Follow this simple rule when you begin practice: *Do not shoot to warm up, warm up to shoot.*

Use the Five-Spot Warm-Up Drill to warm up your body as well as your shooting skills (see Figure 2.14). This drill will be the best shooting practice you do all day. It will also provide a proper warm-up for your entire body. Most important, it will reintroduce you each and every day to perfect shooting form, technique, and mechanics. You should never have a bad shooting day if you warm up properly. The Five-Spot Warm-Up Drill will ensure that you develop good shooting habits daily. By practicing and warming up correctly, you will develop an excellent shooting rhythm from all spots on the court. Using Figure 2.14, follow these steps to complete the drill:

1. Beginning at Spot 1, set the ball onto your shoulder pad or shooting pocket, in a triple-threat position.
2. Shoot the ball.
3. Repeat steps 1 and 2. Make a minimum of ten shots before you move away from the rim toward Spots 2, 3, 4, and 5. Make sure you feel good about how your shot is working before moving to the next spot. Upon completing the Five-Spot Warm-Up Drill, you should have made a minimum of fifty shots (ten from each spot) as part of your warm-up.

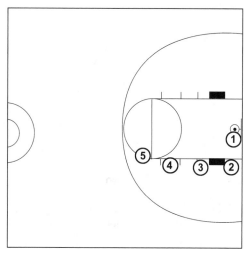

FIGURE 2.14   The Five-Spot Warm-Up Drill

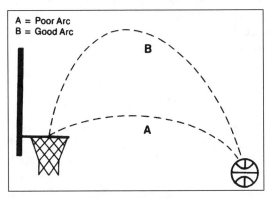

FIGURE 2.15   The Arc of a Shot

The Follow-Through Drill

The follow-through drill is very easy to practice and can be done anytime and anywhere. You may choose it as a warm-up or preparation drill before you begin shooting or even practice it while you watch television. This drill is designed to help players improve the follow-through movement of the wrist and backspin rotation on the ball.

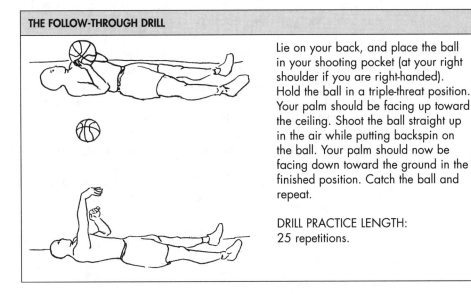

THE FOLLOW-THROUGH DRILL

Lie on your back, and place the ball in your shooting pocket (at your right shoulder if you are right-handed). Hold the ball in a triple-threat position. Your palm should be facing up toward the ceiling. Shoot the ball straight up in the air while putting backspin on the ball. Your palm should now be facing down toward the ground in the finished position. Catch the ball and repeat.

DRILL PRACTICE LENGTH:
25 repetitions.

THE SURE-SHOT SHOOTING SYSTEM

The Sure-Shot Shooting System is a systematic approach to developing more effective, efficient, and consistent shooting skills. This system includes both sound fundamentals and advanced shooting techniques. Its practice principles will help you shoot better and become mentally tougher and more focused as you practice. You will discover how to get into a shooting zone. You will be introduced to key concepts within this system such as the Shooting Lane, the V-Shot Principle, the Short-Shot Principle, the Goal-Shooting Principle, correct target sight, and many other techniques to empower you to shoot perfectly every time.

Three Practice Principles for Shooting Success

The Goal-Shooting Principle.   Goal Shooting means to practice with a purpose. Too many players simply go out and practice without any goals. This concept is simple: you have to have goals if you want to score goals. Goal Shooting means you will have a clear-cut goal for every shooting drill you practice every day. At the end of your practice, you will have achieved success in each shooting drill simply by reaching a series of mini goals. Goal Shooting is a good way to track your progress, gain confidence, build mental toughness, develop determination, increase shooting concentration and rhythm, and so much more.

When using Goal Shooting every day, you will be making a minimum of ten shots from a given game spot or during a shooting drill. Making ten shots from each spot will be more than adequate. The emphasis is on *making* a specific number of shots, not just taking a certain number of shots or shooting for a certain amount of time. Why is this important? You need to practice success. By making a certain number of shots, you will develop a habit of succeeding while increasing your dedication, determination, and concentration. It will do little good to go out and shoot for thirty to sixty minutes just to practice without tracking your progress.

As you practice for the first time using the shooting principles, mechanics, and mental habits explained in this chapter, do not get discouraged. Recognize that you probably will feel a little awkward at first. This is because these techniques are new, not because they are wrong. Understand the difference. Commit yourself to using these principles and to practicing these drills for five or six days a week for a period of two to three weeks. In a short time, you will see great improvement in your shooting skills, confidence, and accuracy. In one month you will be able to sink one hundred or more shots successfully each day in half the time that it took you on the first day you tried this—guaranteed. If you have a bad day, remember this: you have to have goals if you want to score goals.

IF YOU ARE CONSISTENT IN *HOW* YOU SHOOT THE BALL,

THEN YOU WILL BE CONSISTENT IN *HOW WELL* YOU SHOOT THE BALL.

SCOTISM

◾◾ **TRAINING TIP** _____

Where to Aim When Shooting

There are three targets usually taught by coaches for aiming and shooting the basketball at the rim. The first is the front of the rim. Most coaches suggest that players shoot the ball just over the front of the rim. Second, players are taught to aim at the area just over the front of the rim or in the middle of the rim area. Third, players are taught to aim at the back of the rim.

You have to decide for yourself which target area you are most comfortable with. The first two targets are good, but the third target, the back of the rim, is best. Why? It's simple geometry. If you shoot your shot correctly, you will be putting "follow-through" on your shot, which creates a backspin on the ball. Backspin softens the shot and makes the ball spin backward when it comes in contact with the rim. If you hit the front of the rim with backspin, nine out of ten times the ball will spin backward away from the rim. However, if you aim at the back of the rim and shoot with backspin, nine out of ten times the ball will contact the back of the rim, spin backward, and roll into the basket. Experiment for yourself.

The Short-Shot Principle.   To get into the mental habit of aiming at the back of the rim, use the Short-Shot Principle. To do this, count each basket you make during your shooting practice as one point. Your minimum goal is to make ten shots from each spot you practice from. The Short-Shot Principle works like this. If your goal is to make ten shots from a specific spot or ten of a certain type, you will count each made basket as one point out of ten. Whenever you miss a shot short, to the left or to the right, you will subtract one point from the total you need to make. If you miss a shot long, the score will remain the same because it means you aimed at the correct target, which is the back of the rim. If you make a basket, it counts as one point. Here are some examples of the principle at work:

1. A player has a score of 7 made baskets, shoots the ball, and misses by hitting the back of the rim. NEW SCORE: 7.
2. A player has a score of 0 and misses a shot on the front of the rim (or short of the back of the rim without going in). NEW SCORE: –1.
3. A player has a score of 9. On the next shot, the ball hits the front of the rim but still rolls successfully into the basket. NEW SCORE: 10.
4. A player has a score of 3, shoots the ball, and misses the shot on the left side of the rim. NEW SCORE: 2.

Players will usually miss a shot short because they are aiming at the front of the rim. Shots will miss to the left or right for only one of two reasons: either the feet were not lined up to the rim in a correct Shooting Lane, or the player's elbow was too far out or too far in, rather than directly above the knee to form a straight shooting line to the basket.

Using the Short-Shot Principle when practicing shooting will force you to aim at the back of the rim *all of the time*. It will help you to maintain and correct shooting habits, lines, and angles and to increase your mental toughness. The Short-Shot Principle is a shooting principle, not a shooting drill. It can, however, be incorporated into every shooting drill that you practice. This principle can make you a much more effective, consistent, and disciplined shooter.

The V-Shot Principle.   The V-Shot Principle is also a shooting principle. It involves mechanical movements that players should incorporate into their perimeter shooting drills. Most players practice shooting in one of two ways. They either chase their own rebounds and then dribble out to the perimeter and turn around facing the basket to shoot the ball, or they have someone catch the rebound for them and pass them the ball. Unfortunately, when a player practices alone and retrieves his or her own rebound, almost the only part of the practice that simulates a game situation is the follow-through on the shot. Why? In a game, a player does not dribble out, slowly turn and face the basket, and then shoot the ball at a leisurely pace.

The V-Shot Shooting Principle was designed to help players simulate game situations during practice. The V movement is identical to the process a player experiences when receiving a pass from another player while cutting toward the perimeter area. This single principle encompasses four skills needed in actual game situations. The four skills are as follows:

1. *The jump stop.* A jump stop allows a player to make a strong, controlled stop and prevent traveling. It maintains balance and also allows players to establish a pivot foot with either foot.
2. *Pivot and face the basket.* This movement allows the player to see the entire court. Too many players see only part of the court (and therefore only part of the game) because they never completely face the basket. You can become part of all the action by looking at the entire court every time you touch the ball.
3. *Multiple options.* The V-Shot Principle helps players develop the habit of facing the basket in a triple-threat position with the ball already in the shooting pocket. From this position a player can automatically shoot, pass, or drive.
4. *Follow your shot.* All coaches teach players to follow their shot. Who better knows where the shot is going to go than the shooter? The V-Shot Principle develops this habit for you.

▓▌ TRAINING TIP _____

Which Pivot Foot to Use from the Perimeter?

Which pivot foot to use when facing the basket from the perimeter is an important issue. Let's look at the facts. Of hundreds of coaches surveyed, there were only two justifications for using two different pivot feet. First, it's used to create distance between you and the defender: *two pivot feet allow players to pivot with the outside foot away from the defender. This can be useful to create space against an aggressive tight defense that likes to go chest to chest.* FACT: This tactic gains only one extra second. If a defender is taught to "belly up" chest to chest, that player will still come after you if you create space for a moment. So you have not solved the problem; you have only delayed it by one second.

The second justification is that two pivot feet provide multiple offensive options: *two pivot feet can double players' scoring opportunities.* FACT: Two pivot feet require twice as much practice for a player to become only half as effective. A player and team will achieve more by mastering four to five shots and moves than eight to ten for both feet. Quality practice with sound fundamentals will bring quality results. The principles of the game are simple. If someone bellies up to you defensively, relieve pressure by either dribbling toward a teammate or driving toward the basket. The best way to defeat pressure is by attacking the basket. (For information on how to deal with and score on aggressive defenders, see Chapter 6 on the Triple-Threat Scoring System.)

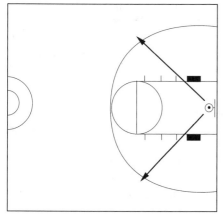

FIGURE 2.16   The V-Shot Principle

The V-Shot Principle is easy to use from any shooting spot on the court. The bottom of the V is always the rim. The top of the V, on both sides of the court, is the spot you choose to practice from (see Figure 2.16). For example, let's say you choose the three-point line wing area. The top of the V would then become each wing on the three-point line, with the bottom of the V being the rim. Continue to work both sides of the V until you have completed your goal of making ten or more shots or points using the Goal-Shooting Principle and the Short-Shot Principle together. Using these shooting principles will make your shooting practices tougher. They will also make you tougher mentally, and that is an added bonus.

(a) The jump stop

(b) Stop on the shoulder pad

FIGURE 2.17   V-Shot Stops

TRAINING TIP

As you practice the V-Shot Principle, it is essential to make two stops (see Figure 2.17):

1. Stop on the jump stop (pivot and face the basket).
2. Stop on the shoulder pad. These stops will improve your balance and shooting mechanics quickly. They will also enable you to read the defender's proximity. If the defender is one arm's length away or closer, pass the ball or drive to the basket. If the defender is two arm's lengths away or more, shoot the ball.

Follow these steps to practice the V-Shot Principle:

THE V-SHOT PRINCIPLE

Begin the drill underneath the rim. Move toward the spot you want to practice from. Pass the ball out away from you putting a reverse spin on it so it will return to you after bouncing.

Make a two-footed jump stop to catch the ball at the spot you want to practice from. You are now at the top of the V.

Pivot on your *left* foot, and face the basket in a triple-threat position with the ball on your right shoulder pad or shooting pocket. (If you are left-handed, always pivot on your *right* foot, and place the ball on your left shoulder pad.)

Stop on the shoulder pad. Read the position of the defender.

Next, shoot the ball and follow your shot to the bottom of the V or rim, get the rebound, and go to the other side of the floor or V. Repeat the process until you have successfully made a minimum of ten shots. It's that simple.

Remember: If the defender is one arm's length away, you would drive to the basket. If the defender is two arm's lengths away or more, shoot the ball.

Practicing Top of the Key and Baseline Shots

What about practicing shots from the top of the key or baseline? No problem. We use the same drills, mechanics, and principles. To practice from the top of the key, you simply practice a straight V (see Figure 2.18). A straight V simply means you are choosing a game spot at the top of the key and going back and forth in a straight line repeatedly.

To practice shots from the baseline, use a flat V (see Figure 2.19). Use the same six steps, just a different location—the baseline. Being able to shoot effectively from any of these perimeter areas means you are prepared to shoot from any position on the court.

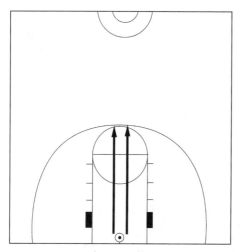

FIGURE 2.18   The Straight V

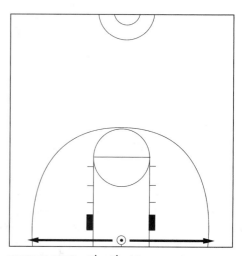

FIGURE 2.19   The Flat V

SHOOTING DRILLS

Perimeter Shooting Drills

Perimeter shots are those whose range extends anywhere past the foul line perimeter area by 12–15 feet or more. Picture an imaginary dotted half-circle at the offensive end of the court (see Figure 2.20). A player's perimeter area is the area farthest from the basket from which he or she can shoot the basketball with consistency (that is, with 40 percent accuracy or better). Perimeter shots can be jump shots or set shots, depending on the preference and abilities of the individual player. All players should develop good perimeter shooting skills.

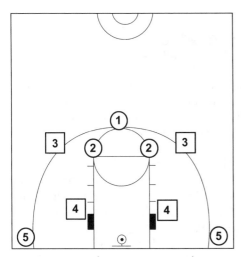

FIGURE 2.20   The Five Perimeter Shots

As shown in Figure 2.20, there are five basic perimeter shots to practice for game situations: (1) shots straight away from the rim (all other perimeter shots will have two spots—one on each side of the court), (2) foul line corner shots, (3) wing shots, (4) bank shots, which are banked in off the backboard, and (5) baseline shots. *Note:* bank shots are usually not good shots from outside the three-point line because players seldom practice from that spot; however from 15 feet and closer, a bank shot is a higher-percentage shot from this angle.

When practicing perimeter shots, make a minimum of ten shots each day using the Short-Shot Principle. Also use the V-Shot Principle when practicing shooting. It will help you obtain greater shooting consistency. You can and should practice shot variations from each game spot: the catch and shoot; jab, step back and shoot; shot out of triple threat, jump shot off the dribble, and so on.

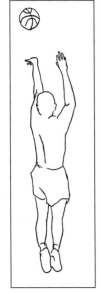

FIGURE 2.21
A Jump Shot

> **TRAINING TIP** _____
>
> For an extra challenge, after making at least ten shots or points from each spot using the Goal-Shooting Principle, try making three shots in a row, and later four or five in a row, before moving on to your next shooting spot or drill.

Jump Shot Drills

Several variations of shots are considered jump shots (see Figure 2.21). There are jump shots on the fast break, jump shots off the dribble, jump shots from a triple-threat position, jump shots out of a catch and shoot, and jump shots coming off screens. Listed next are several drills that will give you the ability and skill to use a jump shot in any game situation.

> **TRAINING TIP** _____
>
> When shooting a jump shot, always try to release or shoot your shot on the way up as you are reaching the top of your jump, *not* on the way down. This will make your shot quicker and stronger as well as harder to block.

The Catch and Shoot.   The catch and shoot is a jump-shooting skill seldom used at the beginning levels or often even at the high school levels of basketball. However, it is a vital skill, especially at the college and professional levels. The catch and shoot allows a player to release the shot within one second of catching a pass. It is virtually impossible for a defender to block it. The catch and shoot is a zone buster. This means you can use it effectively and quickly against any zone defense. It will allow you to shoot the ball one full second faster than you could a set shot and not allow the defense enough time to recover. It is a shot that is taken in rhythm, so once learned, it is easy to use.

Like all shooting skills, the catch and shoot requires practice. It is one of the most effective and valuable shooting skills you can develop as a perimeter and three-point shooter. This shot is also extremely effective when playing against zone defenses. To learn how to catch and shoot, begin by practicing the technique close to the basket until you are comfortable with the shot.

Begin practicing the mechanics of the catch and shoot at the bottom of the circle below the foul line. Shoot the ball on the way up on your jump to keep from pushing the ball toward the basket. Pushing the ball typically happens when a player shoots the ball on the way down. Once you become proficient with the catch and shoot from close range (see Figure 2.22), extend your range back to the foul line corners and then past the three-point line. Always begin practicing the catch and shoot by making at least ten shots close to the basket. The catch and shoot can also be used in fast-break situations.

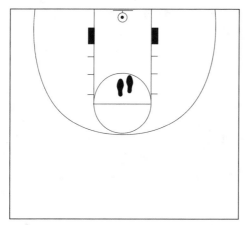

FIGURE 2.22   Location for Practicing the Catch and Shoot at Close Range

Follow this procedure to practice the catch and shoot:

THE CATCH AND SHOOT

1
Pass to yourself by spinning the ball backward, or have someone pass the ball to you.

2
Have your hands ready to receive the ball. Simply catch it while you are jumping in the air so that you land with both feet in a jump stop and automatically recoil, quickly springing back up into the air for a jump shot.

3
Shoot the ball on the way up on your jump shot for greater strength and accuracy.

When catching the ball, make sure you square your shoulders to the rim as you shoot.

Jump Shot Off the Dribble, to the Right.   Another important type of jump shot is the jump shot off the dribble. This shot is used to maneuver past a defender to a clear spot on the floor for an open shot. To perform jump shots off the dribble, to the right, follow these steps:

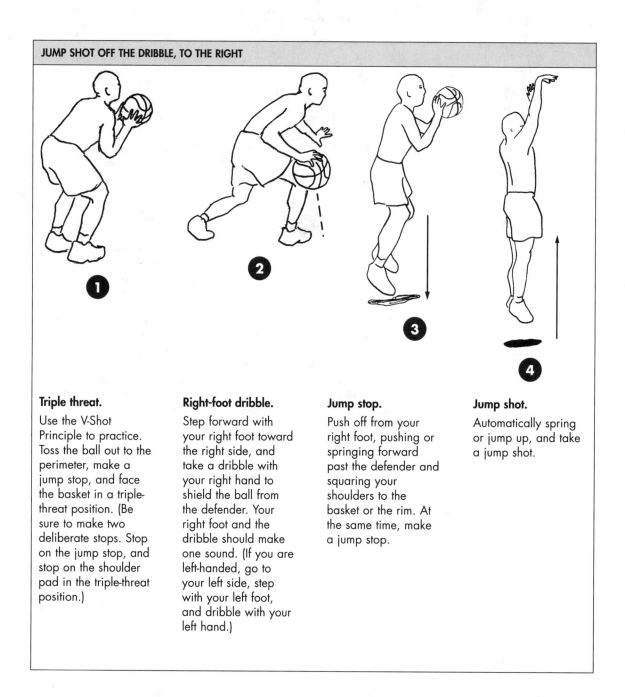

JUMP SHOT OFF THE DRIBBLE, TO THE RIGHT

Triple threat.

Use the V-Shot Principle to practice. Toss the ball out to the perimeter, make a jump stop, and face the basket in a triple-threat position. (Be sure to make two deliberate stops. Stop on the jump stop, and stop on the shoulder pad in the triple-threat position.)

Right-foot dribble.

Step forward with your right foot toward the right side, and take a dribble with your right hand to shield the ball from the defender. Your right foot and the dribble should make one sound. (If you are left-handed, go to your left side, step with your left foot, and dribble with your left hand.)

Jump stop.

Push off from your right foot, pushing or springing forward past the defender and squaring your shoulders to the basket or the rim. At the same time, make a jump stop.

Jump shot.

Automatically spring or jump up, and take a jump shot.

When Losing Hurts Enough to Make You Go and Practice,

Then You Know You're a Player.

Jump Shot Off the Dribble, to the Left.   To perform jump shots off the dribble to the left, follow these steps:

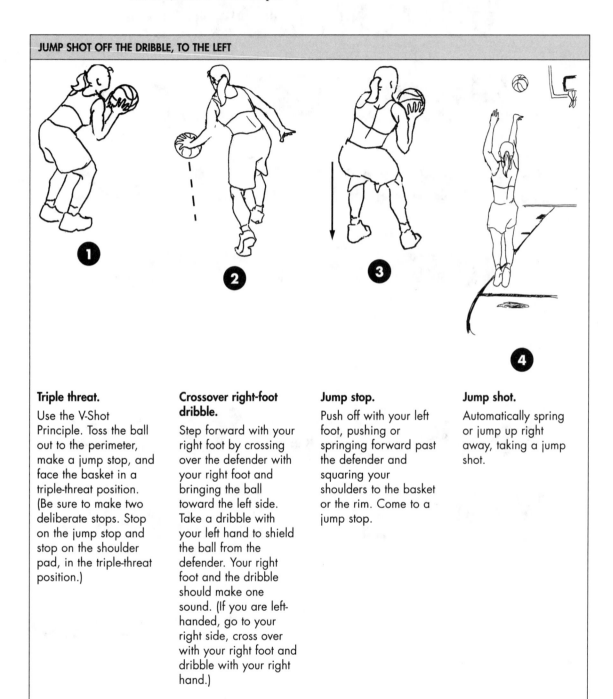

JUMP SHOT OFF THE DRIBBLE, TO THE LEFT

Triple threat.

Use the V-Shot Principle. Toss the ball out to the perimeter, make a jump stop, and face the basket in a triple-threat position. (Be sure to make two deliberate stops. Stop on the jump stop and stop on the shoulder pad, in the triple-threat position.)

Crossover right-foot dribble.

Step forward with your right foot by crossing over the defender with your right foot and bringing the ball toward the left side. Take a dribble with your left hand to shield the ball from the defender. Your right foot and the dribble should make one sound. (If you are left-handed, go to your right side, cross over with your right foot and dribble with your right hand.)

Jump stop.

Push off with your left foot, pushing or springing forward past the defender and squaring your shoulders to the basket or the rim. Come to a jump stop.

Jump shot.

Automatically spring or jump up right away, taking a jump shot.

Shot Faking.   You will want to add a shot fake to your repertoire of jump shot routines. A shot fake draws a defender toward you to get him or her off balance so that you can gain advantage for a better shooting position. You can also use this as a defender is aggressively running toward you if you are not comfortable with the time or distance you have to take a clean shot.

To shot fake, make sure the ball comes above the shoulder pad and ear on the fake. You must "sell" the defender on the idea that you are going to shoot the ball. To practice good mechanics, stand in front of a mirror and practice twenty-five repetitions to see yourself do the fake the correct way (see Figure 2.23).

(a) Correct position   (b) Incorrect position

FIGURE 2.23   Faking a Jump Shot

Use these steps to practice shot fakes:

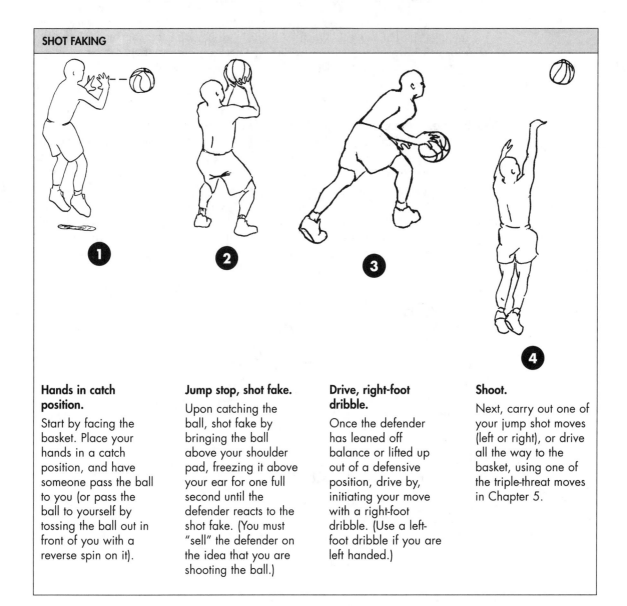

SHOT FAKING

Hands in catch position.

Start by facing the basket. Place your hands in a catch position, and have someone pass the ball to you (or pass the ball to yourself by tossing the ball out in front of you with a reverse spin on it).

Jump stop, shot fake.

Upon catching the ball, shot fake by bringing the ball above your shoulder pad, freezing it above your ear for one full second until the defender reacts to the shot fake. (You must "sell" the defender on the idea that you are shooting the ball.)

Drive, right-foot dribble.

Once the defender has leaned off balance or lifted up out of a defensive position, drive by, initiating your move with a right-foot dribble. (Use a left-foot dribble if you are left handed.)

Shoot.

Next, carry out one of your jump shot moves (left or right), or drive all the way to the basket, using one of the triple-threat moves in Chapter 5.

Low-Post Shooting Drills

Having the ability to shoot the ball in the low-post area is important for every player. For low-post players it is vital. In many shots taken in and around the low-post areas, a player's front side is not squared to the rim in order to use the body as a shield against defenders. Next we discuss several fundamentally sound and easy-to-use low-post shooting drills.

The Drop-Step Move. This is an excellent offensive move for players in the low-post area. In offensive basketball the court is divided into two post areas, a low post and a high post (see Figure 2.24). A low-post player is usually one of the taller players on the team and typically plays close to the basket. Such players often are positioned with their backs to the basket when in the low-post area, but may also play up around the high-post areas.

The drop-step moves involve both footwork and shooting choreography. To practice the drop step, stand to the side of the lane above the first hash mark closest to the baseline. Hold the ball under your chin in a Power Pocket Position so it cannot be stolen from you (see Figure 2.25). In this position, you can make a drop-step move to either side, depending upon which side your defender is playing. If the defender plays on your right side, drop-step to the left. If the defender plays on your left side, drop-step to the right. Practice from both sides of the foul lane so you'll be comfortable all around the basket.

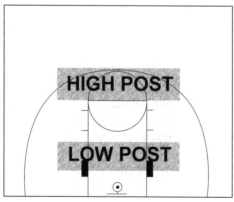

FIGURE 2.24 Low-Post and High-Post Areas

FIGURE 2.25 The Power Pocket Position

▌ TRAINING TIP _____

When setting up position in the low-post area, try to stand where your two feet split the second hash mark. This will give you room to go both to the baseline and to the middle of the lane. If you post on the block when going for the baseline, the backboard will serve as a second defender.

Drop Step to the Left. To perform a drop step to the left in the low-post area, do the following:

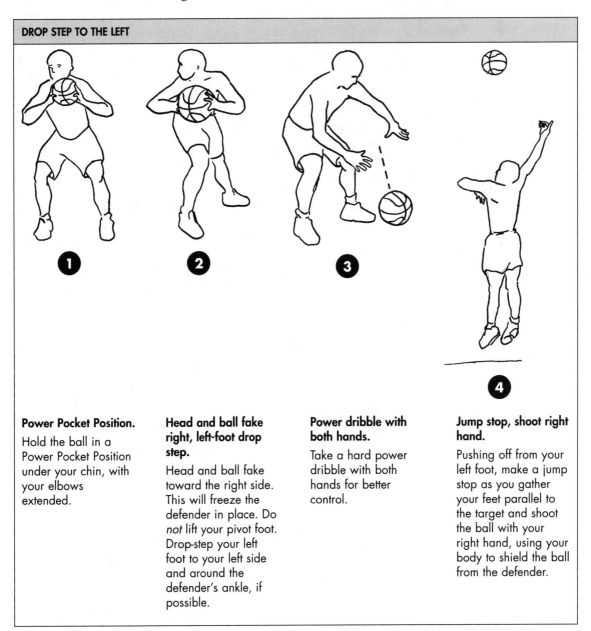

DROP STEP TO THE LEFT

①

Power Pocket Position.

Hold the ball in a Power Pocket Position under your chin, with your elbows extended.

②

Head and ball fake right, left-foot drop step.

Head and ball fake toward the right side. This will freeze the defender in place. Do *not* lift your pivot foot. Drop-step your left foot to your left side and around the defender's ankle, if possible.

③

Power dribble with both hands.

Take a hard power dribble with both hands for better control.

④

Jump stop, shoot right hand.

Pushing off from your left foot, make a jump stop as you gather your feet parallel to the target and shoot the ball with your right hand, using your body to shield the ball from the defender.

Make ten shots, then practice a drop step to the right, going in the opposite direction but on the same side of the court.

Drop Step to the Right. To perform a drop step to the right in the low-post area, do the following:

DROP STEP TO THE RIGHT

Power Pocket Position.

Hold the ball in the Power Pocket Position, with your elbows extended.

Head and ball fake left, right-foot drop step.

Head and ball fake toward the left side. This will freeze the defender in place. Do *not* lift your feet. Drop-step your right foot to your right side and around the defender's ankle, if possible.

Power dribble with both hands.

Take a hard power dribble with both hands for better control at the same time that you lift your left foot to avoid traveling. This is *not* a double dribble.

Jump stop, shoot left hand.

Pushing off with your left foot, make a jump stop on both feet as you gather yourself parallel to the target. Shoot the ball with your left hand, using your body to shield the ball from the defender.

▌▌ TRAINING TIP

Every day, practice on a different side of the lane. This will enable you to be effective from both sides of the court. In a game, the direction you pivot in will always be to the side opposite that a defender is playing. You may want to use a chair to represent a defensive player as you practice.

The Mikan Drill

George Mikan, a former NBA legend, all-star, and member of the Basketball Hall of Fame, made this drill popular. It is a simple hook shot drill, close to the basket. This drill will also help you to develop excellent footwork for layups and reverse layups. All players at any position should practice this drill every day; it only takes a few minutes but is an invaluable tool close to the basket.

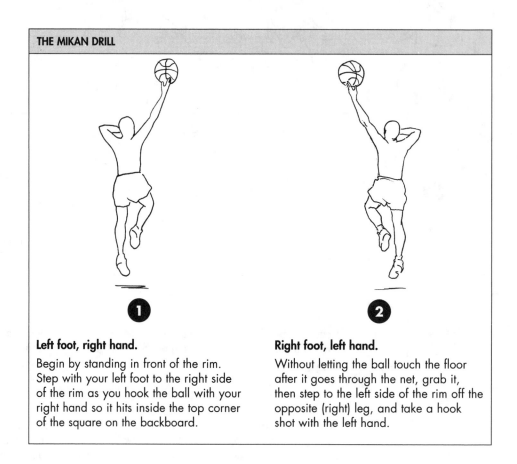

THE MIKAN DRILL

①

②

Left foot, right hand.

Begin by standing in front of the rim. Step with your left foot to the right side of the rim as you hook the ball with your right hand so it hits inside the top corner of the square on the backboard.

Right foot, left hand.

Without letting the ball touch the floor after it goes through the net, grab it, then step to the left side of the rim off the opposite (right) leg, and take a hook shot with the left hand.

Repeat the drill in a continuous motion, moving "left foot, right hand; right foot, left hand," repeating the same footwork without stopping until you have made ten successful shots each day. Do not let the ball touch the ground, and do not dribble the ball while doing this drill.

▌ TRAINING TIP _____

The Mikan drill is excellent to use when learning to practice reverse layups. Simply start on the second hash mark up from the baseline, facing the basket. Use the same mechanics and footwork as in the three-step layup, except on your last step, go under the rim and shoot the ball with your opposite hand off the backboard. If you start on the left side, you will shoot a reverse right-handed layup. If you start on the second hash mark on the right side, you will shoot a reverse left-handed layup.

Hook Shot Drills

The hook shot was commonly used by players in the 1940s through the 1960s. In fact, it was the number one offensive weapon of Kareem Abdul-Jabbar when he played in the 1970s, 1980s, and 1990s. Jabbar is the NBA's all-time leading scorer in history, with 38,387 points and an NBA career scoring average of 24.6 points per game.

The hook shot has become a lost art in the midst of slam-dunks and three-point shots. It is a great shot for any player to learn. It is extremely difficult to defend and almost impossible to block. It is a great weapon to use when playing against taller players as well. If mastered, the hook shot can be as valuable to a low-post player as a three-point shot is to a perimeter player. The shot basically finishes in the same way as the Mikan drill but from farther away, and therefore it requires more practice (see Figure 2.26).

Each day, alternate the side of the court from which you shoot hook shots. This move is not simply a shot; it also involves choreographic movement and footwork, just like dancing. Unless you are willing to practice this shot hundreds and even thousands of times, you will not perform it well. If you practice it a little each day, it will become second nature to you over time and easier to perform.

FIGURE 2.26 The Hook Shot

Right-Handed Hook Shot.   To execute a right-handed hook shot, perform the following steps:

RIGHT-HANDED HOOK SHOT

Power Pocket Position.

Post up on the second hash mark in the lane, holding the ball in the Power Pocket Position. Pretend you just received the ball from a teammate.

Head and ball fake right.

Head and ball fake to the right to move or unbalance the defender.

Left-foot drop step, right-hand dribble.

Move to your right, taking a dribble with your right hand and stepping with your left foot. The foot and the dribble should be done simultaneously and make one sound.

Right-foot shoulder pad.

Take the next step on your right foot without a dribble as you bring the ball up toward your right shoulder pad.

Left-foot step, right-hand hook shot.

Take your last step (left foot), and take a hook shot with your right hand. In the same motion extend your left arm toward the defensive player to protect your shot. This stage must be done in one motion.

Left-Handed Hook Shot.   To execute a right-handed hook shot, perform the following steps:

LEFT-HANDED HOOK SHOT

Power Pocket Position.

Post up on the second hash mark in the lane, holding the ball in the Power Pocket Position. Pretend you just received the ball from a teammate.

❶

Head and ball fake left.

Head and ball fake to the left to move or unbalance the defender.

❷

Right-foot drop step, left-hand dribble.

Move to your left, taking a dribble with your left hand and stepping with your right foot. The foot and the dribble should be done simultaneously and make one sound.

❸

Left-foot shoulder pad.

Take the next step on your left foot without a dribble as you bring the ball up toward your left shoulder pad.

❹

Right-foot step, left-hand hook shot.

Take your last step (right foot), and take a hook shot with your left hand. In the same motion, extend your right arm toward the defensive player to protect your shot. This stage must be done in one motion.

❺

DEVELOPING CONFIDENCE IN YOUR SHOOTING SKILLS

Shooting is the most important skill to master in basketball. The name of the game is putting the ball in the basket. Anything that you practice on an individual or team basis is oriented toward getting possession of the ball and scoring points. Many of the skills of basketball, such as rebounding, defense, passing, and cutting, are called "habit skills." Once you have mastered them, you no longer have to practice them regularly because they have become a habit. Habit skills require only the use of the muscle known as memory to tell your body when and how to perform the necessary skill. That is why, before basketball games at every level, you do not see players spending 75 percent of their warm-up time in practicing rebounding, passing, or defense. They practice shooting! Confidence in performing habit skills comes from knowing when and how to perform the skills correctly. Confidence, success, and consistency in shooting a basketball can come only from a combination of two things:

1. Regular practice.
2. Proper execution of correct shooting techniques and mechanics.

Shooting is not only a skill but an art. To shoot a basketball well requires use of your motor memory, confidence, motor skills, and a basketball. Anyone can learn how to shoot a basketball correctly. But to shoot with proper technique, confidence, consistency, and accuracy in a game under pressure—this is an art, and it requires regular practice.

Concert pianists practice for hours every day. Singers, entertainers, artists, and professionals of all kinds have all developed a repertoire of skills. But if they do not practice, they will not perform well. Millions of people know how to play a piano but cannot perform in front of a large audience. They have knowledge, but they are not proficient in the *art* of playing the piano. If you had practiced a song hundreds of times a week for two months, would you be more willing to play in public? Yes, you would. With your skill and knowledge, you would have added art and confidence in performing through your consistent practice.

This principle applies to shooting a basketball. How many basketball players have you seen hesitate to take an easy shot in a game? How many hesitate to take a last-second game-winning shot? They know how to shoot, and they have made those shots in practice, so why do they hesitate? The answer is simple: they have not developed the *art* of shooting a basketball. Developing the art of shooting in game situations comes from regular practice and correct repetition of proper technique to shoot well.

There are five fundamental shots all players should learn and master. All five will prepare any player for a whole range of game situations:

1. Layup shot (right- and left-handed).
2. Mikan hook shot (close to the basket with both hands).
3. Foul shot out of a triple-threat position (this also simulates game shot mechanics).

4. A regular shot or jump shot from the triple-threat position.
5. The catch and shoot (a jump shot from a catch position).

Tips to Increase Your Shooting Percentage

If you take the time to study shooting fundamentals and techniques in great detail, two things will become apparent very quickly. First, good teams have lost games because players got rushed into taking too many shots prematurely when, with a little bit of patience, a better opportunity would have presented itself. As a player, live by this rule: *the only good shot is an open shot.* Learn to get yourself open for good shot opportunities and to make moves that free you of a defender so you can get an open shot. Take open shots whenever possible.

Second, do not be afraid to shoot the ball. The best players in the world only shoot 50 percent from the field in game situations (this includes layups and field goal attempts that do not count when fouled on a shot attempt). Actually, 45 percent is a more realistic percentage for the average player, even in the pros. This means players fail more often then they succeed. The best way to increase your shooting percentage is to practice shooting—a lot of shooting on a regular basis. Here is a helpful principle: *practice leads to confidence. Confidence leads to success. Success leads to more confidence, and the cycle goes on and on.*

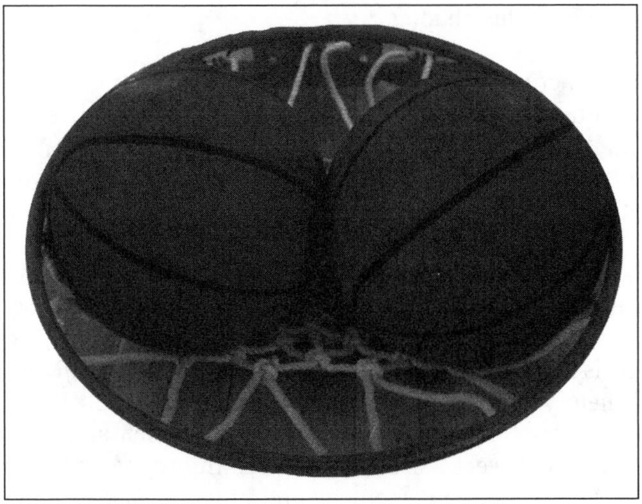

The more of anything you do in life, the more confidence you will have in doing it. If you are confident with playing the piano, working on the computer, or shooting a basketball, you will be successful at it. Consistent practice is vital. Define what and how you will practice. The drills you practice will depend upon what positions you play: center, forward, or guard. It will do little good for guards to spend a lot of time practicing shots close to the basket or for centers to spend most of their time shooting 20-foot perimeter shots. Practice what you will need and use in game situations.

FIGURE 2.27   Two Basketballs in a Rim

▊▊▋ TRAINING TIP

To see how easy it is to make a basket, look at how big the rim actually is. You can fit two balls through the rim at the same time (see Figure 2.27). The moral is, never pass up a shot-portunity.

A shot-portunity is when an offensive player has a wide-open shot for which the player has a 45 percent success rate or higher. In such cases, he or she should take the shot!

Since centers and power forwards spend most of their game time close to the basket, they should spend most of their time in shooting practice close to the basket. A good ratio would be 60 percent of shots around the basket and 40 percent away from the basket, for times when they need to play in a high-post area. These percentages are similar to those of game situations.

Small forwards are required to perform well both inside and outside. It is recommended that such players break down practice time, spending 75 percent on outside shooting and 25 percent on inside moves and shooting. Guards should focus heavily on perimeter shooting since that is where they will spend most of their time. A ratio of 90 percent of perimeter shooting and 10 percent of inside shooting drills is a good ratio for shooting guards and point guards. A few daily repetitions of interior shots for a guard will be enough to develop the mental and physical habits and skills to succeed close to the basket when needed.

Remember to practice where you will be playing. Too many post players want to spend their practice time outside when their coach will never let them play from that area in game situations, and the same is true of guards wanting to play inside. And unless you can make (not take) two or three three-point shots a game consistently, a coach doesn't care if you can hit one occasionally as a center or power forward. Your coach will need and want some inside scoring.

Follow these rules to maximize the effectiveness of your practice. They summarize many of the points made in this chapter.

Five Rules for Shooting Practice

1. *Warm up properly.* Warm up to shoot, and do not shoot to warm up. Use the Five-Spot Warm-Up Drill.
2. *Practice success.* Make a specific number of shots for each shooting drill you do. Use the Goal-Shooting Principle when you practice to achieve success on each drill.
3. *Shoot the ball consistently.* Shoot the ball the same way every time. Use correct shooting lines, lanes, and angles. If you are consistent in how you shoot the ball, you will be consistent in how well you shoot the ball.
4. *Rest on free throws.* This is a great way to rest in between shooting drills. Make five in a row. This will help you learn to concentrate on the foul shot. It will also allow you to practice free throws when you are tired, which simulates game situations. At least once a week, also take ten free throws at a time in between drills and track your shooting percentage and progress. Take a minimum of one hundred total free throws during your practice.
5. *Practice sound shooting principles.* Use principles such as the Short-Shot Principle, the Goal-Shooting Principle, and the V-Shot Principle to create game situations and habits during your shooting practice.

COACHES' CHALK TALK: TEAM SHOOTING

As a coach in a team setting, you can practice shooting drills in several different ways:

1. *Have players practice individually.* Set 8–10 minutes on the clock in practice. Have your players use the V-Shot Principle during shooting drills to practice game shots from all areas of the court. This will best simulate game situations. You will be surprised at the results by simply requiring that your players make shots in sets of ten for several different game shots. It really does bring game pressure, game situations, and game results.
2. *Have two players use one ball.* Player A rebounds and player B shoots. Do not switch until B makes 10 shots; otherwise, it will be difficult for B to develop a good shooting rhythm or "feel" from the practice spot. After B makes ten shots, B rebounds and A shoots. Then the players move to the next practice spot (see Figure 2.28).
3. *Have three players use two balls.* Player A shoots ball 1; player B rebounds and passes to player C; C passes ball 2 to A, then receives ball 1 from B. Keep this going until A makes 10 to 20 shots. Then the three players rotate. This is the fastest way to get numerous repetitions when doing shooting drills in a team practice (see Figure 2.29).

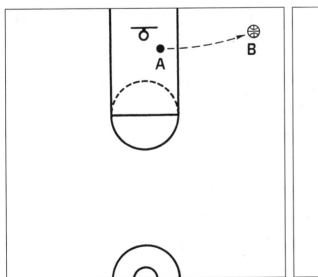

FIGURE 2.28 Two-Player Drill with One Ball

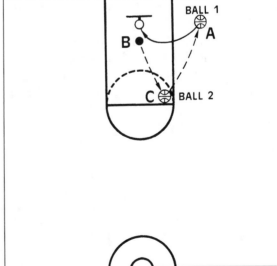

FIGURE 2.29 Three-Player Drill with Two Balls

It is better to have players make a specific number of shots. This will make them concentrate more and put a little pressure on them not to slow down the other players. If they are allowed to shoot for three to five minutes, often they will not work hard or have time to develop a shooting rhythm.

The drills you use as a player or coach to fulfill your needs are up to you. Whatever you do, however, keep this thought in mind: quality time is more valuable than quantity time. You are better off practicing so that you become excellent in a few areas rather than average in many. Thirty minutes of practicing specific drills is more valuable than two hours of "just shooting" or playing in uncompetitive scrimmages. Too many players go to the gym to shoot and spend one to two hours taking trick shots or playing in pick-up games against lesser competition. You will gain more and go farther if you spend one or two hours a day practicing specific drills for shooting and other areas of your game at full intensity and with a purpose.

If you want to develop the *art* of shooting or any other skill in basketball, spend quality time. Be willing to do what the unsuccessful basketball player is not willing to do—practice with a specific purpose.

CHAPTER QUESTIONS

1. List the four essential elements involved in proper shooting fundamentals.

2. Including the reverse layup, how many different variations of a layup are there? List each one.

3. Explain three benefits of the Five-Spot Warm-Up Drill.

4. Describe how the V-Shot Movement simulates game situations when you practice.

5. What is the purpose of using the Goal-Shooting Principle when practicing, and how will it help?

6. Explain how the Short-Shot Principle works.

7. What are the two offensive post areas of the court, and where are they located?

8. Where should a player aim when shooting the ball, and why?

9. How can a player and team increase their shooting percentages?

10. What are the five rules to follow when practicing shooting?

Foul-Shooting Fundamentals

IN THIS CHAPTER YOU WILL LEARN:
- Proper techniques and shooting mechanics for greater success at the foul line
- Ten common mistakes made by players when shooting free throws
- The value of good free-throw shooting to players and teams
- Correct mental mechanics and habits of foul shooting
- The three stages involved in shooting free throws correctly for greater consistency and success
- How to hit pressure free throws when a game is on the line
- The secrets to becoming a 90 percent free-throw shooter
- Foul-shooting progression chart, standards, records, and tips

THE IMPORTANCE OF FREE-THROW SHOOTING

"Free throw"—that is what the shot is called, and it is free. Yet most players at all levels fail to take advantage of the free-throw opportunity. Any player who works on and develops good shooting technique and mechanics can be a good free-throw shooter. Anyone.

But there is much more involved in free-throw shooting than just taking the shot. It involves both physical technique and mental mechanics. Having a sound shooting technique and shooting routine is important, but they are only two-thirds of the puzzle. A mental technique for concentrating on the mechanics of the shot instead of the many distractions of a game situation is equally important.

The key to successful foul shooting is combining physical and mental techniques in consistent practice. Practice means repetition. And you must practice not just free throws, but free-throw-shooting technique while simulating game situations. Statistics verify that most athletes will shoot 70 percent or less most of the time from the free-throw line at the high school and college levels of basketball. In fact, even most pro teams typically achieve a success rate lower than 75 percent, and they are supposed to be the best in the world. During a regular season, fewer than 1 percent of players at every level, including the pros, succeed at shooting 90 percent or better from the free-throw line. And on the average, a high school or college team will lose two or three games each season because, as a team, they missed 30 percent or more of shots taken from the line. Did you also know most players at every level could raise their scoring average by up to two full points per game if they achieved an 80 percent success rate from the free-throw line? For example, if you currently average fifteen points a game but make only 60 percent or fewer of your shots from the foul line, you could boost your average to seventeen points a game or more by shooting free throws better. That is a big difference.

Too many players underestimate the power of the foul line over the course of a game and a season. One year while I was coaching in high school, my team's star player averaged eighteen points per game but achieved only 64 percent from the line. Because he was frequently fouled and shooting a lot of free throws, he could have averaged twenty-one points per game if he had shot 80 percent or better from the free-throw line. He could have done this by practicing free throws daily. This might have significantly affected his career. He went on to play college basketball but did not get as much recruiting attention as he had hoped for because his statistics, both in scoring and free-throw shooting, were not high enough. College coaches study all of a player's statistics.

Not only would more practice have helped the star player, but also the team would have won two additional games that season just from improved free-throw shooting, and this difference would have provided a chance for the conference championship. To be fair, that player was not to blame that the team did not win the championship that year; in fact, without him the team would not have even had a chance. But, with better free-throw shooting, they may have taken home a title.

As a coach, try to have all of your players shoot a free-throw shot in the same way. (However, if a player can already shoot successfully over 80 percent in games from the line, leave that player alone!) Usually, all players should learn to shoot free throws in the same way. The techniques in this chapter have proved to be consistently effective over the years. Listed next is a simple but effective breakdown of what it takes to shoot free throws at a higher level. Each stage of foul shooting will be explained one step at a time.

TEN COMMON MISTAKES IN SHOOTING FREE THROWS

- The shooting foot, knee, elbow, arm, and ball are not in a straight line to the middle of the rim.
- The shooter's knees are not bent, but straight and stiff.
- The ball is pushed forward on the shot, not shot in an arc toward the front of the rim.
- The shooter does not put backspin on the ball or follow through on the shot.
- The shooter's eyes follow the flight of the ball and do not stay focused on the back of the rim.
- The shooter has poor habits, or no habits, of mental concentration and thinks about something other than shooting the free throw.
- The shooter does not practice enough foul shots to be confident at shooting free throws.
- The shooter has not developed a pre-shot routine to follow when taking free throws.
- The shooter has not practiced shooting free throws when tired or fatigued.
- The shooter does not value the importance of a free throw in the early or middle part of the game.

▌ TRAINING TIP

Think about these facts as you decide on how much free-throw practice you need and the importance of such practice.

1. A player's game free-throw percentage typically averages from 10 to 15 percent lower than the percentage achieved in shooting practice.
2. The higher a free-throw percentage you shoot from the free-throw line in a game, the lower the differential percentage is between practice free-throw percentages and game free-throw percentages. Practice makes a difference.

THE THREE STAGES OF FOUL-SHOOTING DEVELOPMENT

Stage 1: Learn Proper Shooting Mechanics

To shoot 60 percent or higher from the free-throw line, a player must have basic proper shooting mechanics and form. Most basketball players attain this basic level. For greater success, you must adjust your technique and shooting rhythm, and work at it. A basic and effective guideline for shooting free throws is the BEEF principle, which involves four specific mechanics. Take time to develop all four shooting mechanics of BEEF. They promote a more consistent shot and greater confidence.

Technique + Consistency = Success.

THE BEEF PRINCIPLE

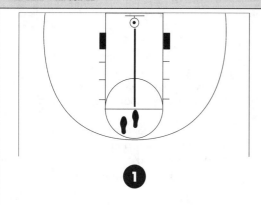

1

2

B—Balance/Bend Your Knees.

For proper balance, stand with your feet shoulders' width apart. A wider foot stance will take strength away from your shot, making most shots too short. If your foot stance is too narrow, your body may lean to the left or right as you shoot, causing you to miss the shot off to the side. Place your shooting foot (the right foot if you are right-handed) at the center of the foul line, making an imaginary straight line from the back of the rim to your shooting arm. (**Tip:** Almost every free-throw line has a nail hole directly at the center of the foul line to help you line up with the middle of the rim.) You can place your feet parallel along the foul line or bring your non-shooting foot slightly behind your shooting foot, as shown in the illustration. Decide which foot position is most comfortable for you. In either position, your shooting foot should line up with the middle of the rim.

Placing the shooting foot slightly in front of the nonshooting foot allows you to shoot the ball with the entire right side of your body (if you are right-handed) without turning your shoulders sideways.

E—Elbow In.

Tuck your elbow in before shooting so that it is directly above your knee and directly below the ball. Toe, knee, elbow, shoulder, and ball should all be in a straight line pointing to the middle of the rim. The shortest distance between two points is a straight line. By tucking your elbow in, you will eliminate many misses. You should never miss a shot to the left or to the right side of the rim. If you miss a free throw, always miss it straight and long.

Knowing this will also help your teammates. If you miss a shot, the ball will come off the rim straight and not to the side. If they do not know, tell them about this. It may be worth an extra four to six points for your team each game, especially if all of your teammates shoot with proper mechanics every time.

THE BEEF PRINCIPLE *(continued)*

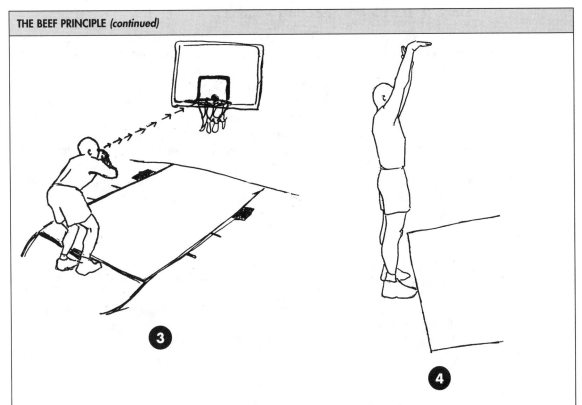

E—Eyes on the Target.

Your visual focus and concentration should be centered on the middle hook on the back of the rim. *Never* follow the flight of the ball with your eyes. Always stay focused on the rim and see the shot through the net.

F—Follow Through.

Always put proper rotation and backspin on the ball. A good follow-through will soften (not shorten) your shot and give the ball a greater chance of going in. If you have trouble developing a good follow-through, review the chapter on shooting and work on the Five-Spot Warm-Up Drill each day. Also talk to your coach and get some additional drills that may help.

Stage 2: Develop a Shooting Routine

All players should develop a pattern or routine to use when shooting free throws and then stick with it. Some players wipe perspiration from the forehead; others like to take two or three dribbles. Some wipe their shoes off and still others spin the ball or take a few deep breaths before shooting. Although the routine itself seldom has any effect on the actual mechanical shot, it does have an effect on the mind-set, which you established during practice.

Whatever you use as a routine, do it the same way every time, both in practice and in games. At the end of the routine, make sure that you take a deep breath before executing the shot. Using a set routine will also help make your shot easier and more routine in games. Remember, if you are consistent in *how* you shoot the ball, you will also become consistent in *how well* you shoot the ball.

▮▮▮ TRAINING TIP _____

When learning to shoot using new routines and mechanics, recognize that the new habits will feel somewhat awkward and different at first. This is because the routine, mechanics, and habits are new, *not wrong*. Understand the difference.

Stage 3: Use Mental Concentration

This simply means to think certain thoughts or words as you shoot. Better yet, actually say the words in your head while you are shooting. It is a form of self-talk that allows your mind and body to communicate and work together in order to make a successful shot. It will help you focus only on the shot. Larry Bird, who every year was one of the NBA league leaders in free-throw-shooting percentage, always said "nothing but net" to himself as he was shooting the free throw. The verbal self-communication frees the mind of all other thoughts. Don't repeat to yourself the taunts of the crowd or the opposing players as you shoot. Don't think about cheerleaders, parents, the score of the game, or that "I have to make this shot." None of these thoughts will help you make your free throw.

What you think about is exactly what you will get, good or bad, whether you are shooting a bonus one-on-one situation or a game-winning (or -losing) foul shot, or even if you are up by twenty points. If you do not concentrate on shooting the free throw, it usually will not go in. Numerous distractions can occur when you shoot a foul shot; if you think about them instead of about the shot itself, you are not concentrating. A shooter must learn to block out all noises and distractions. Engaging in verbal commands and self-talk about the shot itself is the only way this can be done. So how does it work?

PRACTICE
IS
REPETITION.

SCOTISM

Come up with words to think about as you shoot—words that will help you concentrate on your shot, and only your shot. Use key words related to the mechanics and routine for the shot itself. For example, "Elbow in, bend, follow through." Say these five words as you execute the mechanics of the shot, as follows.

ELBOW IN, BEND, FOLLOW THROUGH

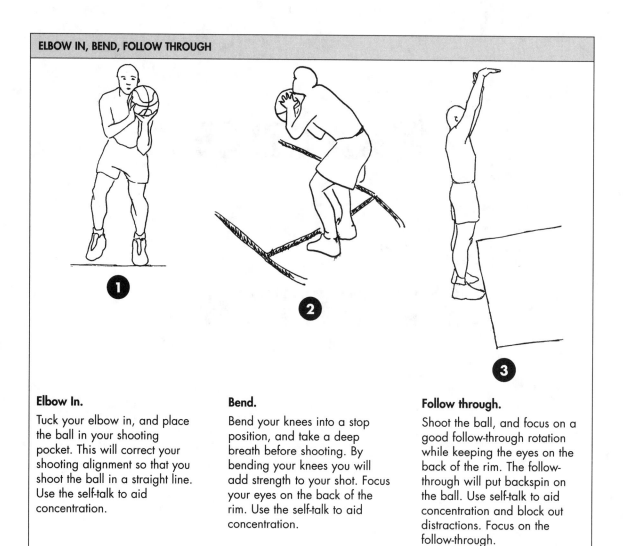

Elbow In.

Tuck your elbow in, and place the ball in your shooting pocket. This will correct your shooting alignment so that you shoot the ball in a straight line. Use the self-talk to aid concentration.

Bend.

Bend your knees into a stop position, and take a deep breath before shooting. By bending your knees you will add strength to your shot. Focus your eyes on the back of the rim. Use the self-talk to aid concentration.

Follow through.

Shoot the ball, and focus on a good follow-through rotation while keeping the eyes on the back of the rim. The follow-through will put backspin on the ball. Use self-talk to aid concentration and block out distractions. Focus on the follow-through.

Why is it important to use self-talk as verbal shooting commands as you shoot? Your mind can concentrate on only one thought and action at a time. If you do not believe it, try this little experiment to prove the point. Attempt to scratch your head and shoot the ball at the same time. It sounds silly, but it is very difficult to do. Your mind cannot focus on two functions very well at the same time. And the key to shooting free throws is to focus only on the shot.

When you practice foul shooting by yourself, get in the habit of saying these five words, "elbow in, bend, follow through" out loud as you do the actual mechanical steps. As you practice this way, you will develop a real feel for the free throw and begin to take pride in how well you shoot.

Stage 4: Practice Free-Throw Shooting

The free throw is not only the easiest shot in all of basketball to practice, but also the best shot. If you don't practice any other shooting drills, then at least practice free throws. A few obvious benefits are that you can practice them alone and you don't have to break a sweat when shooting. And by practicing foul shots, you can significantly increase your shooting skills from all other areas of the court. Practicing free throws is also one of the best drills for working out problems you may be having with shooting the basketball during typical game situations from the field. Really.

What is hard about practicing free throws is that it takes time and commitment. To get to the top level of foul shooting (90 percent or better), you will have to do what other great players have done: take a minimum of one hundred free throws daily—and not just during the basketball season. It will take only thirty to forty minutes each day. Make the commitment. It's far better to be great at making free throws than to be a "foul shooter."

▌ TRAINING TIP _____

The most consecutive free throws a player will ever take in a game is three to five. So when you practice, make three, four, or five in a row between drills. To further simulate game situations, if you miss before making three free throws in a row, do a defensive slide from the foul line to the baseline or five repetitions of jumping up to slap the backboard with the ball quickly each time. This will wind you and force you to shoot free throws again when you are tired. That is a game situation. If you want to add additional pressure, make three shots in a row in under one minute. Now you are really learning to shoot free throws under pressure.

FOUL-SHOOTING PROGRESSION CHART

Level	Success Rate	Criteria
1	60%+	Player usually has good shooting form and mechanics.
2	70%+	Player has a consistent shooting routine, plus good shooting technique and mechanics.
3	80%+	Player uses mental concentration and verbal commands to focus on the shot. Player also has a consistent shooting routine, plus good shooting technique and mechanics.
4	90%+	Player practices a minimum of one hundred free throws daily. Player also meets all criteria for levels 1, 2, and 3.

▌ TRAINING TIP _____

1. *Chart your progress:* Keep track of how many free throws you make out of one hundred each day (see Figure 3.1). Keep your record in a notebook so that you can track your progress and percentages daily over time, or make copies of Figure 3.1 to assist you. You will usually see improvement on a monthly, though not a daily, basis. If you have a bad day, don't get discouraged.
2. *Make a specific number of consecutive shots to end practice:* Make a specific number of consecutive free throws to end your practice each day. Whether you are practicing ball handling, shooting, or defense, end with free throws. Set a goal, and stay until you accomplish it. Begin with a small number, such as five or ten. As you get better, work your way up to twenty-five or even up to fifty in a row before you quit.

▌ FREE-THROW-SHOOTING RECORD AND STANDARDS

The current world record for most consecutive free throws is held by Dr. Tom Amberry. He is in the *Guinness Book of World Records* for having shot 2,750 consecutive free throws without a miss, and he did it at the age of seventy-one. Tom was a podiatrist by trade and fifty years earlier had played college basketball. Upon retiring from his practice, he wanted to stay active, so he decided to take up free-throw shooting. Tom began practicing five hundred or more free throws every day. After a few months, he developed a severe case of tendinitis in his left shoulder (he shot left-handed). It was impossible for him to continue practicing left-handed, so he decided to start shooting right-handed. Lacking confidence in his abilities to shoot adequately with his opposite hand, he decided to do some homework. That is how we met. He learned the same principles from me about foul shooting that I am teaching you. Dr. Amberry used the same fundamental techniques found in this chapter to break the world record, and he did it while learning to shoot with his opposite hand! This is one more proof that if the fundamentals are good, the performance has to improve. It's that simple.

MONTH	1	2	3	4	5	6	7	8	9	10	11	12	13	14	15

MONTH	16	17	18	19	20	21	22	23	24	25	26	27	28	29	30

FIGURE 3.1 Free-Throw Tracking Chart

FREE-THROW-SHOOTING STANDARDS

Success Rate	Shooting Level
50% or below	Below average
60–69%	Average
70–74%	Good (top 25% in the world)
75–79%	Very good (top 10% in the world)
80–89%	Excellent (top 5% in the world)
90% and above	Superb! (top 1% in the world)

▊ TRAINING TIP

Did you know that when you practice free throws, you are also practicing and improving your shooting skills for game situations? Here is why. When you shoot a free throw or a game shot (a set shot, layup, or jump shot), you are using the exact same mechanics that you would for a normal shot—mechanics that bring the ball into your shooting pocket before you release the ball. Practicing the V-Shot drill in Chapter 2 provides a perfect example. You always end up facing the basket in a triple-threat position. *A perfect triple-threat position is exactly the same as a correct foul-shooting position!* If you take the time to develop proper shooting mechanics, every time that you practice a free throw, you will also be practicing a game shot. Likewise, every time you practice a game shot, you will also be practicing the exact same mechanics for a free throw. Basketball is a simple game—don't complicate it! FACT: Practicing foul shots is a great way to improve your three-point-shooting skills and to develop a better shooting rhythm.

▊ COACHES' CHALK TALK: TEAM FOUL-SHOOTING DRILLS AND FUNDRAISER

Good free-throw shooting is essential to the success of any team at every level. It is to basketball what putting is to golf—critical. Did you know that, on the average, free-throw points make up 15 to 20 percent of a team's entire point totals for a game? If you doubt this, track the box scores in your sports paper for a few weeks, and you will discover the same results. The following suggestions concern improving a team's free-throw shooting, both as a group and as individual players.

Create a Free-Throw System

It is important to develop and implement a system of teaching and practicing free throws. Make sure you are comfortable with it, or your players will not buy into it. Base your system on sound fundamentals. Use an existing system or develop your own—just make sure it works. The fundamentals taught in this chapter do have proven results and are simple for coaches to teach and for players to use.

Plan Your Practice Time

Free-throw shooting does take up valuable practice time. A great way to spend less practice time and still develop players' concentration and confidence in shooting free throws is to require three, four, or five shots in a row during practice breaks or rest periods. Simply put two to three minutes on the score clock. If players miss during the two to three minutes, have them do five push-ups, five sit-ups, a defensive slide, or five backboard touches. Do something short to wind them before they go back to the free-throw line to shoot again, so they can try to make their shots before time expires. The players that don't make three to five in a row before the time period is up have to do a sprint.

Players will develop mental toughness from the added pressure of having to shoot free throws within a certain time period. They will gain extra confidence as they start to hit five shots in a row consistently in practice every time. Thus, making one or two in a game will be much easier. You might require that for every time players do not make their five in a row during practice, they owe you an extra set of ten consecutive free throws after practice or on their own time. Requiring that players make a specific number of free throws in a row before they can leave is also a great idea and provides its own kind of pressure. Ability to achieve two sets of five in a row or, once in a while, ten in a row (the optimum number) will take work and a lot of concentration in a consistent shooting routine. And that is the goal—consistency.

Free throws can also serve as an excellent warm-up drill before practice or before taking more difficult shots that require more exertion and movement. Here are a few more practice ideas:

1. Have players take ten, twenty, or twenty-five free throws after completing the primary warm-up drill(s). They should be shot in sets of five in a row, not just ten, twenty or twenty-five total shots. You will find that players' concentration levels really improve.
2. In the off-season, have your players *make* five free throws in a row between each drill they practice one day. On the next day have them *take* ten free throws between each drill they practice. Record the total number of "makes" to get a free-throw percentage.
3. At the end of practice each day, your players should shoot twenty-five free throws. More than this is not necessary, especially if players have to make five in a row at a time. You're trying to build confidence, concentration, and good habits, and twenty-five free throws can accomplish that. Ideally, you want your team to be able to make over 70 percent of your free throws in games as a team. If they can't do so yet, keep practicing.
4. After every set of five successful free throws in a row, have your players switch or rotate baskets. During practice, when you have free-throw/water breaks, have them shoot at a different basket each time.

Set Up an Annual Competition

Hold a Free-Throw-athon to raise money or as an annual competition during each preseason. This will help players develop a better shooting touch as well as have fun. Charge a nickel to sponsors for every free throw made by a player, and have players shoot one thousand free throws in a single day. It will take four to six hours for each player to finish. If you perfer a preseason competition involving only your team, then give away a pair of shoes or sweats to the top two shooters at the end of the competition.

Whatever type of competition you use, players will be motivated to gear up for it as it approaches. They will no doubt practice on their own before the season begins. You can also raise a lot of money for your program with such a competition. If each player gets a minimum of ten sponsors, you will raise an average of $350–$400 per player for your program. How many players do you have? See—practicing free throws can pay off!

Keep Records

Establish and keep free-throw records for your team, and put them on a wall in your gym or locker room. You might post major achievements such as these:

1. Best percentage from Free-Throw-athon: 924 out of 1,000 (92.4%)/Jim Newbold/ 1998
2. Most consecutive makes in practice: 78 in a row/Chris Miller/1987
3. Most consecutive makes in games: 22 in a row/John Lee/1999
4. Best season free-throw percentage: 89% (25 shots minimum)/Andy Wildauer/ 1985
5. Best career free-throw percentage: 84% (100 shots minimum)/Mike Garcia/ 1988
6. Best team free-throw percentage in a game: 18 out of 20, 90% (10 shots minimum)/2001
7. Best team free-throw percentage in a season: 72%/2004

With teams, as with individual players, focus is the key. Put the goals and the records in front of your players and they will respond, at least the ones that want playing time. Teach proper shooting techniques as well as habits for mental concentration, and you will see the results. As a coach, also recognize that the majority of basketball games are lost by ten points or less. Free throws really do have an effect on the outcome of games.

CHAPTER QUESTIONS

1. What are five common mistakes made when shooting free throws?

2. Briefly describe the three stages of foul-shooting development.

3. What is the BEEF principle?

4. Why is it important to have a foul-shooting routine?

5. What are the three mechanical steps to use when taking a free throw?

6. Why is it important to chart your progress while practicing foul shots?

7. List two ways to practice free throws in order to simulate game situations.

8. What would be considered a good free-throw percentage for a high school player?

9. What is a correct foul-shooting position identical to?

10. Describe two ways in which a coach can set up free-throw practice to help the team shoot better in game situations.

Three-Point-Shooting Fundamentals

IN THIS CHAPTER YOU WILL LEARN:

- Ten different three-point shots for game situations to give you opportunities to take and make more three-pointers
- The history of the three-point shot and how it originated
- Five three-point-shooting fundamentals to make you a more consistent and effective shooter
- More than a dozen three-point-shooting tips for greater success
- Principles and concepts that teach *when* to shoot three-pointers, how to know when you're open, and how to get defenders off balance with shot fakes and reads
- The difference between *taking* a good shot and *making* a good shot

THREE-POINT-SHOOTING BASICS

Three-point shooting is a skill that is seldom practiced by most basketball players. It can be a great equalizer for players who are limited in size or athletic skills. To learn how to shoot from the three-point range is quite simple. Practice is the first building block. All of the shooting mechanics for three-point shooting are identical to those of most other shots. The only major difference is that three-point shooting will require more practice—a lot more. Do not try to make one hundred shots from the three-point area the first day you begin. Start with making ten to twenty-five shots each day. In a week, increase the number to twenty-five to fifty, then in a month, fifty to seventy-five. After three to six months, you may be ready to move up to one hundred a day. If you are serious about being a great three-point shooter, you will have to progress to making a minimum of one hundred shots a day and also should use the Short-Shot Principle and the Goal-Shooting Principle.

One of the best three-point shooters whom I ever saw or worked with was Kari Gallup, who played collegiately at Brigham Young University. Kari was from Canada and had not had access to the training and facilities that many players in the United States have. She did, however, have plenty of interest and dedication.

Kari won the NCAA three-point-shooting competition during her senior year in college and went on to play professional basketball. She understood the importance of making one hundred three-point shots a day and having the ability to shoot a variety of three-point shots in game situations.

When you practice three-point shots, plan your practice so that you take different shots from different spots in sets of ten, as in other shooting drills. That is why you need a minimum goal of how many shots you will *make* for each drill. Making ten shots from each practice spot is a good goal. The minimum number of shots you should make every day if you want to become a good three-point shooter is fifty. If you want to be a *great* three-point shooter the minimum is one hundred. This will take a lot of discipline, dedication, and determination, especially during the first few weeks that you begin practicing from this distance.

This chapter will show you how to become a good, or even a great, three-point shooter. You will also learn how to shoot correctly from the three-point line and beyond. You will begin making shots that are better, stronger, more consistent, more frequent, longer, and faster than you have ever shot before. Last but not least, you will also learn about the history of the three-point shot, as well as dozens of fundamental tips, concepts, and ideas that will improve your performance.

THE HISTORY OF THE THREE-POINT LINE

Did you know that in the early days of basketball, field goals were worth three points? When the game of basketball was first invented by Dr. James Naismith in December 1891, the original field goal was worth one point, and there were no free throws. After two years, in 1893, the rules were changed so that a field goal was worth three points. In 1897, the current system, in which any field goal is worth two points and a free throw is worth one point, was adopted, and it remained that way until the implementation of the three-point line.

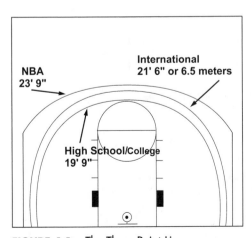

FIGURE 4.1 The Three-Point Line

In 1961, one of the game's great innovators, Abe Saperstein, established a new league called the ABL, or the American Basketball League, in order to compete against the NBA. Years earlier, Mr. Saperstein had also organized, founded, and promoted the original Harlem Globetrotters, the most financially successful and popular traveling, or barnstorming, team in the history of the game. Saperstein wanted his new league to have something different from what the NBA offered, so he came up with the idea of the three-point line at the distance of 23 feet, 9 inches, which is what the NBA now uses (see Figure 4.1). The shot from the three-point line was nicknamed "the 25-footer." Although the three-point line and shot were a new sensation in the ABL, the league was not, and it folded after only a season and a half, as did the three-point line, for the time being. Then in 1967 another rebel league, the ABA, or American Basketball Association, adopted the shot. The ABA, equipped with the three-point shot, fancy uniforms, and red, white, and blue basketball, woke up the basketball world and shook up sports conservatives, bringing about a new and exciting style of play. The game of basketball was never the same again, and it was only a matter of time before the game at all levels would embrace the fans' favorite, the three-point shot.

In 1981, the NBA began using the three-point line as a permanent fixture of the game. Other organizations would soon follow. During the 1983–84 basketball season, Idaho became the first state whose high school organization used the three-point line. In 1987, the rest of the high schools in the United States, under the direction of the National High School Federation, followed Idaho's lead and adopted the three-point line. But high schools chose to use a shorter distance of only 19 feet, 9 inches from the basket. Internationally the three-point line also caught on and was officially adopted by the World Basketball Congress in Munich, West Germany, on June 23, 1984. The international three-point line was set at a distance of 21 feet, 6 inches, or 6.6 meters, from the rim. It was officially used for the first time in the 1988 Olympics.

In college basketball, the ACC (Atlantic Coast Conference) experimented with the three-point line during the 1984–85 season. The rest of the NCAA adopted the three-point line during the 1985–86 season. The NCAA chose to use a distance of 19 feet, 9 inches, the same as the distance established by the National Federation of High Schools in the United States.

The three-point line has restored the game to shorter and less athletic players alike. It has opened up the key, or lane, areas of the court. It has made the game more explosive and enjoyable and has changed the way in which coaches strategize as well as how players practice. The three-point line has made the game more exciting and fun for players and fans alike. The three-point line is here to stay, and the game is better for it.

FIVE FUNDAMENTALS OF THREE-POINT SHOOTING

Fundamental 1: Shot-Put Shooting

Shot-put shooting refers to a shooting location for the three-point shot. It is not a set position that must be held, but a location involved in the process of the shot. In shot-put shooting you bring the ball directly above the elbow, in the shoulder pad area, shooting it almost as if it were a shot put (see Figure 4.2). As you release the shot, be sure your knees are sufficiently bent and that you finish the shot with follow-through and arms above your head, not forward toward the front of the rim. This will help you shoot the ball in a straight line more consistently and add shooting strength and range to your shot.

FIGURE 4.2   Shot-Put Shooting

Fundamental 2: Target Sight: Aim for the Back of the Rim

Always aim for the back of the rim. More specifically, you should focus your eyes on the middle hook on the back of the rim. And the farther away from the basket you shoot, the more important it becomes to aim there. The back of the rim makes a good target for several reasons:

1. Aiming at the back of the rim forces a player to physically arc the ball more by extending the arms directly over the head, rather than pushing the ball toward the basket. This also makes the defender have to jump toward a shooter to try to block the shot. Aiming at the front of the rim, however, physically carries the shooter's arm toward the defender, which makes it much more difficult to get a shot off.
2. Late in a game, a player's and a team's shooting percentages typically go down because of fatigue. By aiming at the back of the rim, players open up a larger target area (18 inches larger) because backspin will allow the ball to spin backward into the cylinder if it hits the back of the rim. This will increase your opportunities for success.
3. If you shoot a ball with backspin and aim at or hit the front of the rim, nine out of ten times the ball will hit the cylinder and spin away from the basket. But if you shoot a ball with backspin and aim at or hit the back of the rim, nine out of ten times the ball will spin backward into the cylinder for a successful shot. That is why it is called "backspin."

Fundamental 3: Lines, Lanes, and Angles for Three-Point Shooting

Shooting Lines.   In three-point shooting, it's critical to shoot in a straight line to the basket. The best way to do this is to make sure the toe, knee, elbow, and ball are lined up straight. This will prevent you from missing to the left or the right and will also strengthen your shot (see Figure 4.2).

Shooting Lanes.   To position yourself in a correct shooting lane, line up your left foot with the left side of the rim and your right foot with the right side of the rim. In an incorrect shooting lane, your feet would be turned away from the rim. Of course, you can shoot the ball in the direction of the rim from such a stance, but by placing your feet and body in the shooting lane, you can eliminate up to one-third of the misses you would normally have from the three-point line. Perfect shot alignment becomes more critical with a three-point shot because the farther away from the basket you shoot, the greater the opportunity for error.

Shooting Angles.   The shoulders, the knee, and the ball of the foot should be placed in a vertical straight line for proper balance and shooting strength. In proper shooting alignment, your elbow should be directly above your knee, and your knee should be directly above your toe. By creating a vertical line for body balance with the shoulders, the knee, and the ball of the foot, you should also end up forming two 45-degree body angles—the first from the shoulder to the hip to the knee, and the second from the hip, to the back of the knee, to the heel of the foot. These shooting angles will add leg strength to your shot and will also keep you from pushing the shot toward the basket instead of shooting it correctly. Review Chapter 2 for details on proper shooting fundamentals.

Fundamental 4: The Short-Shot Principle

As discussed earlier, this is a shooting principle, it is not a shooting drill. You should use the Short-Shot Principle to build your effectiveness as a shooter. It will teach you to aim for the back of the rim. Take a minute to review the Short-Shot Principle in Chapter 2 before you begin practicing three-point shooting.

Fundamental 5: The Goal-Shooting Principle

Using goals is especially important when practicing and shooting shots with a high degree of difficulty, such as the three-point shot. Using the Goal-Shooting Principle will be a great benefit in building shooting confidence and success from the three-point range. A three-point shot is more difficult than most shots because it is farther from the basket. Practicing it will be harder, but it will make you more successful. Review the Goal-Shooting Principle discussed in Chapter 2.

THREE-POINT-SHOOTING DRILLS

Drill 1: The Three-Point Shot Out of the Triple-Threat Position

The first three-point shot to tackle is the shot out of the triple-threat position. This shot simulates receiving the ball on the perimeter area of the court, facing up to the basket. You should face the basket and determine, or "read," where the defensive player or the defensive team is on the floor. If the defender is two or more arm's lengths away from you, shoot the ball. Use the V-Shot Principle to integrate game-situation scenarios into your practice. Review the V-Shot Principle in Chapter 2.

Drill 2: The Catch and Shoot

The catch and shoot allows you to shoot your shot one second quicker than you normally would when taking a set shooting position before releasing the ball. This is a great technique for smaller players to use in order to shoot more quickly against opponents. When practicing the catch and shoot, catch the ball while jumping, with your feet in the air as you receive the pass (see Figure 4.3). On receiving the pass, land on your feet, and without slowing your momentum or motion, spring back into the air while taking the shot (see Figure 4.4). When receiving the pass for a catch and shoot, always put both hands up near your shoulder or shooting pocket. This will prepare you to catch the ball and allow you to automatically spring up for the jump shot. Having your hands up and ready will also give your teammates a good, clear target for the pass.

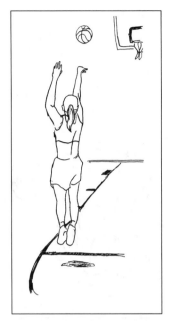

FIGURE 4.3 Catching the Ball in the Air for the Catch and Shoot

FIGURE 4.4 Shooting the Ball in the Catch and Shoot

▮▮ TRAINING TIP _____

For a greater challenge, once you complete ten made shots of a certain drill, develop the habit of making three, four, or up to five in a row to build greater confidence in three-point shooting skills.

Drill 3: The Jab, Step Back, and Shoot

This shooting technique will free you up for a three-point shot when you are guarded closely by a defender. To execute the jab, step back, and shoot, simply face the basket in a triple-threat position. Take a six-inch jab step toward the basket (and defender). Do this by lowering your shoulders and holding the ball below your hip area (see Figure 4.5). Next, if the defender backs away, step back and shoot by quickly raising and shooting the basketball with a jump shot or set shot from the jab position (see Figure 4.6). Retrieve your shot, and repeat the steps. As a drill, make ten shots, practicing from a different spot for each set of ten shots. You can use the V-Shot Principle to practice this drill from both sides of the court.

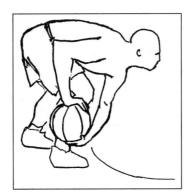

FIGURE 4.5   Taking a Jab Step

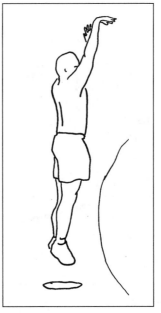

FIGURE 4.6   Completing the Jab, Step Back, and Shoot

▓▌ TRAINING TIP _____

Do not overextend on your jab step. If you do, you will give the defender time to recover while lengthening your own recovery time. You will also throw your body off balance by extending your weight too far forward or sideways.

When performing a jab step, you'll always want to jab low, not long. As with any fundamental, you should practice the jab, step back, and shoot slowly at first. You will develop rhythm and quickness over time. Using proper technique is important. Practice making a quick, short, low, 6-inch jab step, then step back and shoot.

Drill 4: Baseline Three-Point Shots

Rather than a particular shooting drill, this area of practice focuses on a single spot on the court. Practice shooting three-point shots from the baseline corner area of the three-point line. This spot is often neglected by players in their practice routine. You can practice baseline shots by using any of the shooting techniques from the catch and shoot, the shot from the triple-threat position, or the jab, step back, and shoot.

■■ **TRAINING TIP** _____

Rest by taking free throws between shooting drills. One of the best drills you will ever do in order to become a better three-point shooter is to practice free throws. Practicing free throws between drills will also simulate game situations. It will also develop the mental and physical habit of being able to make free throws while tired.

Drill 5: The Shot Fake, Lateral Side Shuffle, Three-Point Shot

In many game situations you will have to make a three-point shot or have the opportunity for a three-point shot while a defender is running toward you. An approaching defender often causes a player to rush a shot. A good alternative is to develop a shot fake with footwork sliding laterally, followed by a good three-point shot.

To execute the shot fake, lateral side shuffle, three-point shot, begin by receiving a pass, and immediately go into a shot fake (see Figure 4.7). (You should use the catch and shoot when catching and shot faking in this drill.) Next, shuffle one step laterally to your right side by pushing off your left foot as you take one dribble with your right hand (this improves the shooting opportunity) (see Figure 4.8). Upon gathering the ball, make a jump stop, springing up into a jump shot (see Figure 4.9).

FIGURE 4.7   The Shot Fake

FIGURE 4.8   The Lateral Side Shuffle

FIGURE 4.9   The Three-Point Shot (Jump Shot)

The 75 Percent Rule

Coaches, when a player can shoot successfully 80 percent of the time or more from the free-throw line in games, or make 75 percent of the three-point shots in regular practice, you might consider giving the player a green light to shoot in game situations.

To practice the shot fake, lateral side shuffle, three-point shot to the left, repeat the same process, but after the shot fake, push off the right foot and shuffle one step toward the left side with a dribble before shooting the ball.

Drill 6: The Jab Dribble, Step Back, and Shoot

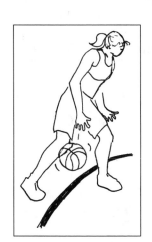 

The jab dribble, step back, and shoot is another weapon to use in a fast-break situation or if the team is in great need of a three-point shot toward the end of a game or a quarter. To perform the jab dribble, step back, and shoot, begin 10 to 20 feet above the three-point line and take two to three dribbles hard toward the basket and the three-point line. Once you near the line, jab with your left foot (if you are dribbling with your right hand) to back off a defender (see Figure 4.10), then step back behind the three-point line by pushing quickly backward with your left foot behind the line. Square up to the rim to take the three-point jump shot (see Figure 4.11). Jab to make the defender retreat, then step back quickly behind the three-point line and shoot the ball. Practice this shot with each foot while dribbling with the opposite hand (dribble with left hand, jab with right foot; dribble with right hand, jab with left foot).

FIGURE 4.10 Jabbing with the Foot

FIGURE 4.11 Stepping Back to Shoot

Drill 7: Three-Point Shots Off Screens or Picks

Many coaches plan set plays that involve screens, or picks, to free up good three-point shooters. In order to shoot three-point shots effectively off screens, come off a screen by rubbing shoulder to shoulder with the teammate who is setting the screen. As you come off the screen looking for the pass, square up to the basket and use the catch and shoot.

The easiest way to shoot three-point shots off screens is to *turn the body to the rim* immediately after coming off the screen and catch and shoot the ball in rhythm. When practicing three-point shots coming off a screen or pick, make sure to practice going off of screens to both the left and right sides.

No One Ever Got Cut from Practicing Too Much.

There's another advantage to taking your shot in a catch-and-shoot position. If a defender does get through the screen, you will have the ability to make a jump stop and stay on balance or make a jump stop from a catch-and-shoot move, make a shot fake, and go by the defender.

▋▌ TRAINING TIP _____

If a player has difficulty in making a shot to one side of the floor or in making a shot out of a specific shooting drill, the player should practice an extra set or two of making ten shots from that drill every day for a week or even up to a month until it becomes more comfortable. At the end of team practice, such players can take an extra set of ten shots or even two sets of ten in order to improve their shooting rhythm from the weak spots or shots from the three-point line.

Drills 8 and 9: The Three-Point Shot Off the Fast Break

To practice shooting the three-point shot off the fast break, begin at half court, explode three to five dribbles to the top of the key, and pull up for a jump shot above the three-point line. Do not go the full distance of the court. The objective is to develop a feel or rhythm for the shot, not to do dribbling sprints. As you practice this drill, dribble exclusively with your right hand for one set of ten made shots. After each shot attempt and rebound, dribble the ball at one-half speed back to the center-court line. When you touch the half-court line with your foot, explode ahead with three to five dribbles again. Be sure to square your feet up to the rim when you make the jump stop; the correct shooting lane will ensure that you shoot the ball in a straight line. Later, work on dribbling with your left hand for another set of ten shots. Learn to shoot off the dribble while dribbling, using either your left or right hand. Always dribble with your eyes up.

▋▌ TRAINING TIP _____

Three-Point-Shooting Tips for Shorter Players

The value of mastering the catch and shoot for shorter players cannot be stressed enough. Such players can gain one second and get a shot off much faster by using this technique.

For shorter players, especially guards, another invaluable shot for three-point shooting is the shot on the fast break. This is a great shot for games because of its rhythm and quickness and its element of surprise. It is easy to master and simple to take.

In general, if you achieve a success rate of 80 percent or better from the free-throw line or can hit 75 percent of your threes during practice, the chances that your coach will give you the green light to shoot are very high. *Practice.*

Drill 10: The Two-Basket Drill

If you practice in a gym, take advantage of its equipment and space. Normally, a side basket and main basket will both have three-point lines. You can work out a simple three-point-shooting drill from the main basket to the side basket by shooting a three-point shot from behind the arc of the main basket, rebounding your shot, and then shooting a three-point shot from behind the arc of the side basket (see Figure 4.12). Repeat the process by going back to shoot at the main basket, then the side basket, and so on, until you have successfully made a minimum of ten shots. This will speed up your shooting practice and get you accustomed to shooting at more than one basket—a double bonus.

Mastering all ten drills will take time and work. Do not expect to develop all these shots during the first day or first week, whether you play at the middle school, high school, college, or professional level. You should be able to develop a shooting rhythm with the drills provided. Make sure you practice each drill using both sides of the floor; when practicing the three-point-shooting drill off the dribble, practice dribbling with both the left and right hands but shoot with your dominant shooting hand only.

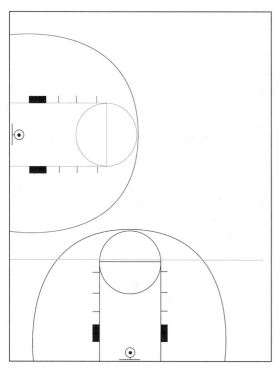

FIGURE 4.12 The Two-Basket Drill (Main Basket and Side Basket)

The 50/100 Rule

In order to be a good three-point shooter, you'll have to *make,* not just *take,* fifty three-point shots per day. If you want to be a great three-point shooter, you'll have to *make* a minimum of one hundred three-point shots per day.

▌ TRAINING TIP _____

The three-point shot is difficult to master, which means it requires a lot of practice. Do not get discouraged. Start with a small goal for the number of shots to *make* each day, and increase the number gradually. Here are three helpful hints:

1. Put a higher arc on the shot to give the ball a greater chance of going in.
2. Bend your knees more deeply. This will increase your shot's strength and distance.
3. Shoot 8–12 inches from behind the line—the degree of difficulty is no higher.

COACHES' CHALK TALK: TEAM THREE-POINT-SHOOTING PRINCIPLES AND SITUATIONS

All three-point-shooting drills can be practiced in a team setting. Refer to Chapter 2, Coaches' Chalk Talk, to find out how to practice team shooting drills. You can also change each drill into two-team competitions or add players to a single-line shooting drill of elimination for a change of pace and fun. As a coach, make sure you prepare for the following:

1. At least two three-point-shooting plays to run during a game when your team may need a big shot against a man-to-man defense
2. At least two three-point-shooting plays to run against a zone defense—one play versus a one-man front, and one play versus a two-man front on the top of the zone
3. At least one out-of-bounds play from the sideline for a three-point shot
4. At least two out-of-bounds plays from the baseline to get a three-point shot
5. A three-point offense strictly designed to get quick scores or three-point shots if your team is down by a lot and needs to get back into a game (There is a huge difference between scoring three points at a time and two points at a time. If the team is down by fifteen points with three minutes left, you need only five possessions from the three-point line; you need eight possessions from two-point range to get back in the game.)

If you prepare players for these game situations, they will develop confidence in you as a coach. Here's another way to add to their preparation. During a game that you know the team simply cannot lose, try turning the players loose for four to five minutes, running the three-point-shooting offense (not the plays) to see how they respond. It will give them a chance to practice it during a game situation.

▌ TRAINING TIP

It is not realistic to familiarize a team with up to a dozen different three-point offensive plays. Pick out the top three to five situations encountered most often, and prepare your team for those.

You can add others during the week of a game against a team that may present different defensive situations, requiring different three-point plays. Scouting these situations and preparing for them are two steps toward winning the game.

CHAPTER QUESTIONS

1. Why is the degree of difficulty for a three-point shot higher than a shot from 12 feet?

2. Who invented the three-point line?

3. In what decade was the three-point line adopted at all levels of basketball competition?

4. Which shooting technique helps a player release the ball one second more quickly?

5. How many three-point shots will a player have to make daily in order to become a good three-point shooter? a great three-point shooter?

6. Up to how many three-point plays should a coach be prepared to run with a team in game situations?

7. List three offensive game situations that may require a three-point-play option.

8. Give at least three tips that can help to improve three-point-shooting skills.

9. What is the NBA three-point shot nicknamed?

10. Is the best target sight for three-point shots the same target sight to be used inside the three-point arc? Why or why not?

Scoring Fundamentals

THE TRIPLE-THREAT SCORING SYSTEM

IN THIS CHAPTER YOU WILL LEARN:
- The triple threat—the game's most valuable offensive scoring tool
- The Triple-Threat Scoring System—seven scoring moves that provide a total of twenty-eight scoring options, which will fit any type of offense
- Two scoring positions for explosive quickness to the basket
- Drills for developing and using moves out of the triple-threat position
- How to increase your scoring by up to ten points per game or more
- Choreography and footwork to make you a serious offensive threat

THE IMPORTANCE OF THE TRIPLE THREAT

The triple threat is a common phrase in the basketball world. You hear about it at camps, clinics, and gyms, in books, and on videos. As a player or coach, I am sure you have heard the expression quite often. The triple threat, as the name indicates, consists of three options: to pass the ball, to shoot the ball, or to drive with the ball to the basket (*not* to dribble—dribbling is not a threat unless you are going to the basket to score). The triple threat is a position, not a move (see Figure 5.1). It can help players be more productive offensively and much more effective.

To understand why the triple threat is so important, recognize the difference between shooters and scorers. Shooters can shoot the ball well and hit shots when they are open. Scorers, on the other hand, can create shots for themselves, or their teammates, *every time they touch the ball*. Very few players can be categorized as scorers. A good shooter typically will average twelve to eighteen points per game, depending on how many shots open up. A scorer, on the other hand, will average from twenty to thirty plus points per game consistently, night in and night out. A scorer has the ability to receive the ball, read the defender or the defense, then make a correct move to throw a defender off balance.

A scorer is also referred to as a "go to" player or a "clutch player"—someone a team will rely on when the game is on the line. Being a "go to" player or "clutch player" does not mean hitting the game-winning shot every time. Instead, it means

FIGURE 5.1
The Triple-Threat Position

being able to take the big shots in the last three to four minutes of a close game and wanting to take them. Like all players, "go to" players will usually make half of their shots and will miss half. The big difference is their ability to create a wide variety of good open shots for themselves or their teammates *every* time they touch the ball. They have a variety of moves to draw from. There are only five ways in which a player can score a basket in a game:

1. A shot or move out of the low-post area
2. A shot or scoring move from the perimeter area of the court
3. A shot or move on the fast break (discussed in Chapter 12)
4. An offensive rebound
5. A free throw

Once you recognize these five categories, you should be more motivated to work on different scoring moves from the low post and perimeter areas of the court. Now let's discuss the elements involved in the triple threat.

THE TRIPLE-THREAT POSITION

Over the past twenty years I have traveled around the United States and the world doing basketball clinics for Converse, Spalding, Rawlings, Sport Court, Nike, and other organizations. From literally thousands of encounters with coaches, players, and various information resources, I have been able to reach some concrete conclusions about the triple threat. Whenever I do a clinic or camp and talk about scoring moves, I always begin by asking the players or coaches to show me a correct triple-threat position. Typically, players will demonstrate one of three positions (see Figure 5.2):

1. A player holds the ball high either above the ear or head in a set position. From this position, it will take up to one full second longer to "load" and shoot the ball because a player typically will have to "reload" to shoot the ball. Reloading involves taking time to bring the ball down into the shoulder pad or to bend the knees to shoot. The cardinal sin of most offensive basketball players is holding the ball over the head. Not only does it take away two offensive options, but it also slows the player down by one second when deciding to shoot or drive.
2. A player holds the ball out in front of the chest, which makes it easy for a defender to hit, knock away, or steal it.
3. A player holds the ball down to the side by the waist or hip area, which allows for only one immediate option—driving to the basket.

Look again at a perfect triple-threat position (see Figure 5.3). From this position a player can immediately shoot, pass, or drive the ball to the basket without having to reposition the ball or make any additional movements. There is no time

(a) Ball above
ear or head

(b) Ball extended too far
from chest

(c) Ball held near hip

FIGURE 5.2   Three Incorrect Locations for the Triple-Threat Position

FIGURE 5.3   The Triple-Threat Position (Back View)

lost for reloading in order to shoot, pass, or drive. All three options of the triple threat can be immediately executed from this single position. By the way, a perfect triple-threat position will be identical to a correct foul-shooting position that employs sound shooting mechanics. (Review Chapter 3.)

▬▬ TRAINING TIP _____

These triple-threat principles apply when playing against a man-to-man defense. When playing against a zone defense, it is not logical to drive to the basket but more effective to shot fake out of a catch and shoot and pass fake with the ball overhead to freeze the defense. Follow these guidelines:

1. *Against a man-to-man defense:* Stay low and balanced with the ball in a triple-threat position.
2. *Against a zone defense:* Use the catch and shoot, and keep the ball up high for pass fakes.

The Jump-Stop Pivot Drill

Which option of the triple threat you use in play will depend on the defense. Always let the defense dictate your choice. Chapter 2 introduced a drill based on the V-Shot Principle, which builds the habit of facing the basket and viewing the entire court as well as a defender. Together with this habit of keeping an eye on the big picture, players must develop the physical skill and game habit of making a jump stop to receive the ball and facing the basket, *using the same pivot foot every time* to pivot into a correct triple-threat position. The ball must be received within the player's perimeter area. A player's perimeter is the farthest distance from the basket from which the player can effectively and consistently shoot. A good shooting percentage consists of 45 percent success or greater. The perimeter should never exceed 20 to 25 feet—each player must decide which area is most effective and comfortable. Receiving the ball outside the perimeter area forfeits one of the options of the triple-threat position—shooting.

A simple drill for developing the habit of pivoting on the correct foot is the jump-stop pivot drill (See Figure 5.4). To practice it, simply begin at a foul-line corner and pass the ball ahead toward the other foul-line corner, 10–12 feet away. Pass the ball to yourself by putting a reverse spin on the ball, and make a jump stop while you catch it. Make sure both feet hit the ground at the *same* time and make one sound on the jump stop. Upon catching the ball, pivot on your *left* foot if you are right-handed and face the basket in a triple-threat position. (Left-handed players will always pivot on the *right* foot.)

(a) Putting a reverse spin on the ball

(b) Jump-stop and pivot to face the basket

(c) Facing the basket in triple-threat position

FIGURE 5.4   The Jump-Stop Pivot Drill

TRAINING TIP

When practicing the jump stop and pivot mechanics, it is essential to make two deliberate stops.

1. Stop on the jump stop.
2. Stop on the shoulder pad. This will help improve your balance and mechanics quickly (see Figure 5.5).

(a) On the jump stop   (b) On the shoulder pad

FIGURE 5.5 Two Stops in the Jump-Stop Pivot Drill

Next, go back to the opposite foul-line corner, repeating the same process. Again make sure you make a jump stop with one sound and pivot on your left foot into a triple-threat position as you face the basket. Repeat this movement, completing twenty to thirty repetitions as a warm-up exercise for your practice. Develop the habit of receiving the ball and facing the basket within your perimeter area—the area from which you can shoot the ball with 45 percent accuracy or better, comfortably and confidently. If you do not receive the ball in your perimeter and are 10 feet past the three-point line, do not shoot the ball. Learn to catch the ball in your perimeter area.

■| TRAINING TIP _____

Which Pivot Foot Should Be Used from the Perimeter?

Which pivot foot to use when facing the basket from the perimeter is an important issue. Let's look at the facts. Of the thousands of coaches I have talked to, I have heard only two arguments to justify using two different pivot feet:

1. *To create distance between yourself and the defender:* The most logical argument given for using two pivot feet is that it allows pivoting with the foot on the outside, away from the defender. This can be useful in order to create space against an aggressive tight defense that likes to go chest to chest. However, this only gains one extra second. If a defender is taught to "belly up" chest to chest, that player will still come after you even if you create momentary space. You have not solved the problem—only delayed it by one second.

2. *To give players more options:* This creates the same problem. Two pivot feet will require twice as much practice to make a player only half as effective. A player and team will be much farther ahead mastering four to five shots and moves off of one pivot foot than eight to ten for both feet. Quality practice with sound fundamentals will bring quality results. The principles for the game are simple. If someone "bellies up" on you defensively, dribble to relieve pressure, either by dribbling toward a teammate or driving toward the basket. The best way to defeat pressure is by attacking the basket.

IF YOU WORK HARD ENOUGH AND LONG ENOUGH, YOU CAN BEAT PEOPLE, BECAUSE THE WORLD IS FULL OF AVERAGE.

PAT SUMMITT
UNIVERSITY OF TENNESSEE
NCAA NATIONAL CHAMPIONSHIP COACH

THE TRIPLE-THREAT SCORING SYSTEM

If you have not mastered shooting skills yet, work on shooting first, then come back to work on these scoring moves. If you have studied and understand what the triple-threat position is and how to use it, then it is time to introduce the Triple-Threat Scoring System (TTSS). Although I did not invent the triple-threat position or its name, through decades of study, research, coaching, and practice, I have designed and developed the Triple-Threat Scoring System. It will help teach players to be more offensively minded and effective. To be offensively minded means only one thing: *to go to the basket!*

The moves and scoring options in this system show how to get there. The concepts and moves involved in the TTSS are advanced moves and techniques. Mastering the fundamentals of the game is strongly recommended before trying to learn scoring moves. The shooting fundamentals in Chapter 2 are compatible with the TTSS and will provide a solid foundation for further development.

The TTSS teaches seven different offensive scoring moves that each involve specific footwork or choreography. The seven moves evolve into twenty-eight different scoring options. Thus seven moves give the appearance of twenty-eight moves, even though they really are only options. These options range from shots to passes that open up as offensive players "read" and attack defenders. The seven moves can be executed from any area from the perimeter and are initiated through two offensive positions that are foundational to the TTSS. The great thing about the TTSS is that players actually need to practice only seven moves in order to execute the twenty-eight options because sixteen of the options repeat the exact same footwork. The difference comes in ways of initiating the moves: from triple-threat position, a rocker step, or a catch and shoot.

The TTSS will fit into any offensive settings or plays. Learning centers on doing the footwork or choreography correctly. If you watch a dance performance and see somebody that is out of synch with other dancers, you know that their footwork is not effective. The same is true for basketball. You must learn the choreography or footwork for these different moves to become a consistently effective and successful scorer.

Position 1: The Triple-Threat Position

By now readers understand what the triple-threat position means, what it looks like, and how to assume that position when receiving the ball on the perimeter. From this position, facing up to the basket, a player can initiate all of the scoring options in the TTSS. Mastering the habit and skill to pivot facing up to the basket on the correct foot, in a correct triple-threat position, is essential. The ability to score consistently will depend on it.

Position 2: The Jab-and-Attack Position

The second position that a player needs to learn is the jab position, or Jab-and-Attack Position (see Figure 5.6). This is part of a jab step, which is a short, quick movement to ward off a defender. You must make a jab step in order to get into a Jab-and-Attack Position. The Jab-and-Attack Position is designed to help you attack your defender quickly and successfully. It is an aggressive offensive position that you hold for one full second as you read the defender's position, and you must get out of your comfort zone to use it. After catching the ball and facing up in a triple-threat position, you need to read how the defender is playing against you. If the defender is two arm's lengths away, a correct decision would be to shoot the ball. If the defender is one arm's length away or closer, automatically move into a Jab-and-Attack Position (see Figure 5.7).

FIGURE 5.6 The Jab-and-Attack Position

To get into this position, take your lead foot (which, if you are right-handed, will be your right foot), and step forward so that the heel is lined up with the toe of your pivot foot (see Figure 5.8). Your lead foot heel moves parallel to the toe of your pivot foot. I also refer to this as the Sprinter's Position because, once you are down low, it allows you to explode to the basket, past the defender. (Sprinters start a race from this position because it gives them an explosive first step.) This is a critical position because it produces an explosive first step no matter how quick a defender is.

FIGURE 5.7 Moving into the Jab-and-Attack Position

When assuming the Jab-and-Attack Position, do not overextend yourself, or your center of gravity will be too far forward. This will cause you to travel by pulling your body forward and picking up your pivot foot, instead of letting you push off your pivot foot for explosiveness. Do this drill every day to avoid the bad habits of overextending and jabbing to the side. Either one of these common habits will make you an ineffective offensive player.

To practice the Jab-and-Attack Position, work with a line and do twenty to thirty repetitions daily. Use the line to keep your body well balanced and in the Sprinter's Position. The lines on the court can be a great tool in mastering the footwork and correct spacing for the jab step.

Once you lower yourself into a Jab-and-Attack Position, read the defender's foot position. If the defender backs away from you when you make a jab step, you can then rise up and shoot the ball, using a set shot or jump shot. You can also come back with a shot fake to draw the defender back toward you. If the defender does not back off once you are in a jab position, simply go by the defender with a low, explosive first step out of the jab position to the basket.

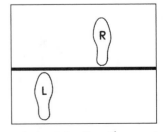

FIGURE 5.8 Foot Placement for the Jab-and-Attack Position

Using a Jab Step

When you use a jab step, jab low and not long. Never jab long, and never jab to the side. Many players have heard of this step and have even practiced it, but they jab to the side or overextend when jabbing low. When executing a jab step, your feet should be shoulders' width apart, and the stride length should be heel to toe or approximately one to two inches apart—a Sprinter's Position (see Figure 5.8). Players need to realize that the basket is straight ahead and so is the opportunity to score. Jab directly at the basket and at the defender. This will give you the results you want—scoring more points.

Benefits of the Jab-and-Attack Position.   Here is a list of the many benefits available through use of the Jab-and-Attack Position.

1. It protects the ball from the defender. In a Jab-and-Attack Position, for right-handers, the ball will always be on the right side of the lead leg. A defender will find it very difficult to reach in and steal the ball. It will force the defender to lean forward and be thrown off balance. Thus holding the ball in this position detours or discourages the defender from reaching in.
2. It enables the offensive player to shoot quickly when a defender backs off. The player can use a "hinge movement." This movement allows a player to rise up and shoot the ball out of the jab position without having to recover or change body position drastically.
3. It gets defenders on their heels. Coaches always recommend watching the waist or crotch area of the offensive player when defending, because this is the hardest part of the body to fake. When a player goes into the Jab-and-Attack Position, the defender loses sight of the waist area of the offensive player. This puts defenders on their heels and off balance, making them ineffective.
4. The offensive player gains an explosive first step by using the Sprinter's Position. In game situations in which the defender does not back off, this step can launch a quick drive to the basket.
5. The jab step forces a defender to back off and release pressure. If the defender does back off, the player can rise and shoot the ball.

▨I TRAINING TIP _____

Use a Chair to Simulate a Defender

The best way to practice jab moves in the backyard or driveway or in the gym, whether as an individual or team, is to set up a chair and pretend it is a defender. Putting a pair of shoes under two chair legs (see Figure 5.9) will make the simulation more realistic.

The top of the back of the chair represents a defender's hip area and helps show how low the offensive player's back should be in the Jab-and-Attack Position.

Shoulders should be level with the back of the chair (as in Figure 5.9). Getting the shoulders down to the level of the defender's hips will throw off the defender and mask the offensive player's waist area.

You will have to practice, practice, practice to get used to making these moves. Once you learn them, you will become a powerful and successful offensive player. Executing the footwork correctly will increase your scoring average by up to ten points a game or more, depending on your ability to work hard.

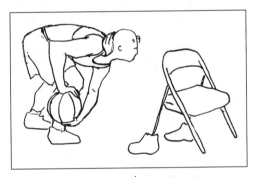

FIGURE 5.9   Using a Chair in Practice

SEVEN SCORING MOVES

As already noted, the TTSS involves two set positions, seven specific moves, and twenty-eight scoring options. That is a lot! However, you need to learn only two set scoring positions (The triple-threat position and the Jab-and-Attack Position) and seven scoring moves. The additional options occur naturally as you use the moves and respond to a defender's actions. This process will make more sense as you learn each move.

Move 1: Shot out of Triple Threat

This is the first move you need to practice on a daily basis. It is already incorporated into your normal shooting practice when you use the V-Shot Principle to face up to the basket. If, upon facing up to the basket, you have an opening, shoot the ball.

Move 2: Jab Step, Step Back, and Shoot

In this move, when you take a jab step and go to a Jab-and-Attack Position. If the defender retreats, quickly rise up and shoot during that retreat (see Figure 5.10). The jab step should be made low, not long. Keep good body balance.

Move 3: Catch and Shoot

This technique has been described earlier. The key to success is constant readiness to receive the ball, placing the hands in the shoulder pad area, and shooting the ball off the catch or pass from a teammate. Review information on the catch and shoot from Chapter 2. This move is typically used when a player is prepared to received the ball with hands ready in a catch position.

Move 4: Go Move

Follow the instructions perfectly to obtain the best results. In this move the offensive player takes four steps and *two dribbles* to the basket, using sound fundamentals to finish the scoring move. By using only one dribble, a player would still end up taking four steps to get on the correct foot for shooting a layup. So, although there is an extra dribble in this move, there is not an extra step. Use two dribbles to keep you from traveling. Begin with the ball on your perimeter, facing the basket in a triple-threat position.

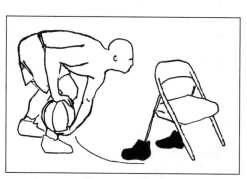 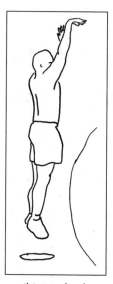

(a) Jab step, Jab-and-Attack Position

(b) Step back and shoot

FIGURE 5.10   Executing Move 2

Triple threat.

Go to a triple-threat position and face the basket. (The pivot foot is always the left foot for right-handers.)

Jab step.

Take a jab step, going into a Jab-and-Attack Position. If the defender does not back off, drive to the basket.

Right-foot dribble.

To drive to the basket, step forward with the right foot and take a dribble with your right hand. The dribble and the step should make *one* sound, not two.

Left-foot dribble.

Take a second step, and dribble toward the basket, stepping forward with your left foot and taking a second dribble with your right hand. Again, the dribble and the step with the left foot should make one sound.

Right foot, shoulder pad.

Step with your right foot while bringing the ball into your shooting pocket or shoulder pad. Gather yourself, and load the ball into your shooting pocket for a strong finish.

Left-foot layup with the right hand.

Step forward with your left foot, lifting your right leg up toward the basket as you jump up and shoot the ball with your right hand to score the layup.

▮ TRAINING TIP _____

Say the commands out loud as you practice the steps: *"Jab, right-foot dribble, left-foot dribble, right foot, shoulder pad, left-foot layup with the right hand."* Learning will be easier.

99

MOVE 4: GO MOVE FOR LEFT-HANDED PLAYERS

1

2

3

Triple threat.

Go to a triple-threat position, and face the basket.

Jab step.

Take a jab step as you go into a Jab-and-Attack Position. If the defender does not back off, drive to the basket.

Left-foot dribble.

To drive to the basket, push off your pivot foot (right foot) and make one sound as you step and dribble.

4

5

6

Right-foot dribble.

Take a second step with your right foot and dribble toward the basket. Again, the dribble and the step with the left foot should make one sound.

Left foot, shoulder pad.

Gather yourself, and load the ball into your shooting pocket for a strong finish.

Right-foot layup with the left hand.

Take your last step, and jump up to score the layup.

IT'S NOT THE SOLE OF THE SHOE THAT MAKES A PLAYER GREAT;

IT'S THE SOUL OF THE PLAYER.

SCOTISM

Move 5: The Crossover Move

In this move, the offensive player attacks the defender by crossing over with the ball and the lead foot (the right foot, for right-handers). The footwork is the same for left-handed players, but the opposite foot and hand positions should be used.

THE CROSSOVER MOVE

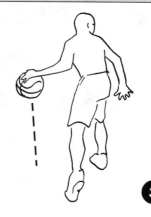

Triple threat.

Begin with the ball on your perimeter, facing the basket in a triple-threat position.

Jab step.

Next, take a jab step, going into a Jab-and-Attack Position. If the defender does not back off . . .

Cross over, right-foot dribble.

. . . quickly step across the defender with your right foot and the ball as you push off your pivot foot and take a dribble with your *left* hand to shield the ball from the defender. (The pivot foot is always the left foot, for right-handers.) The dribble and the step should make one sound, not two.

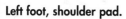

Right-foot layup with the left hand.

Step forward with your right foot, lifting your left leg up toward the basket and shooting the ball with your left hand. Take your last step, and score the layup with your left hand.

Left foot, shoulder pad.

Step forward with your left foot, bringing the ball to your shooting pocket or shoulder pad for a strong finish.

Move 6: Jump Shot Right

Move 6 is the jump shot off the dribble to the right. This shot is used to maneuver past a defender and move to a clear spot on the floor to take an open shot. To perform jump shots off the dribble to the right, follow these steps. The footwork is the same for left-handed players, but the opposite foot and hand positions should be used.

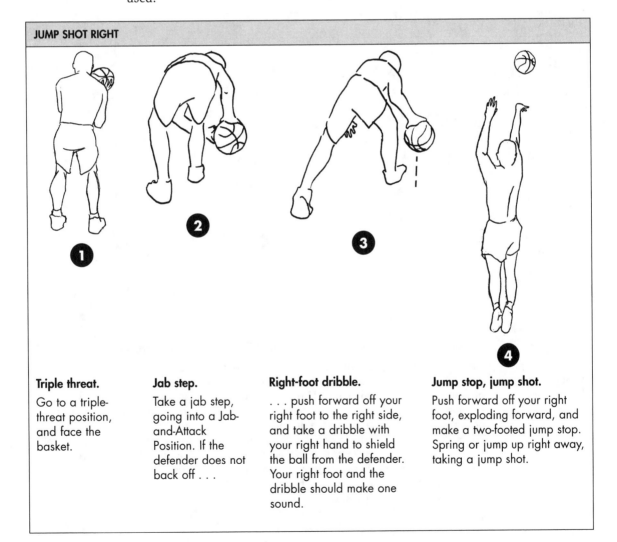

JUMP SHOT RIGHT

Triple threat.

Go to a triple-threat position, and face the basket.

Jab step.

Take a jab step, going into a Jab-and-Attack Position. If the defender does not back off . . .

Right-foot dribble.

. . . push forward off your right foot to the right side, and take a dribble with your right hand to shield the ball from the defender. Your right foot and the dribble should make one sound.

Jump stop, jump shot.

Push forward off your right foot, exploding forward, and make a two-footed jump stop. Spring or jump up right away, taking a jump shot.

> ### ▌ TRAINING TIP _____
>
> When executing and practicing the jump shot, do not jump too far forward, to the side, or fade away as you come to a jump stop to shoot. These habits will cause your shot to go off line. Try to square up to the basket on your jump stop, then jump up and come down in as close to the same spot as possible.

Move 7: Jump Shot Left

To perform this move, do the following:

JUMP SHOT LEFT

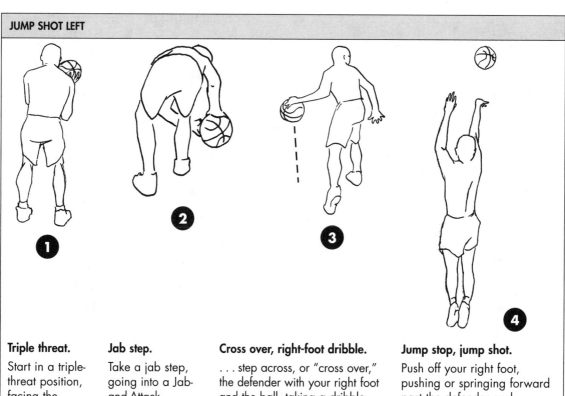

Triple threat.

Start in a triple-threat position, facing the basket.

Jab step.

Take a jab step, going into a Jab-and-Attack Position. If the defender does not back off . . .

Cross over, right-foot dribble.

. . . step across, or "cross over," the defender with your right foot and the ball, taking a dribble with your *left* hand to shield the ball from the defender. The dribble and the step should make one sound, not two. As you cross over with the ball, keep the ball below your knees, and jerk it through quickly from right to left.

Jump stop, jump shot.

Push off your right foot, pushing or springing forward past the defender and squaring your shoulders to the basket while making a two-footed jump stop. Immediately spring or jump up, taking a jump shot.

HOW TO DOUBLE YOUR MOVES: THE CATCH AND SHOOT, SHOT FAKE

The catch and shoot, shot fake is an invaluable tool to use against both zone and man-to-man defenses. It allows you to fake the defender into getting out of position or off balance. Here's how to practice it. Upon catching the ball, make a jump stop and immediate shot fake, freezing the ball above your ear while keeping your feet on the ground (see Figure 5.11).

After the defender runs by you or leans off balance, initiate Move 4, 5, 6, or 7. All of these moves begin the very same way, with the command "right-foot dribble" (see Figure 5.12). For a solid practice routine, complete five to ten repetitions of each of these four moves.

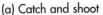

(a) Catch and shoot   (b) Shot fake   **FIGURE 5.12** The Right-Foot Dribble

FIGURE 5.11 The Catch and Shoot, Shot Fake

HOW TO TRIPLE YOUR MOVES: THE ROCKER STEP

The rocker step is a faking move that pushes the defender backward and then draws the defender toward you, throwing the defender off balance. The principle behind the move is based on the fact that a defender cannot move in two directions at the same time. By drawing a defender toward you with the rocker step, you are trying to make that player commit to one location.

To use the rocker step, begin in a triple-threat position, facing the basket. Back off the defender by using a jab step. If you don't have enough room to shoot or if you are not comfortable with the spacing, draw the defender toward you with a shot fake to throw off his or her balance. Then go by the defender for the easy shot or move (see Figure 5.13).

If the defender does not come back toward you, you are open to shoot the ball.

(a) The triple-threat position

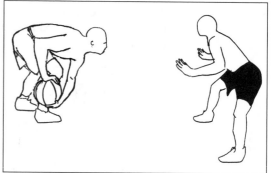

(b) Taking a low jab step

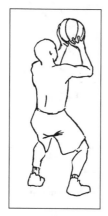

(c) Making a
shot fake

(d) Right-foot dribble

FIGURE 5.13   Using the Rocker Step

HOW TO CHOOSE A SCORING OPTION

As mentioned earlier, the TTSS breaks down into two positions and seven moves. The only variable is the option of adding an extra fake by using the rocker step (before executing a move to draw the defense off balance) or the catch and shoot, shot fake. Either one can draw the defense off balance, allowing the offensive player to drive and pass the ball to a teammate (called a "draw and kick"). These moves can create more offense for the team.

Average players will *take* an open shot. Good players can *make* open shots. Great players can create (and make) open shots for themselves or their teammates every time they touch the ball. Through daily practice and repetition, you will begin to recognize instinctively which move is best for a given situation. In addition to individual practice of the scoring moves, you will need to play a lot of one-on-one to develop a feel for the moves and scoring options and how to use them. Use the directions outlined in this chapter to play one-on-one correctly.

PLAYING ONE-ON-ONE

Playing one-on-one is an excellent way to practice the triple-threat moves for game situations. To play correctly, use the following pro rules:

1. The offensive player must let the defensive player check the ball in to initiate play from the perimeter area of the court.
2. The offensive player is allowed to take no more than two dribbles to attack the basket. If more than two dribbles are taken, treat it as a turnover. The purpose of this rule is to teach you to get to the basket quicker. It will also help to neutralize help side defense (help coming from a defender's teammates). In a game situation, if you take more than two dribbles, help side defense will be there to take an offensive charge. Learn to attack the basket quickly. This will also force you to use and develop the moves in the TTSS correctly; none of the moves require more than two dribbles.
3. Check the ball in at the perimeter area after a defensive rebound.
4. The ball changes possession after each score.
5. Play an offensive rebound "live," simulating a game situation. Score the rebound if you can.
6. If you score a basket, the offensive player then becomes the defender. This will force you to also work on your defensive skills.

As you play one-on-one, take care to learn to read the defender's foot position. You must learn what moves to use correctly and when to use them in order to be an effective scorer and creator with the ball.

 TRAINING TIP _____

One-on-One Play-Off Series

An excellent way to improve offensive moves and skills is to play one-on-one daily, using the "two dribbles" rule noted earlier. Try the play-off version of one-on-one. In this series, the first player to win four out of seven games is the play-off champion. Both players can rest between each game by shooting and recording ten free throws. Alternate who gets to shoot ten free throws first after each game. The player who makes the most shots out of ten gets the ball first in the next game. If it is a tie, they can shoot it off from the three-point line. This form of practice provides two different competitions daily: a one-on-one competition and a free-throw competition. It also prepares players for game situations by having them shoot free throws while tired.

One-on-one can be played to seven points or to eleven points, by counting a three-point shot as two points and a normal field goal inside of the three-point line as one point. After a score, a player moves to defense. Thus the game includes both offensive and defensive opportunities and practice.

How to Read and Attack a Defender

Most players in a game either predetermine a move to make or have no game plan at all. Attaining a higher level of offensive play requires both physical and intellectual skills, in addition to poise. Most basketball experts agree that one thing that made Larry Bird special and Michael Jordan great was their ability to hold the ball for four to five seconds before making a move. Some called this poise; some said it was composure. What they did was read the defender: looking at the body position to see where the defender was off balance, reading weakness in the opponent, and then attacking the weakest area or countering with jabs and shot fakes to get the defender off balance.

There's a simple formula that dictates how to respond to a defender. If the defender is two or more arm's lengths away, shoot the ball. If a defender is only one arm's length away, go to a Jab-and-Attack Position, and attack the defender's lead foot. Here are a few simple examples of how to attack a defender:

READING A DEFENDER	DEFENDER'S POSITION	MOVE TO USE
 **1**	Two arm's lengths away.	Shoot the ball.
2	Defender is one arm's length away or closer.	Make a jab step, going to a Jab-and-Attack Position. Then read and attack the defender with a scoring move unless the defender is obviously retreating.
3	Defender's left foot is forward and closest to you.	Drive to your right side. The defender has to drop-step, losing one full second before recovering to defend your drive.
4	Defender's right foot is forward and closest to you.	Drive to your left side by crossing over the defender's lead foot, forcing the defender to drop-step in order to stay with you.

SUMMARY OF THE TRIPLE-THREAT SCORING SYSTEM

Use the following table as you master the moves of the TTSS. It will remind you of the many options available to you once you've learned the positions and the moves. Having twenty-eight scoring options will make you "offensive-minded."

TRIPLE-THREAT SCORING SYSTEM

The Two Positions

1. The triple-threat position
2. The Jab-and-Attack Position (Sprinter's Position)

The Seven Scoring Moves

1. Shot out of triple threat (Use the V-Shot Shooting Principle to practice this.)
2. Jab step, step back, and shoot
3. Catch and shoot
4. Go move
5. Crossover move
6. Jump shot right
7. Jump shot left

Three Variations for Practicing Scoring Moves (Practice the moves using each two days weekly.)

1. Out of the triple-threat position
2. Out of a catch and shoot
3. Out of a rocker step

Twenty-Eight Scoring Options

Option 1/Move 1	Shot out of triple-threat position
Option 2	Pass out of triple-threat position
Option 3/Move 2	Jab step, step back, and shoot
Option 4/Move 3	Catch and shoot

From the Jab-and-Attack Position (To Go by the Defense)

Option 5/Move 4	Go move out of Jab-and-Attack Position
Option 6/Move 5	Crossover move out of Jab-and-Attack Position
Option 7/Move 6	Jump shot right out of Jab-and-Attack Position
Option 8/Move 7	Jump shot left out of Jab-and-Attack Position

From the Catch and Shoot, Shot Fake (To Draw the Defense to You)

Option 9/Move 4	Go move out of catch and shoot, shot fake
Option 10/Move 5	Crossover move out of catch and shoot, shot fake
Option 11/Move 6	Jump shot right out of catch and shoot, shot fake
Option 12/Move 7	Jump shot left out of catch and shoot, shot fake

From the Rocker Step (To Back Off the Defense and/or to Draw the Defense to You)

Option 13/Move 4	Go move out of the rocker step
Option 14/Move 5	Crossover move out of the rocker step
Option 15/Move 6	Jump shot right out of the rocker step
Option 16/Move 7	Jump shot left out of the rocker step

Options 17–28

To add an additional twelve options to your scoring repertoire, simply recognize that once you beat your defender and another help defender picks you up, one of your teammates will be open. Pass, and get an easy assist. The pass adds another twelve options to your arsenal when used with the moves from Options 5–16.

A Daily Workout Based on the Triple-Threat Scoring System

The following practice program is designed to put the entire scoring system into a daily workout. It will take less than an hour a day to complete. The first three to four weeks may take a little bit longer as you get used to executing the shots and moves correctly. Use the workout program as your road map to better scoring skills.

The moves are arranged in three parts, so that you work the moves out of the triple-threat position with the jab step, Jab-and-Attack Position two days a week, with the catch and shoot, shot fake two days a week and the rocker step two days a week. This will cut down on the number of repetitions each day but will bring similar results while tripling your scoring options.

▪▎▎ TRAINING TIP _____

As you practice shooting, you have a goal to *make* a certain number of shots, not to *take* a certain number. The rule is the same when you practice scoring moves. The workout calls for a minimum number of shots to be completed for each move (usually five to ten). Practice each move and *make* five to ten shots of each move. This discipline will improve your concentration, dedication, conditioning, and determination. That's what real practice is all about. For the first few months, make a minimum of ten shots with each scoring move. Once you become familiar with them and can use them in game situations, then you can reduce the number of makes you complete for the TTSS workout to five repetitions per day. Always practice footwork and moves perfectly and at full intensity. Full intensity means as fast as possible while still maintaining control.

THE TRIPLE-THREAT SCORING SYSTEM (TTSS) WORKOUT PROGRAM

Practice Moves

(Complete 5–10 repetitions of each move daily.)

I. Five-Spot Warm-Up Drill

(Make 10 shots from all 5 spots.)
Take and record 10 free throws (10 total).

II. Jump stop and pivot drill (10 Repetitions)

Take and record 10 free throws (20 total).

III. Jab step, Jab-and-Attack Position (Sprinter's Position) (10 Repetitions)

Take and record 10 free throws (30 total).

Move 1:	Shot out of triple threat (Using the V-Shot Shooting Principle, make 25 shots.) Take and record 10 free throws (40 total).	
Move 2:	Jab step, step back, and shoot Take and record 10 free throws (50 total).	
Move 3:	Catch and shoot off the pass (Use one of the three move variations on alternating days: Mon./Wed.—triple threat, Tues./Thurs.—rocker step, Wed./Sat.—catch and shoot.) Take and record 10 free throws (60 total).	
Move 4:	Go move (Right-foot dribble, left-foot dribble, right foot, shoulder pad, left-foot layup) Take and record 10 free throws (70 total).	
Move 5:	Crossover move (Right-foot crossover and dribble with left hand, left foot, shoulder pad, right-foot layup with the left hand) Take and record 10 free throws (80 total).	
Move 6:	Jump shot right (Right-foot dribble, push off right foot, jump stop, jump shot) Take and record 10 free throws (90 total).	
Move 7:	Jump shot left (Right-foot crossover and dribble with left hand, push off right foot, jump stop, jump shot) Take and record 10 free throws (100 total).	

More Tips for Practice

Applications for Game Situations.   To use the TTSS correctly, you must receive the ball within your shooting perimeter and always face up to the basket. Your perime-

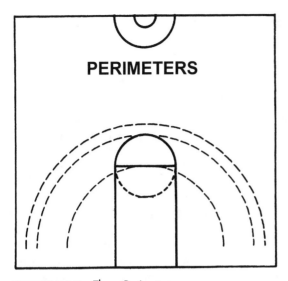

FIGURE 5.14   Three Perimeters

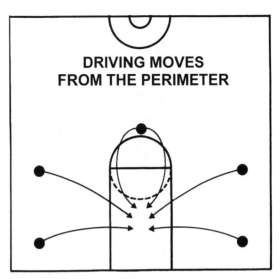

FIGURE 5.15   Spots for Practicing the Scoring Moves

ter is the farthest distance from the basket from which you can effectively and consistently shoot the ball. In general, there are three perimeter areas in which players are most comfortable and effective (see Figure 5.14). The first is an appropriate perimeter for all centers and power forwards as well as beginning players at the junior high level and under. The outer perimeters are proper for guards and small forwards at the junior high, high school, and upper levels of competition all the way to the pros. Low-post players should also use these perimeters if they have developed good three-point-shooting skills.

TRAINING TIP

A playing skill or move will never become second nature to you until you have practiced it ten thousand times *correctly.*

Using Areas of the Court.   The five areas or "spots" on the court shown in Figure 5.15 are realistic locations for receiving the ball on offense. Practice from different spots each day. Although the moves and footwork will not change, the area you practice from should.

Common Mistakes in Using the TTSS.   Avoid these common mistakes when executing triple-threat moves:

1. *Holding the ball above the head:* This takes away two options—to shoot and to drive.
2. *Overextending the jab step:* This forces the body off balance and creates traveling problems. It will also make you slower.
3. *Holding the ball on the inside or in the middle front of the body when in the Jab-and-Attack Position:* This exposes the ball to the defender and creates control problems for you.
4. *Not getting low enough in a Jab-and-Attack Position:* If you do not get low enough, you will not break the eye level of the defender, and you will lose your explosive first step. You will also make it easy for a defender to cover you.

The TTSS will unify and maximize all the offensive skills you develop. It is truly an offensive weapon. It will increase an individual's scoring and benefit any team. The TTSS will, however, require a great deal of practice and rehearsal. Stick with it, and do not get discouraged. Practice each move and position a minimum of ten times each day for at least a month. Practice can and will improve performance. The more time you put into practicing, the more playing time you will get!

COACHES' CHALK TALK: IMPLEMENTING THE TRIPLE-THREAT SCORING SYSTEM

As coaches, no one condones selfish play. But being a good one-on-one player and being a selfish ballplayer are two different things. As a coach, you rely on your best offensive ballplayer for an important basket. Being familiar with the triple threat and being good at one-on-one will not make your players selfish. It will help all of them improve as offensive players.

From a coaching viewpoint, trying to teach an entire team the triple threat during the season is impractical. But if you can take only five to ten minutes each day, you can build one move at a time by adding one per week. The triple threat can be useful and should be taught when circumstances permit or necessity dictates. On less intense levels of basketball, such as youth league and junior high school teams, it can be a very beneficial tool. A lot will depend on the level and the abilities of your players. The easiest way to begin is by teaching the two positions and seven basic scoring moves. Take ten minutes of practice time each day to let the players practice the moves. You will be amazed at the results you receive within three to four weeks.

Once your players have learned all seven moves, put five to ten minutes on the clock in the gym daily, and have your players practice the seven moves, completing five repetitions of each move within the time period. They will have to work hard to get all the repetitions in. Alternate the catch and shoot with the rocker step and shot fake every other day. If you have an extra five minutes, have the team play one-on-one using the pro rules with only two dribbles. Have the players keep score to make it more competitive. When practice is particularly sluggish, have a one-on-one tournament for the team.

If you want to integrate the Triple-Threat Scoring System into your team practices (or to teach it to an individual player), the best way is to play one-on-one, using the rules outlined in this chapter. This will give your players live experience with the triple threat. The best time to introduce it to the team is at the beginning of the season, for fifteen to twenty minutes a day during your two-week preseason preparation. Have your players play one-on-one to seven or eleven points. At the end of each week or month, take an hour for a team tournament to break up the monotonous routines of daily practice. At the end of the season, have a team one-on-one championship. It will be fun for the players and good practice in using the triple threat. It is also excellent practice for preparation against a man-to-man defense.

Another excellent time to introduce the Triple-Threat Scoring System and moves is during summer camp with your team. This will give you and the players some quality time to learn the footwork and change old physical habits. Regardless of how you decide to implement the system, be patient. Invest a little time each day, and you will see results one step at a time.

One last thought: when a player has a lot of difficulty in learning, follow this simple rule. If a player messes up the footwork when practicing, repeat the move again *twice as slow, twice in a row*. Slowing down the steps and the process will allow a player to better assimilate the footwork and choreography. It is hard to break old habits and develop new ones; force-feed improved habits by practicing the move twice as slow, twice in a row.

CHAPTER QUESTIONS

1. Explain the triple-threat position and its importance in basketball.

2. List the seven scoring moves in the Triple-Threat Scoring System.

3. What are the benefits gained from the Jab Step and the Jab-and-Attack Position? What is the difference between the two?

4. How do the Catch and Shoot and the Rocker Step help a player increase the number of available moves?

5. Why is it important to play one-on-one using pro rules?

6. How can a player determine how far out from the basket is an appropriate shooting perimeter?

7. What are three common mistakes made when using the triple-threat position?

8. How can a team benefit from practicing and using the Triple-Threat Scoring System?

Passing Fundamentals

IN THIS CHAPTER YOU WILL LEARN:
- The most neglected fundamental of the game of basketball
- Unselfish basketball passing, the key to good teamwork
- A repertoire of passing techniques and drills
- Dozens of fundamental and advanced passing skills and drills
- Four key passing techniques
- Five advanced drills for improving peripheral vision
- Passing drills for team practices
- Three abilities needed to be a great passer

THE SIGNIFICANCE OF A GREAT PASS

At only 6 feet 1 inch, Nate "Tiny" Archibald attained every possible accomplishment in basketball. He was an all-star at the NCAA Division I level of basketball for the University of Texas–El Paso. He went on to a stellar NBA career and won an NBA championship with the Boston Celtics. Individually, he also, *in the same season* (1972–73), led the NBA in both assists (11.4 per game) and scoring (34.0 points per game). This amounted to a phenomenal achievement, considering Archibald's size. Also, no other player in the history of professional basketball, before or after Tiny, has ever accomplished that feat. Nate Archibald, a great scorer, to his credit also understood the powerful potential of a great pass.

One of the most enjoyable things to watch in a basketball game is passing. Nothing picks up a team or a crowd faster than a basket made possible by an exceptional pass. It gives that team an emotional lift and breeds a spirit of unity, enthusiasm, and teamwork. A good pass is really worth three points: two for the basket made and one "invisible point" for the momentum and unity it brings to teammates and the fans.

A great pass is not necessarily a fancy trick pass or a "hot dog" pass. A great pass is simply one made to the right location, to the right player, at the right time. John Stockton, the all-time NBA assist leader, throws basic, fundamental passes—

nothing fancy. And yet he is the greatest passer in basketball history. And it is doubtful that his record will ever be broken. What is truly amazing about Stockton's record is that in his first three NBA seasons, he played only rarely, as a substitute.

Any player can develop the ability and skill to be a great passer by developing three abilities:

1. You must be able to see the whole court and all that is happening at all times.
2. You must develop, through practice and repetition, a repertoire of passes suited to many different game situations and opportunities.
3. You must be able to deliver the ball to the right person, in the right place and at the right time, at all times. This takes perfect vision and perfect timing (which comes from accepting nothing less than perfect performance in practice).

There are different kinds of passes. A pass that leads directly to a basket *or* a pass that leads to a score that could not have occurred without the pass is called an assist. One example is a lead pass to a teammate who is alone over half court but must dribble to score a layup. Some passes are more difficult than others. A behind-the-back or no-look pass will obviously be more difficult than a simple chest pass. But advanced passes may be appropriate in certain game situations. Basic arithmetic is less difficult than geometry, but both can be effective and useful if mastered. The same goes for passing the basketball. Both fundamental and advanced passes can be effective and useful in game situations when mastered correctly (they are defined and described later in this chapter). You're not a "hot dog" or show-off if you have mastered a skill and do it correctly in the right game situation. Showing off is trying to do something fancy that you have not mastered.

Passing is a vitally important skill because basketball is a team game. By developing your skills as a passer, you will show individual creativity and talent as well as improve and support your team.

PASS PLACEMENT AND LOCATION

Different game situations call for making a pass to different locations. This is perhaps one of the least taught and understood fundamentals of passing. A pass to a teammate should always follow these two guidelines:

1. A pass should travel in the direction in which the player is moving or toward the spot where the player calls for the ball (see Figure 6.1).
2. A pass should always be thrown to the side of your teammate opposite of the defender. This is true whether your teammate is posting

FIGURE 6.1 Player Calls for the Ball with Hand Up

FIGURE 6.2   Pass to Teammate away from Defender

up, cutting through the lane area, or cutting outside to the perimeter (see Figure 6.2).

As a passer, you should also recognize where on the court you want your teammate to receive the ball or the spot to which you'd like to deliver the ball. Obviously, the best location will be close to the three-point-line perimeter, which provides three good options to the receiver of the ball: to drive, to shoot, or to pass. If your teammate receives the ball too far from the basket, the only real option will be to pass. As the passer, your primary responsibility is to deliver the ball to the right location and at the right time. Maximize your team's scoring opportunities by developing the habit of proper pass placement when you pass the ball to your teammates.

This principle applies to passes to players coming off screens for a shot, passes to the low post, fast-break passes, point-guard-entry passes, backdoor passes, and lob passes. The same fundamental concepts are applicable when making an entry pass to a high-post player or low-post player.

Pass placement and position are vital to providing more scoring opportunities for your teammates. Make every possession count.

The exact placement of a pass as it reaches a teammate also determines its success. A pass that forces a teammate to stretch, overextend, or get off balance is not a good pass. Always try to pass the ball to a player's shooting pocket or shoulder area if the teammate is a stationary receiver, such as a post-up player or a perimeter player working against a zone defense. This will allow the player to catch and shoot quickly from the perimeter or, if in the post, will allow your teammate to pin a defender and hold position while receiving the pass.

With a teammate on the move, always aim for the target hand or to the outside, away from the defender. Try to anticipate the direction of your teammate's movement and determine where he or she will be when the pass arrives. This will minimize the defender's opportunity to steal the ball.

The next section shows how certain game situations demand different pass locations.

PASSES IN GAME SITUATIONS

Point-Guard-Entry Passes, Fast-Break Passes, and Lane Passes to Cutters

These passes are all moving-target passes. Figure 6.3 shows where they occur on the court. A good pass location to aim for with a moving target is either the hand target a teammate provides or the shoulder or chest area of the player to whom the pass is directed. Your teammate should not have to lean down, backward, or sideways to receive your pass, especially while moving. The ball should be easy to catch on the move without slowing down the player. The same is true of passes made to players who are cutting quickly through the lane to get open. Such cutters need to catch the ball at the chest area in preparation for shooting or passing. Then they will not waste an extra second or excess movement in bringing the ball up to

GIVE COACHES A REASON TO KEEP YOU, NOT A REASON TO CUT YOU.

SCOTISM

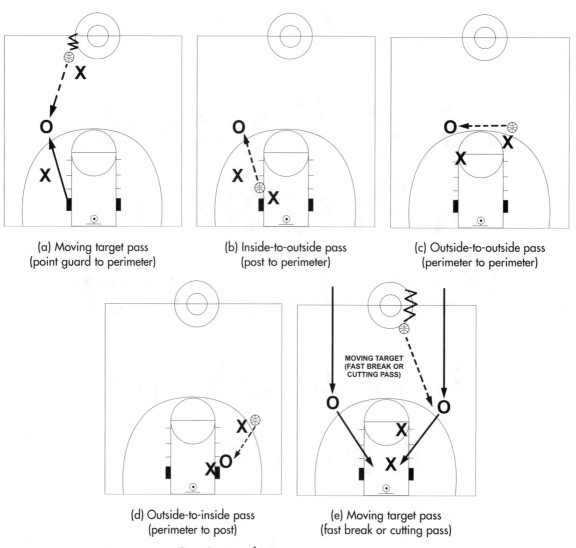

(a) Moving target pass
(point guard to perimeter)

(b) Inside-to-outside pass
(post to perimeter)

(c) Outside-to-outside pass
(perimeter to perimeter)

(d) Outside-to-inside pass
(perimeter to post)

(e) Moving target pass
(fast break or cutting pass)

FIGURE 6.3   Court Positions for Passes

the shooting pocket, and they will be able to react more quickly to what is happening on the court. The only exceptions to the chest pass location are these:

1. A high lob pass for a tip-in or a dunk
2. A pass to a teammate ahead of you on the fast break.

In the case of a lob pass, you should either lead the player toward the backboard or rim (if they cannot dunk) or (if a player can dunk) place your pass directly on top of or by the rim on the side that the player is coming from.

Passes to the Low Post

There is much debate among coaches as to where a pass should be made when entering a pass to a low-post player with a defender playing behind him or her. Such a pass should be easy to catch and targeted to an area difficult for a post defender to reach in order to knock away or tip the ball from the team member making the catch. One thing is certain: the bigger and better the offensive post player, the easier the pass will be to make. Some coaches advocate a direct chest pass to the low post, which works if the post player is agile, strong, and capable of catching a quick pass while also holding off a defender. However, a bounce pass to the low post is recommended for several reasons:

1. A defender will have to reach farther to tip the ball away from the teammate making the catch.
2. A bounce pass makes it easier for the offensive post player to follow the path of the ball and pick it up.
3. A bounce pass forces the offensive post player to bend into a lower stance, adding physical strength and balance while the player receives the ball.
4. A defender will momentarily lose sight of the ball as it is being passed.

If a defender is fronting the post (in which a defender plays between two teammates, one of whom is the post player), a lob pass will be the best pass. A lob pass must be high in order to travel over the defender, who is playing outside the lane area and in front of the offensive post player. Whether a bounce pass or a lob pass is thrown, the post pass should be aimed so that it is received on the player's side opposite the defender. Targeting this location forces the defender to go twice as far to tip or steal the ball.

▐ TRAINING TIP _____

Before making a lob pass to a fronted post player, it's a good idea to make a pass fake away from the post to another teammate. The fake pass will freeze, relax, and reposition help defenders as well as provide extra space and time to enter the lob pass into the post.

Perimeter Passes

Perimeter passes can be made by a point guard and directed to a teammate on the perimeter, thrown from one perimeter player to another perimeter player, or even passed from the low post back outside to a perimeter player. In each of these situations, the receiver should catch the ball with the outside hand, away from the defender. You can use a bounce pass or a chest pass in this situation. A chest pass is usually quicker.

PASSING PRACTICE

Passing is an easy skill to practice with a partner. It is also easy to do alone—all you need is a wall. By practicing passing drills for only a few minutes each day, you will add another dimension to your overall game. Working on passing drills for five to ten minutes each day can also serve as a great warm-up before training hard, playing, or practicing drills or moves.

To practice passing, use a partner, a wall, or even a toss-back. Pick a target high enough to represent the chest area of a teammate. You can use tape or paint a big "X" or "O" about the size of the basketball on the wall. Remember, the only good pass is a completed pass. Good intentions do not help score baskets; good passes do.

Begin by practicing the fundamental passes from 10 feet. Get to the point that you can hit a small 1-foot target ten times in a row before you move back in distance. Then, as your passes become stronger and more accurate, practice from 20, 30, and then 40 feet respectively. All of your passes should be sharp and quick. Once you can hit your target from 40 feet every time with all the fundamental passes, you are ready to move on to the advanced passes. Practice the advanced passes in the same way. Begin from 10 feet, and practice until you can make all passes effectively and without ever missing; then continue to move farther back, 5 to 10 feet at a time, until you can hit the target at 20, 30, and 40 feet. A good idea is to spend a minimum of one to two weeks at each distance before moving on to the next one. Do this for both the basic and advanced passes. In only twenty weeks you will have developed excellent passing abilities and gained a large repertoire of passes.

▌ TRAINING TIP

If you need two to four weeks to perfect passes from each distance, then use that amount of time. Anything worth doing is worth doing right. Do not move to a greater distance until you have mastered your current distance. A greater distance and more difficult passes take more time to perfect. Take the time to practice if you want to earn game time.

CATCHING PASSES

You can catch or receive a pass in one of two ways: with a two-handed catch (see Figure 6.4) or with a one-handed stop (two examples are shown in Figure 6.5). The younger and smaller the athlete, the more likely that a two-handed catch will work better. To make a two-handed catch, make sure that the thumbs and two inside fingers of both hands touch. This lessens the chance that a hard pass will go through the hands and be lost.

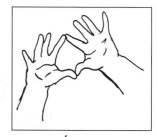

FIGURE 6.4   The Two-Handed Catch

A one-handed stop is a more advanced technique for receiving the ball. It allows a player to stop the ball with one hand, then quickly bring the other hand onto the ball after it has been stopped. You can practice both ways. Use what is comfortable for you. Your comfort zone will dictate your catching technique. Whichever catch you use, make sure to receive the ball with your shooting hand placed immediately behind the seams of the ball. This will prepare you to shoot the ball quickly.

Low-post players should catch passes using the one-handed technique. This will allow them to fight off defenders with the other arm until they can catch the ball.

FIGURE 6.5 Two Examples of the One-Handed Stop

TYPES OF BASKETBALL PASSES

In this chapter, passing drills are divided into two categories: fundamental passes and advanced passes. You must learn fundamental passes in order to become a good all-around player. The advanced passes are more showy and will take longer to learn, but they can be very useful in numerous game situations. They also make the game more fun to play and more exciting to watch.

TRAINING TIP

Before you try to learn advanced passes, make sure you have mastered the fundamental passes. Basketball is a game of fundamentals. A pass is only good when it is successfully completed.

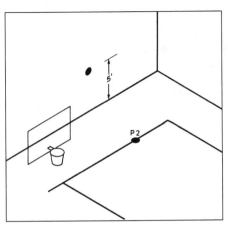

FIGURE 6.6 Focusing on a Target

Fundamental Passes

Fundamental passes are as important to master as correct shooting skills. In basketball, every possession counts, and the best way to get the most out of every possession is to make good passes, which in turn will provide a better shot selection. For all fundamental passes, do these three things as you practice:

1. Pick a target, and keep your eyes on it at all times. See your pass through to the target (see Figure 6.6).
2. Take a step in the direction of the pass.
3. Make sure your fingertips are the last thing to touch the ball. (Do not let the ball touch your palms.)

The Two-Handed Chest Pass.   Follow these steps to execute the two-handed chest pass:

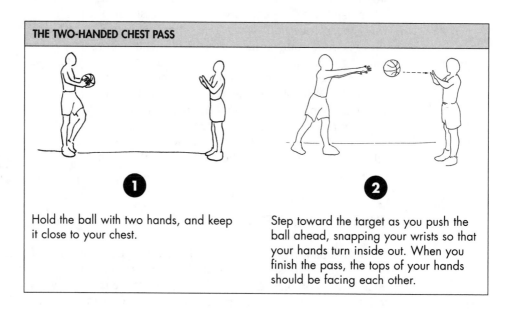

THE TWO-HANDED CHEST PASS

1 Hold the ball with two hands, and keep it close to your chest.

2 Step toward the target as you push the ball ahead, snapping your wrists so that your hands turn inside out. When you finish the pass, the tops of your hands should be facing each other.

The Two-Handed Bounce Pass.   Use the same motion as with the chest pass, but bounce the ball hard on the floor two-thirds of the way to your target. The pass should bounce up and be received in the chest area of your teammate.

The Two-Handed Overhead Pass.   This pass is good to use for lob passes (discussed later in the chapter), outlet passes for fast breaks, and passes against a zone defense. Follow these steps to execute the two-handed overhead pass:

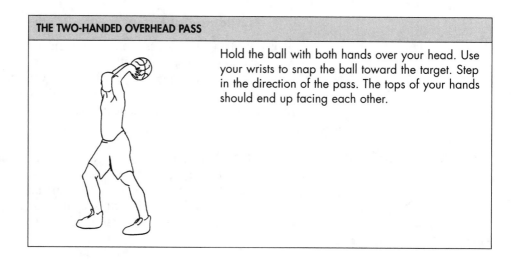

THE TWO-HANDED OVERHEAD PASS

Hold the ball with both hands over your head. Use your wrists to snap the ball toward the target. Step in the direction of the pass. The tops of your hands should end up facing each other.

The One-Handed Shuffle Pass, or Flip Pass. This is a good pass for a teammate cutting close by you, or it can be a soft, easy pass you give off when you drive to the basket. Practice it with each hand, only from 5, 10, and 15 feet. Follow these steps to execute the one-handed shuffle pass:

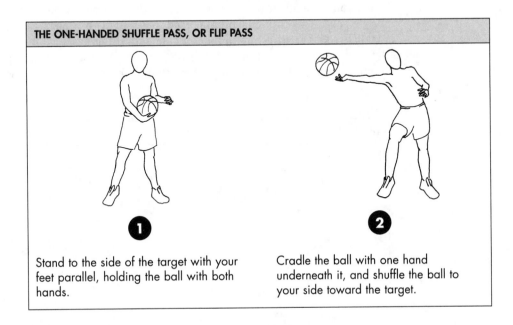

THE ONE-HANDED SHUFFLE PASS, OR FLIP PASS

1 Stand to the side of the target with your feet parallel, holding the ball with both hands.

2 Cradle the ball with one hand underneath it, and shuffle the ball to your side toward the target.

The Baseball Pass. Begin practicing this pass from 20 feet, and practice it in place of the shuffle pass. Practice with each hand. Follow these steps to execute the baseball pass:

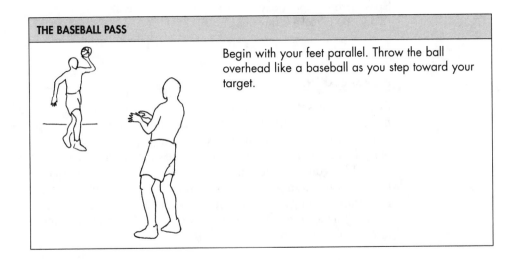

THE BASEBALL PASS

Begin with your feet parallel. Throw the ball overhead like a baseball as you step toward your target.

The Pivot Pass.   This is one of the most important fundamental passes yet perhaps the least-practiced pass by both individuals and teams. The pivot pass allows offensive players to create passing space and physical distance between themselves and the defender. By creating more passing space, you will be able to make an easier, more accurate pass, and experience fewer turnovers in passing situations, especially when you have already used your dribble. Use this pass when closely pressured by the defense. This drill can be practiced alone or with a partner/defender. Practice making passes from pivots to the left side and, if the passing lane is covered by the defense, pivoting back to the right side. Stay low on the pivot, and practice making the pass from both sides. Follow these steps to execute the pivot pass:

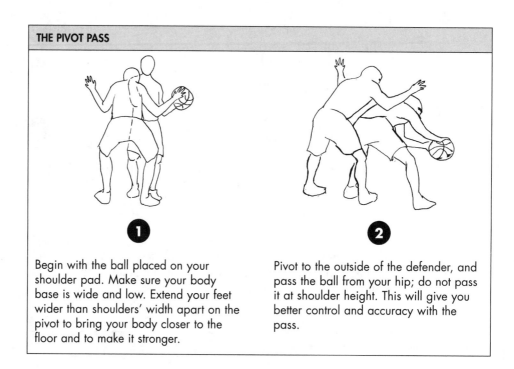

THE PIVOT PASS

1
Begin with the ball placed on your shoulder pad. Make sure your body base is wide and low. Extend your feet wider than shoulders' width apart on the pivot to bring your body closer to the floor and to make it stronger.

2
Pivot to the outside of the defender, and pass the ball from your hip; do not pass it at shoulder height. This will give you better control and accuracy with the pass.

Advanced Passes

Advanced passes are more difficult and therefore will take more time and effort to master in order to use them effectively. To perform advanced passes correctly, you must be willing to spend a good deal of time practicing them. Concentrate on using peripheral vision, looking to either side of your body without turning your head. Each drill requires different abilities and takes time to perfect. Be able to hit your target ten times in a row. Do not move farther from the practice target until you have mastered a pass from shorter distances. Advanced passes are reaction passes: as you practice them, you will automatically begin to use them as you react to different game situations.

The Off-the-Dribble Pass.   Work on this pass in a stationary dribbling position first, then begin practicing it with a dribble on the move. Practice it with both hands. Follow these steps to execute the off-the-dribble pass:

THE OFF-THE-DRIBBLE PASS

Keep your eyes on the target. Step in the direction of your pass. Pass off the dribble with one hand. Do not pick up the ball with two hands to pass it; this is a reaction pass and should come right off the dribble.

The Wrap-Around Pass, or Hook Pass.   This is a variation of the pivot pass. Be sure to practice this pass using both hands and pivoting in both directions. It will enable you to extend an additional 1 to 2 feet farther around a defender to make a pass. Follow these steps to make the wrap-around pass:

THE WRAP-AROUND PASS, OR HOOK PASS

Follow the preceding instructions for the pivot pass, except instead of using two hands, you will use only one to release or pass the ball. You must extend farther and lower when pivoting away from the defense to wrap the pass around a defender.

▮▮ TRAINING TIP

Remember this simple rule: the higher the degree of difficulty, the more repetitions you must practice in order to master the skill.

The Behind-the-Back Pass.   This pass is made by swinging the ball around the back to the target. Practice this pass with each hand, until you have mastered the skill with both hands equally well. This is a quick, sharp pass; do not float the ball or pass it softly. Follow these steps to execute the behind-the-back pass:

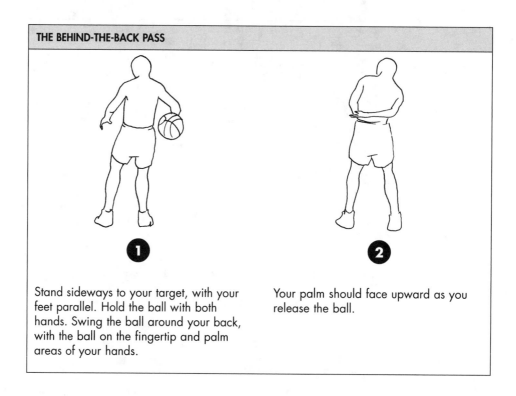

THE BEHIND-THE-BACK PASS

1. Stand sideways to your target, with your feet parallel. Hold the ball with both hands. Swing the ball around your back, with the ball on the fingertip and palm areas of your hands.

2. Your palm should face upward as you release the ball.

The Behind-the-Back Bounce Pass.   This is performed the same way as the behind-the-back pass, except that as you swing the ball around your back, you bounce it two-thirds of the way to the target with a hard bounce. Practice the drill with both hands.

THE ONLY GOOD PASS IS AN OPEN PASS.

THE ONLY GOOD OPEN PASS IS A COMPLETED PASS.

SCOTISM

The No-Look Pass, or Blind Pass.   Practice this pass with each hand, sending the ball in both directions. Follow these steps to execute the no-look pass:

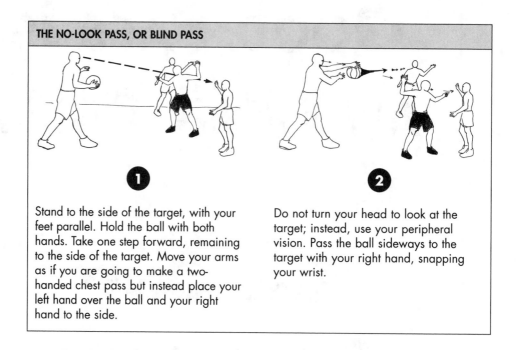

THE NO-LOOK PASS, OR BLIND PASS

1

Stand to the side of the target, with your feet parallel. Hold the ball with both hands. Take one step forward, remaining to the side of the target. Move your arms as if you are going to make a two-handed chest pass but instead place your left hand over the ball and your right hand to the side.

2

Do not turn your head to look at the target; instead, use your peripheral vision. Pass the ball sideways to the target with your right hand, snapping your wrist.

The Behind-the-Head Pass.   This is a great pass to use in order to freeze the defender, who will more than likely be watching your eyes to see whom you will pass to. Use peripheral vision to be successful and accurate with this pass.

Practice it with both hands and only from 10 and 15 feet. This is not a long-distance pass; at greater distances use the lob pass.

Follow these steps to execute the behind-the-head pass.

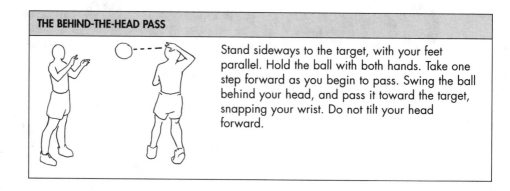

THE BEHIND-THE-HEAD PASS

Stand sideways to the target, with your feet parallel. Hold the ball with both hands. Take one step forward as you begin to pass. Swing the ball behind your head, and pass it toward the target, snapping your wrist. Do not tilt your head forward.

The Lob Pass.   Begin practicing this pass at 20 feet and beyond, using it in place of the behind-the-head pass.

A human target is not necessary as the passer must learn to pass to a spot up above or by the rim, not to a moving teammate. (If you do not have a backboard at home, use the side of a house or a building or even a tall ladder.) Follow these steps to execute the lob pass:

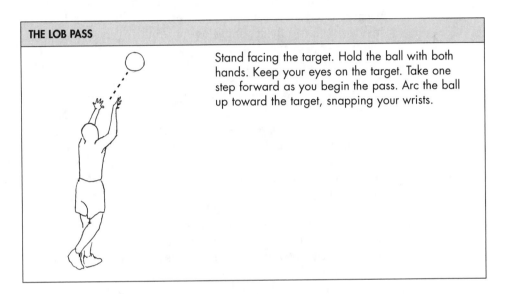

THE LOB PASS

Stand facing the target. Hold the ball with both hands. Keep your eyes on the target. Take one step forward as you begin the pass. Arc the ball up toward the target, snapping your wrists.

THE MENTALITY OF A PASSER

Most basketball players believe that if you do not score a lot, then you are not a good player. This is not always accurate. The beginning of this chapter mentioned Nate "Tiny" Archibald and the fact that he led the NBA in both scoring and assists in the same season. Wow! And yet Archibald spent most of his NBA career playing a backseat role to other scorers. When he won an NBA championship with the Boston Celtics, he focused almost entirely on setting up other people by passing the ball. He had a teammate at the time who was a pretty good player as well, named Larry Bird. Archibald focused on being a "creator," using his skills and talents to create shots for other players.

Never underestimate the power of a pass. If you know that you aren't the top scorer on your team, try to develop the mentality of a creator or passer. You do not have to be a point guard to be a great passer. Just develop your passing skills. Some of your best games will be memorable because you made a "double double"—ten or more assists and ten or more points in a single game.

No one can consistently get ten assists in a game without practicing and developing superb passing skills, as well as mental and physical skills. Take time to study and review what constitutes a good pass: choice of the receiver, location on the court, and the details that make each type of pass unique. All these little things will increase your totals.

Don't underestimate the usefulness of the moves presented in Chapter 5 (the Triple-Threat Scoring System). If you can break down a defender from the perimeter and draw a second defender to you, then you will discover a lot of open teammates, translating into more assists for you.

Anthony Duricy was only 5 feet, 6 inches tall with his shoes on, but he understood the power of a good pass. Duricy had worked really hard and during his senior year in high school he was in position to be a starter and possible all-star. But because the team was in a "rebuilding year," the high school coach decided to play his two seniors only sparingly, as substitutes. This was a real setback for Anthony, who had hopes of playing college basketball. But his hard work still paid off. He got tryouts with college teams as a walk-on, and he went on to play college basketball at North Shore Junior College and then at Western State College, an NCAA Division II college, on a basketball scholarship. Did Anthony ever score more than twenty points in a single college game? No. But he does hold North Shore's single-game record for assists—twenty-six in one game. He also scored fourteen points in the same game—a double double! Anthony developed the mentality of a creator, and he was very good at it. He worked hard every day on developing the passing skills and mentality of a creator. He passed everything, including his classes, and he got to play college basketball.

Passing is also a habit skill: once soundly developed, it is committed to memory. But the fact remains that most players are not good passers. They have not learned to look at the whole court with their head and eyes up, nor do they understand how to throw the correct pass and when to throw it. Yet you need only ten minutes a day to practice passing.

You can become a good passer too. Develop the desire to *want* to set other people up for easy shots. Look for passing opportunities. Take pride in the pass. Make players around you better by setting them up. No matter what your size, you can play a role on any team if you can create shots and pass the ball well. Practice passing and study great passers. Don't let the game pass you by.

▌ TRAINING TIP

An average assists-to-turnover ratio for a guard who handles the ball a lot at the high school or college level is two assists for every turnover (2:1). If your ratio of assists to turnovers is equal to or less than this, practice. If your ratio is 3:1, you're considered a good passing guard. If your ratio is 4:1 or higher, you're on your way to stardom.

▌ COACHES' CHALK TALK: PASSING DRILLS AND TEAM PRACTICE

As a coach, do not try to teach an entire team advanced passes. Players must want to learn and develop these skills on their own. The only passes to drill as a team are the fundamental ones. Here are three simple ways you can develop a team's passing skills.

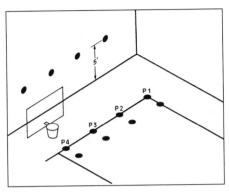

FIGURE 6.7 Setup for the Wall Drill

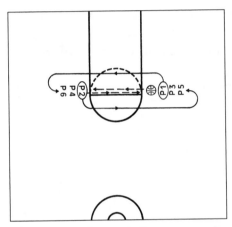

FIGURE 6.8 The Line Drill

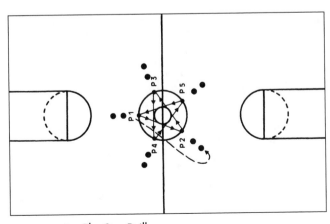

FIGURE 6.9 The Star Drill

The Wall Drill

Along one of the walls in the gym (or locker room), put up "passing spots," 10 to 15 feet apart. Use tape, paint, or a marker. The spots should be about 5 feet high. Put your players in five or six lines facing the spots (see Figure 6.7). Preferably place two, and no more than three, players in each line. Use one ball for each line. Practice the basic passing drills. Have players make each pass five to ten times, then move back 10 feet. They should practice all passes from 10, 20, 30, and 40 feet.

The Line Drill

Put three to four players in one line facing a line of three to four other players. Using one ball, have player 1 pass to player 2; player 1 then proceeds to the end of the opposite line (see Figure 6.8). Player 2 immediately passes to player 3. The drill continues likewise right to the end of the opposite line.

Continue this pattern with the same pass until all players have made five passes. Then practice the same pass 10 feet farther apart. Practice all passes at 10, 20, 30, and 40 feet. Passes should be sharp and quick.

The Star Drill

At center court or at the foul-line circles, have the players form five lines in a star design (see Figure 6.9). Put two or three players in each line. Player 1 passes to player 2 and follows the pass by moving on the right to the end of player 2's line. Player 2 passes to player 3 and goes to the end of player 3's line, and so forth. All players should complete two to three full rotations in the star. This is also a good pregame warm-up drill.

It is better to have players practice a specific number of passes, as indicated in these three drills, because this will make them concentrate more. They will not feel that they have lined up merely to toss the ball around and use up practice time. Have them work to hit their targets accurately with various passes for five minutes daily. Your players will stay familiar with each skill without getting bored with the drill. "Pass" it on.

███ **TRAINING TIP** _____

In the line drill and the star drill, you can have your players practice the V-cut (see Chapter 11) move at the same time. Player 1 will pass the ball and make a V-cut, planting left and going right to the end of the line. Player 2 will do the same thing. Once the drill moves 10 feet farther back or has gone through two sets of repetitions for each player, have the players change the direction of their V-cut from right to left. Get the benefit of two drills in one.

CHAPTER QUESTIONS _____

1. What are three abilities needed in order to be a great passer?

2. Define an assist in basketball.

3. What are two rules for good pass placement?

4. List the five variations of passes that occur during game situations.

5. List four reasons why a bounce pass to a low-post player is recommended.

6. In what two situations is it appropriate to throw a lob pass?

7. In what area of the court is it best for a teammate to receive a pass on the perimeter?

8. Explain the two ways in which you can catch and receive passes.

9. What two criteria determine whether a pass is good?

10. Define an assist-to-turnover ratio. What is considered a good ratio?

Defense Fundamentals

IN THIS CHAPTER YOU WILL LEARN:
- How playing good defense gets you off the bench and into the game
- The value of great defensive skills
- Eight ways to make defense easier to play
- Ways to disrupt your opponents' rhythm
- Man-to-man and zone drills for team practice
- What the two levels of defense are
- What to look for when scouting opposing players and teams
- How to become one second quicker on defense

Defender—one who asserts, guards, prohibits, opposes.
—Webster's Collegiate Dictionary

THE BENEFITS OF PLAYING GOOD DEFENSE

It is possible to write an entire book just on defense. Many have already been written. Since this is a fundamentals book for all areas of the game, the purpose of this chapter will be to define and present fundamental defensive principles. But first, it is important to have a solid understanding of why playing good defense is beneficial.

In a game of basketball (lasting thirty-two, forty, or forty-eight minutes), approximately one-half of a player's time will be spent at the defensive end of the court. Because of this, it's a good idea to develop defensive attitudes and habits that will benefit the team and improve its chances of winning games. For example, if you score thirty points in a game and the player you defend scores twenty-five points, the only thing you have accomplished is neutralizing your opponent. However, if you score twenty-five points and hold an opposing player who is averaging twenty-five points per game to only ten points, you have really accomplished something.

Likewise, if you average only ten points per game but you hold an opposing player who is averaging twenty-five points per game to only ten points, you have also made a great contribution to your team. In both situations, you have decreased the opposing team's offensive output by fifteen points. That is significant.

Offense Wins Games; Defense Wins Championships.

Here's an example. Your team is the Fairborn Flyers, and tonight you play against the Canyon Cougars. You are assigned to defend their top scorer, Sam Shooter, who averages twenty-four points per game, and you average ten points per game. Both the Flyers and the Cougars are averaging eighty points per game as a team. When you defend Sam, if you hold him to twelve points, you will cut the other team's scoring by twelve points, or 15 percent. This also means your team has a 15 percent better chance of winning the game.

If you hold Sam to twelve points, the final score will be 80–68 in favor of your team, with all other players scoring their normal average. If you instead defend Mike, who gets only eleven points per game, and hold him to six points, you have cut the opposing team's score by 5 points. The final score of the game would probably be 80–74 in your team's favor. This should demonstrate the importance of playing defense and being a complete player.

THE FLYERS VS. THE COUGARS

Your Team: The Flyers

Player	Average Points per Game	% of Team Output
You	10	12%
Joe	18	22%
Chris	15	19%
Mark	12	16%
Eric	25	31%
Team total	80	100%

The Opposing Team: The Cougars

Player	Average Points per Game	% of Team Output
Sam	24	30%
Mike	11	14%
Pedro	16	20%
Andy	14	17%
Jim	15	19%
Team total	80	100%

It is not usually possible to stop great shooters from scoring any points in a game. However, good defenders can severely limit their output. You can harass, badger, hound, impede, and frustrate your opponent for the entire game. Defense can actually be more fun than you may think. Playing great defense creates true competition. When you play good defense you can take away from your opponent all the things they normally like to do. What shots does your opponent normally take? Where does he or she like to catch the ball? Does your opponent like to cut to the basket? Does he or she shoot three-point shots? Asking questions like these will help you know and defend your opponent better. Remember, most games are won or lost by fewer than ten points. Your efforts can make a big difference.

It does not take natural ability or great talent to play good defense. It only requires that you work hard and play with your heart. In basketball, on offense you must play with control and poise to be effective. On defense, you should play with aggressiveness and noise to get your opponent out of control and frustrated. This chapter will teach fundamentals first, then advanced defensive concepts.

THE TWO LEVELS OF DEFENSE

There are two levels of defense. Take a moment and look at both.

Level 1: Defend the Basket

This level involves playing sound fundamental defense, which means staying between your opponent and the basket at all times. This is the way that most players and teams play defense. At level 1, you must always react or respond to what the offensive player wants to do because you are playing more of a passive defense to protect the basket.

Solid fundamentals such as footwork, help side defense, watching your opponent and the ball at all times, not allowing an easy shot to go uncontested, boxing out, and rebounding are all part of level 1 defense. Its goal is containment of your opponent, always keeping him or her from getting to the basket and preventing open shots, easy layups, or open three-point shots.

Level 2: Attack the Opponent

This level involves a great deal of physical aggressiveness and mental toughness. At this level of defense, you are going to attack your opponent to get a reaction from the offensive player. You will still defend the basket, but this also creates defensive pressure. The goal is to put more pressure on your opponent in a game than he or she is ever used to in practice.

Examples of level 2 defense include denying the ball or pass, denying cuts to the ball, fronting the low posts, bellying up on the opponent as he or she receives the ball, and yelling to create confusion. Contest everything, deny everything. You will be amazed at the results you get and the confusion you create. Good defenders attack their opponents and take away what the opponents want to do and block them from their favorite spots on the court.

In the next section we apply these defensive concepts and philosophies in defensive fundamentals and drills. There is an old basketball proverb about defense that states, *"You play defense with three things—your head, your heart, and your feet."*

THREE ELEMENTS OF DEFENSE

Playing Defense with Your Head

The fact that you want to play defense means that you are using your head. You realize its important role in winning games. To use your head in playing defense, find the best ways to defend an opposing player or team. Playing offensive basketball is a matter of rhythm-habits, offensive plays, and patterns—a repertoire of individual shots, moves, and skills that a player has practiced over and over. Every team develops several plays that work extremely well, and all players have their favorite shots and moves. In fact, most players have only two or three shots or moves with which they are really comfortable. Scout out these shots or moves, and you will hold the key to their game. It will make your job on defense much easier.

The goal of good defense is to stay between your opponent and the basket. But the goal of *great* defense, whether for an individual or a team, is to disrupt and change the offensive rhythm of the opponent and block their favorite offensive moves and plays. You need only assert effort and prohibit your offensive opponent from doing what they normally like to do. Ask questions like these about the opponents you encounter:

- What are their favorite shots? Where are they made from?
- In what area do they like to get the ball?
- Are they right- or left-handed? In which direction do they like to move, and on what side of the court? Do they make use of the weak hand?
- What are their two favorite moves or plays?
- Is a particular opponent a bad dribbler and a good outside shooter?
- Is the person a good dribbler and a bad outside shooter?
- Do they like to cut to the basket a lot?
- Do they try to go to the offensive boards and rebound?
- Do they do well in the low post?

These questions can help you scout your opponent and play better defense. Defense is hard work, but it also is good basketball. Use your head and play intelligent defense.

Playing Defense with Your Heart

You do not need to be a great athlete or have stunning natural ability to be a great defensive player. You only need to have heart. Having the heart to play defense means two things. First, you have the desire to play defense. You want to play it well, and you take pride in it. Second, you are willing to work hard, to exert all your effort in order to defeat your opponent first mentally and then physically. An old adage states, "Where the mind goes, the body will follow." Good defenders can disrupt, frustrate, and upset opponents' rhythm and get them out of their comfort zone and routine; they capture the minds of their opponents. Opponents will break down and quit mentally, and then their bodies, shown through their actions and frustrations, will follow. Their eyes will show their frustration; their actions will show that they have quit working for the ball on the court. They will also play less aggressively on defense, which will make it easier for you to score.

Anybody can play defense. You do not need to be a great jumper or have speed, strength, quickness, or long arms. You only need the courage to try, to work hard, and to play hard. For most players, this means stepping out of their own comfort zone and stepping into that of their opponents, literally. Here are two ways to become a better defensive player:

1. *Practice the fundamentals:* Develop great fundamental footwork for defense, and practice defensive footwork for a few minutes each day. It's amazing that most players never practice defensive fundamentals on their own during the off-season, yet they play half the game at that end of the court. Simply practice the defensive lateral slide movement. Drill each day for one to two minutes.
2. *Improve your conditioning and athleticism:* Improve your overall conditioning and athletic skills. By developing greater endurance, strength, speed, and agility, you will naturally become a better defender and overall player. To become a better player, you have to become a better athlete.

How will you know when you have become a great defensive player? That's simple. When it's time for a game or scrimmage, the opponent you cover casually says, "Ah, don't cover me. Go cover someone else!" When that happens, you'll know you have arrived. Anything out of the ordinary makes a coach take notice. Playing aggressive, hard-nosed defense is out of the ordinary, especially during team practice and during the off-season. Coaches will notice; in fact, they will notice in a hurry. Players who work hard on defense every day, whether in the schoolyard, at practice, or in a game, will gain the attention and respect of their coach and peers, *guaranteed.* Many players with little talent can make a team and develop into good players only because they had the desire and courage to play aggressive, intense defense. They simply outworked and outhustled the other players. They played great defense, and their actions stated, "If I am not going to score a lot, then neither are you!" So accept the challenge: play with heart.

▌TRAINING TIP

Defend the Best Player Every Time

Resolve to cover the best player on the opposing team every time you play, whether on the playground or in the gym, in team practice or in games. It will not be fun or easy at first. Like any other skill, playing defense correctly takes time to learn. Defense must be learned through mistakes and constant practice. Be determined to succeed. With time and work you will gain confidence and ability and, most important, your opponents' respect.

Playing Defense with Your Feet

Playing defense with your feet means that you do not reach in to steal the ball. Reaching in is lazy and costly, and it often results in a foul or an easily scored basket for the opponent. Reaching in also moves the body forward and off balance. If you lean forward to reach in, you cannot be balanced enough to move laterally or backward at the same time. It takes intelligence and discipline to hold back from reaching in. Also, recognize that 90 percent of all steals take place when the ball is stolen in a passing lane, not off the dribble—so your goal is to contain your opponent. Make them take tough shots.

Playing defense with your feet also means using the correct fundamentals and footwork. Just as a dancer must use the right steps to perform a specific dance, so defensive players must use footwork in order to play sound defense with their feet.

Now we move on to specific discussions of important concepts, footwork, fundamentals, steps, tips, and tools for defense.

LEVEL 1 DEFENSE: DEFENDING THE BASKET

The Defensive Stance

To play defense well, place yourself in a good defensive stance. A correct defensive stance is identical to a correct Sports Position. In this position, an athlete stands with the feet a little wider than shoulders' width apart. The knees are bent, the shoulders are above the knees, and the athlete stands on the balls, or "push pads" (not toes), of the feet (see Figure 7.1). This is a universal position used in almost every sport: a fielder or batter in baseball, goalkeeper in soccer, linebacker or running back in football, and *any* player in basketball. The Sports Position is perhaps more applicable to basketball than to any other sport, considering it is used at both the offensive end (in the triple-threat position) and at the defensive end of the court.

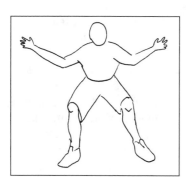

FIGURE 7.1 Correct Defensive Stance (The Sports Position)

A good defensive stance involves all of the elements of a correct Sports Position, with the addition of a couple of key elements: the arm/hand positions and the head position. The best use of arms and hands involves shadowing the ball and passer without reaching in (see Figure 7.2). Pretend there is an imaginary wall you cannot cross; don't attempt to cross it by reaching in at an offensive player. It will take you forward and off balance. A good fundamental position for a defender is no more than one arm's length away from the offensive player after that player receives the ball (see Figure 7.3). This is close

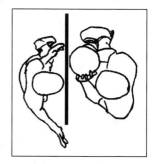

FIGURE 7.2 Shadowing without Reaching In

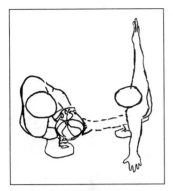

FIGURE 7.3 Fundamental Defense Position: An Arm's Length from the Opponent

enough to discourage an open shot but far enough off to allow you to successfully contest a driving move to the basket.

Chin Level

What is Chin Level? It refers to the height at which a defender should stand when facing an opponent who holds the basketball. Coaches at all levels are constantly reminding their players to "stay down" or "get low" on defense. But a player's definition of *low* and a coach's are usually not the same. A defender is low enough when he or she can react quickly to contest an offensive player from successfully driving to the basket *without* having to drop lower before moving laterally.

For a consistent definition of *staying low,* coaches should teach players the term "Chin Level." The top of the defender's head should always be lower than the chin of the offensive player (see Figure 7.4). This position makes the defender one full second quicker. Here is why. When your opponent has the ball, you must wait to move until you can see what direction they are going. Once you know, you have to react quickly. If your head level matches that of the offensive player, you must drop down to react (taking one second), then slide or even drop-step and slide (taking another full second). However, if the top of your head is lower than the chin of your opponent, you will save one full second because you are already in a low moving position and ready to slide your feet. All you have to do is step laterally. You are not in a standing position, which would require dropping into a moving position to defend the drive. Chin Level is a term that simplifies the principle of how low you should go while making you one second quicker. To use your head when playing defense, play at Chin Level.

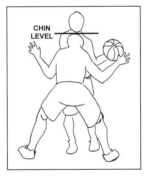

FIGURE 7.4   Chin Level

Focus Sight: On-the-Ball Defense

Another important element of good defense is knowing where to focus your eye on the offensive player. When playing on-the-ball defense, if you follow the path of the ball (ball fakes, shot fakes, and so on), you will be in danger of pursuing a ball fake and getting caught off balance. When defending on the ball, focus your eyes on the hip or crotch area of your opponent. This is the one area of the body that can't be moved in a fake.

Focus Sight: Off-the-Ball Defense

When playing off-the-ball defense (when your opponent does not have the ball), you should use peripheral vision and play somewhere between the player holding the ball and your opponent. Use peripheral vision to see both. For body positioning when playing off-the-ball defense, read the section on Pointers later in this chapter.

Defensive Footwork: The Lateral Slide Movement

Defensive footwork is a key element in playing great defense. To move your body defensively, bend your knees low and stand on the balls of your feet, not on your toes, with your feet a little more than shoulders' width apart (see Figure 7.5). Your hands should be open and your arms extended to the sides; this will keep you from reaching in and will help block the passing lanes. Your palms should face out, and your thumbs should face up, making your hands level with your shoulders.

FIGURE 7.5   The Balls of the Feet

To slide laterally (sideways) on defense, stay low on the balls of your feet and step to your right by pushing off your left leg explosively (see Figure 7.6). Quickly recover your balance with a short step in the same direction with your left foot. This short recovery step should place your feet no closer than shoulders' width apart (see Figure 7.7).

FIGURE 7.6   The Lateral Slide Movement

Too many players incorrectly pull the body to the right with the right leg instead of using the left leg to push the body to the right and explode laterally. *Pulling* the body sideways is much slower than *pushing* it. The momentum of a pull naturally forces you into a more erect position, thereby slowing you down. By pushing off your left leg when you go right, you are using the strongest and largest muscle in your entire body to propel yourself laterally. This will work to your advantage and make you quicker. Another benefit is that you will stay lower, more level, and more balanced in your defensive stance.

Foot movement should follow this exact pattern: explode with a long step, recover with a short step, long step, short step, long, short, and so on. By not bringing your heels together you will accomplish three things. First, you will be able to drop-step and change direction more quickly. Second, you will be able to stay lower in your stance (at Chin Level) at all times. Third, you will make quicker, more explosive movements and be able to defend better and faster.

FIGURE 7.7   Recovery Step after Lateral Slide

The same process will accomplish a move to the left, except this time you push off your right leg explosively and recover with a short step with your right foot. *Your feet should never get closer than shoulders' width apart. Never allow your heels to touch.*

To practice, simply work in a triangle pattern (see Figure 7.8). Once you slide to the corner, drop-step and slide, moving in the opposite direction. When you come back to the middle of the court on the baseline, jog or walk back to the starting point. If you are on a basketball court, stand at the top of the key and go in both directions three times, moving as quickly as possible. Always complete the first repetition on each side at a walk or half-speed pace. Even look down at your legs and feet to make sure your footwork is correct and that your heels do not touch. By doing your first repetition of three at half-speed, you will allow your body to warm up and run less risk of getting injured. *Always warm up and stretch be-*

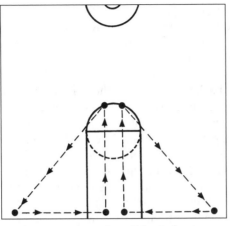

FIGURE 7.8 Triangle Drill for Defensive Footwork

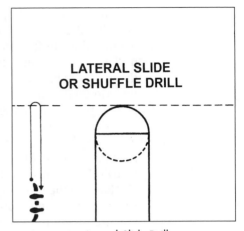

FIGURE 7.9 Lateral Slide Drill

fore you begin any exercise program or workout to avoid injuries. If you do not have a basketball court to practice this drill, then use a driveway, a sidewalk, or a lawn. You can also perform this drill by sliding laterally 15 to 20 feet side to side, completing four to six repetitions in each direction (see Figure 7.9).

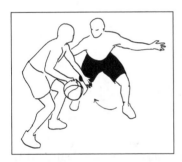

FIGURE 7.10 Executing a Drop Step

FIGURE 7.11 Finishing the Drop Step

The Drop Step

The drop step, as the name indicates, means dropping the leg and foot backward in order to retreat and change direction against an opponent who is dribbling forward. The drop step is the quickest maneuver for changing direction when playing defense because it does not require turning the entire body around to recover to a spot in front of the dribbler and then face the dribbler again. All of that takes a lot of time and energy. A drop step is performed out of the defensive slide movement, which was just discussed.

To execute a drop step as you move in a defensive slide, simply change direction by pivoting backward off your back foot or the foot farthest from the offensive player (in this case, the left foot) and dropping your right foot behind you (see Figure 7.10). You should also "pull" yourself to the right with your right arm and elbow, which will quicken your momentum. The total move should work as follows: (1) slide left, pushing off your right leg; (2) quickly move several steps to the left; (3) pivot to the right off your left foot, and pull yourself backward with right arm at the same time (see Figure 7.11); (4) immediately push off your left leg, sliding laterally to your right and staying low in a good defensive stance.

To drop-step to the left, repeat the same movements but with the opposite feet and hands.

To practice the drop step, begin at the baseline or end line of the court. Slide laterally three to four steps to your left, and drop-step to the right. Quickly slide another three to four steps, drop-step to the left, and repeat. You can practice this drill with or without a dribbler to defend. Repeat this move until you have gone all the way from baseline to baseline. Turn and repeat the drill back to the original end line. Go up the court and back two times. By the way, you do not need a full-court gym to practice this drill. You can use your driveway or yard.

Both the defensive slide footwork drill and the drop-step drill are excellent for daily practice, even during the off-season. They will build defensive quickness, toughness, and endurance, as well as improve overall conditioning for playing basketball. Both drills will take only two minutes a day to complete.

Practice the drills on your own. You will be amazed at how much your defensive quickness and footwork improve, which can only lead to more playing time. Practice. If you think practicing is boring, try sitting on the bench.

◼️ TRAINING TIP

You can even practice these drills during commercial breaks in your favorite TV program. (You have to do things that your competition is not willing to do if you want to get ahead of your competition.) Just hop off the couch and run outside to do the drills. They will only take two minutes.

Pointers

In defensive basketball, your Pointers are your hands. They should be used for only three things:

1. To maintain eye contact with both your opponent and the ball by pointing at and watching both at the same time, using peripheral vision (see Figure 7.12)
2. To deny the ball and discourage easy passes by taking up space in the passing lanes
3. To grab defensive rebounds

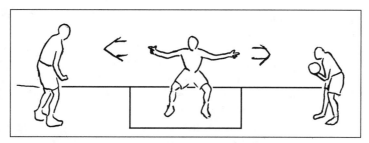

FIGURE 7.12   Using Pointers to Maintain Eye Contact

Here's how to use your hands as Pointers to keep eye contact with both your opponent and the ball:

1. Use peripheral vision to see both. You should be positioned between your opponent and the ball, with your eyes looking straight ahead. Peripheral vision is the range of sight available to you from the sides of your forward gaze. If you turn your head to look directly at the ball, you will lose sight of your opponent. If you turn your head to look directly at your opponent, you will lose sight of the ball. You can keep both in view with peripheral vision.
2. Point one hand toward your opponent; fully extend your arm.
3. Point the other hand to the ball; extend your arm.

By using your hands as Pointers, you will be a better team and individual defensive player. You will know where both the ball and your opponent are at all times. You will also take up space in the passing lanes with your arms up. This will make it more difficult for the offensive team to function effectively.

Where you position yourself will depend on how many passes away from the ball you are. Take one step backward (toward the baseline) and one step toward the ball (sideways) each time the ball moves one pass farther away from the player you are defending (see Figure 7.13).

FIGURE 7.13   Positioning Based on Passing Distance from the Ball

Four Objectives of Level 1 Defense

Level 1 defense (protecting the basket/containment) is about losing a battle once in a while, but trying to win the war. As you protect the basket and lane area and keep opponents from getting easy shots, you must give something up occasionally—usually medium-range and long-range jump shots. Just don't give up wide-open three-point shots or easy layups. When an offensive player is on the "golden arch," or three-point line, move in very close in order to force the player off the three-point line or take his or her shot away.

The four major objectives of Level 1 defense are as follows:

1. *Achieve containment:* Contain and frustrate the offense by prohibiting easy shots and layups. To do this, stay between the opponent and the basket at all times. Never let an offensive player get all the way to the basket for an easy layup.
2. *Force tough shots:* Make your opponent take tough shots. Did you know that most teams score an average of 50 percent of their points from layups? (Offensive rebounds generally translate into layups.) Twenty percent of points come from the foul line, and 30 percent from other shots made farther than 7 feet from the basket. Interestingly enough, the farther out a player or team has to shoot the ball from the basket, the lower the shooting percentages become (see Figure 7.14).
3. *Allow only one shot per possession:* Always hold your opponent to only one shot every time you run down the court. This will further limit opportunities to score. Never give up an offensive rebound. An offensive rebound is usually a layup or easy shot for your opponent. Giving up offensive rebounds is the easiest way to lose a game.
4. *Protect the lane area:* Since most successful shots are taken in the lane area, or the "gold box," the defense individually and as a team must get tougher as the ball gets closer to the basket. The following percentages show typical success rates in game situations:

> 4 feet and in: 90 percent
> 5–10 feet: 80 percent
> 11–15 feet: 60 percent
> 16–18 feet: 50 percent
> 19–22 + feet: 40 percent

These percentages represent wide-open shots, not tightly defended shots in game situations or forced shots taken by offensive players. When guarded closely by defenders, percentages may drop by up to 5 to 10 percent or more from each designated area. Thus, shooters and teams typically average 40 to 45 percent success in shooting field goal percentages.

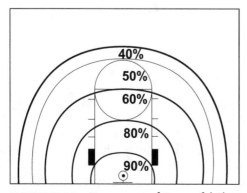

FIGURE 7.14 Percentages of Successful Shots Made from Different Areas of the Court

LOSERS PRACTICE LOSING, WINNERS PRACTICE WINNING.

SCOTISM

Transition Defense

Transition defense is played during a retreat from the offensive end of the court to the defensive end. To play good transition defense, build your defense from the inside out. This means to sprint back on defense ahead of the ball and protect the rim at the defensive end of the floor. First, take away the easy shots by getting deep into the lane area. Second, locate the ball and your opponent. By building your transition defense from the inside out, you eliminate easy driving lanes for layups to the basket. You will be amazed at how many easy baskets you take away from your opponent by doing this simple thing as an individual and team. Just sprint back to the rim, stop the ball, then find your opponent.

It is always shocking to watch players at all levels of basketball (even professionals) who try to defend the ball at half court when a team is fast-breaking against them. Ridiculous! How many shots do players ever take from half court? Get in the habit of playing sound, fundamental transition defense. Protect the basket first at all costs, then find the ball and the player you are covering. A simple rule—if you are coming back on defense and the ball is ahead of you, sprint to get ahead of the ball. Beat the ball to the paint. This extra effort will take away easy baskets.

Team Drill for Transition Defense.   Start with two lines on the opposite baseline: one offense, one defense. The defender must race to the other end of the court and protect the basket, then turn and find the dribbler (see Figure 7.15). Be sure to practice this drill from both sides of the court.

Strong Side/Weak Side: Playing Team Defense off the Ball

In a team defensive situation, even if you are playing a man-to-man defense, it is critical to know where the ball is at all times. Using Pointers (your hands) will help you be a better team defender. When playing team defense, be aware of two parts of the court: the weak side (side of the court without the ball) and the strong side (the side of the court with the ball). You should be closer to your opponent when guarding a player on the strong side of the court. When you are defending a player

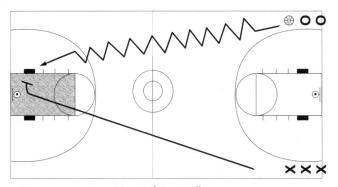

FIGURE 7.15   Transition Defense Drill

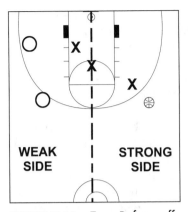

FIGURE 7.16   Team Defense off the Ball

on the weak side of the court, as you move farther into the lane you should be in a better help position to assist your teammates in case they get beat by their opponent (see Figure 7.16).

Communication on Defense.   This area is often overlooked. Communicating is a vital part of team defense, helping players to do the following:

1. They can stay more focused on what is happening, allowing players to react more quickly.
2. They can improve team defense and inspire teamwork.
3. Together they can break down opponents mentally and then physically as offensive players hear the defenders talking and see them in the passing lanes, stopping cuts, helping out, and so on. It makes the opponents realize they are in for a tough, long game without easy baskets.

How do you communicate on defense? When a teammate is defending a dribbler, call out screens: "Watch the pick," "Screen left," or "Screen right." Yell "shot" so teammates know when to box out, or even when to call out which offensive player to defend on a fast break ("You take the dribbler," "I have number 22," and so on). Communication becomes a mandate when playing in a zone defense. The closer you play to the basket on defense, the more you need to communicate and know where all the players are on the court. This is because defensive players closer to the rim have a greater peripheral view of all players on the court. Keep your words brief: "Watch the cutter left," "Shooter is in the corner," and "Two players on the right side" are a few examples. The more you learn to talk on defense, the better individual and team defender you will be, and therefore the more valuable to your team and coach. Coaches need to emphasize the value of and need for communicating on defense. Most players have never been taught this responsibility.

LEVEL 2 DEFENSE: ATTACK YOUR OPPONENT

The following drills and concepts will enable you to attack your opponent, forcing the individual and the offensive team to react to what you are doing. This is serious defense. This section offers advanced defensive techniques for successfully attacking your opponent and getting the reaction you want.

Defensive Denial Principles

For attacking defensive purposes, assume these two premises:

1. *Individual defense:* A player who does not have the ball cannot score.
2. *Team defense:* If the other team's players cannot get the ball in a comfortable position (a position they have practiced), they will have more difficulty in scoring.

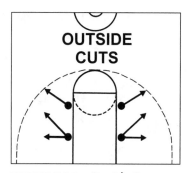

FIGURE 7.17   Outside Cuts

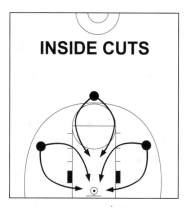

FIGURE 7.18   Inside Cuts

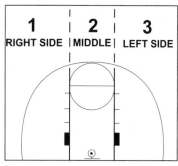

FIGURE 7.19   Dribbling
Avenues

In defense, do those things that will give you the greatest chance of succeeding. The first step is to stop opponents from scoring by denying them the ball where they want to receive it. When they do get the ball, make sure they get it only in places unfamiliar and uncomfortable to them, such as too far away from the basket on the perimeter to shoot, and too far out of the low post (the blocks) to be comfortable.

All offensive movement in basketball is based on two maneuvers. The first is an outside cut, in which a player tries to get open to receive the basketball in the perimeter area, usually around the three-point line (see Figure 7.17). The other is an inside cut, in which a player tries to get open to receive the ball in the lane or post area (see Figure 7.18). To play effective defense and to disrupt your opponents' rhythm, you must stop or at least detour these two types of movement at all times. Make the offensive players get the ball in inconvenient locations whenever possible. You can do this by using three defensive tools: denying the avenue, denying the ball, and denying the cut.

Denying the Avenue.   If the other team does not have the ball, it cannot score. Although it is impossible to keep a team from ever getting the ball, it is possible to limit where it is received. It is also possible to keep a player from getting the ball most of the time, which can become very frustrating for an offensive player. What does it mean to "deny the avenue"? It means to take away a dribbling avenue. The offensive court is generally broken into three lanes, or avenues, in which a dribbler can operate (see Figure 7.19). Did you know that most teams run over 80 percent of their offensive plays to the right side of the court? (This is because most guards are right-handed.) Most players and teams consistently allow dribblers to start their offense to the right side of the floor. Take this away, and force everything to the left. It will automatically take players and teams out of one of their comfort zones and get them rattled.

This one simple decision can actually mess up the offensive team's entire rhythm. Players are not used to operating from the left side of the floor. Most post players like the right side better. Shooters like the right side better. Drivers like the right side better (there usually is little or no help defense baseline). To deny the avenue, simply turn or force the dribbler to the left side of the floor at all times. This will also force the dribbler to use the left hand, which more often than not is also uncomfortable. Individual players and teams should both get used to playing this way. Dictate what you want the offense to do. Do not react to them. Make them react to you.

FIGURE 7.20 Chest Position for Denying the Ball

Denying the Ball. You deny the ball when your opponent is within one pass of it. Here's how to do it:

1. Your chest should be facing your opponent's chest (see Figure 7.20).
2. Turn your head so you can see both the ball and your opponent at all times, using peripheral vision.
3. Use the footwork for the defensive slide. Move your feet using the defensive lateral slide step. The only difference is location: you are as close as an arm's length to the offensive player when you deny the ball.
4. When playing defense on the left side of the court, situate yourself between the player you are guarding and the ball. Be one step closer to the lane than the offensive player is. Your right foot should line up to the opponent's right foot (toe to toe).
5. Your outside hand should be in your opponent's chest area, with your arm fully extended up high to deny the ball and discourage the pass. Deny the ball with your hand, *not* with your body. Your body needs to be one step closer to the lane area at all times to protect against a quick back-door cut to the basket. Players will hesitate to pass if your hand is in front of the passing lane.

When you successfully deny the ball, even if the player you defend does get the ball, you will have forced the pass to occur outside of their normal perimeter area and comfort zone. You will have extended the offense and broken up their normal offensive spacing. You will also have taken away one of their options—shooting. Remember, it is a lot easier to defend a player who does not have the ball because then the player must adjust to what you are doing. If you let the offensive player get the ball, you must adjust to what he or she wants to do.

Denying the Cut. By denying the cut, defenders prevent offensive players from going where they want to go, need to go, or have been trained to go. Make them go in the direction you want them to, which should always be away from the heart of the offensive court, or the middle of the lane (see Figure 7.21). Look closely at the middle area of the three-second lane. Keep your opponent from this area at all costs. Here is how to deny the cut:

1. Use your Pointers to watch both your opponent and the ball.
2. As your opponent begins to make an inside cut into the heart of the lane *or* toward the ball, step into his or her path. Force the opponent to go left or right, preventing a direct cut through the lane or to the ball. Step into the passing lane to stop the player from receiving a pass.
3. Once you have stopped an opponent's cut to the ball and the player moves in another direction, deny the ball.

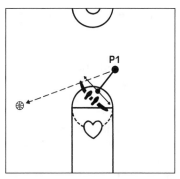

FIGURE 7.21   Keeping an Offensive Player Out of the Middle of the Lane

Examples of Denying the Cut

- To defend player 1, allow the opponent only to cut away from the ball (see Figure 7.21).
- To defend player 2, allow the opponent to cut only to the baseline or above the foul line (see Figure 7.22).
- To defend player 3, allow the opponent to cut only to the baseline or above the foul line (see Figure 7.23).

The Belly-Up Defense

The belly-up defense is another aggressive tactic of Level 2 defense (see Figure 7.24). Use it to put additional pressure on an offensive player who has received a pass. As the defense's name implies, you position yourself belly-to-belly with the offensive player without reaching in or fouling. Feet must be set wide apart and on the outside of both the offensive player's ankles. This locks the opponent in "jail" for you, making it difficult to drive or get free to pass or shoot. In this defense, you must shadow the movement of the ball with movements of your arms and hands, setting up an imaginary wall between you and your opponent. Yell *"Ball, ball, ball."* Position yourself less than one arm's length from the ball. You have now stepped into your opponent's comfort zone.

FIGURE 7.24   The Belly-Up Defense

Do not cross the imaginary wall with your arms. Do not reach in as you shadow the ball.

This defense puts great pressure on the offensive player, breaking his or her concentration. Bellying up on the offensive player takes away two offensive options: the shot and the easy pass to a teammate. This defense also creates another problem for the opponent. That player has to to do something with the ball and do it quickly.

Most offensive players have mastered only two to three basic moves or shots. Most have not been trained in practice situations that involve constant attack and harassment by a defender using belly-up pressure defense. Few offensive players know how to react, and this makes them uncomfortable. And that is what Level 2 defense is all about: breaking out of your comfort zone and breaking into theirs.

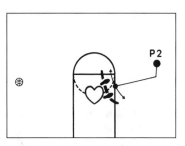

FIGURE 7.22   Example of Denying the Cut

Defending the Post

Defending the post well is essential in defensive basketball. There are several things that you can do to become a better post defender. First, recognize that if you allow an offensive post player to catch the ball

FIGURE 7.23   Example of Denying the Cut

in the blocks or post area, they will have a 50 percent chance, or better, of scoring as well as a great opportunity to pass out to set up teammates when double-teamed by two or more defenders. If you want to win, you need to prevent this from happening. Here's how to deny these opportunities for a good low-post player on offense:

Four Ways to Neutralize a Low-Post Offensive Player

1. *Deny the cut to the low post:* Anticipate when and where the offensive player wants to move, which is usually toward the ball. Step into the path between the ball and the offensive player. You may even intercept a few passes this way.
2. *Deny the space in the low post:* This means denying the area in the blocks at which a low-post player likes to receive the ball. For example, if a player is used to receiving the ball in the low post 6 feet from the basket, force that player to receive the ball 8 to 10 feet from the basket. This will disrupt the player's usual pattern of offense, confidence, and rhythm. In fact, it will upset the entire offensive team's rhythm and play patterns.
3. *Front the post:* This is similar to denying the ball to a wing player or perimeter player. The goal is to detour the offensive player from easily receiving a pass. Fronting the post is an aggressive attacking move. It creates frustration for the offensive player. When you front the post on defense, do not allow yourself to get pushed off the blocks too far and away from the lane area. This could lead to an easy lob pass and layup for the offensive player. Fronting the post is a full-time job and will require a lot of energy, determination, and effort. Like practicing any basketball skill, working at fronting the post will slowly build your confidence. In order to front the post well, you must stay active and respond physically to the opponent at all times. You should also ask for help defense on the lane side or back side, so communicate.

▌ TRAINING TIP _____

Study Your Opponents

What are their tendencies—making a hook shot? a drop step at the baseline? a fade-away jump shot to the right? Whatever the habits of the offensive player, learn them and know them. Force offensive players to do the opposite of what they are accustomed to.

Stick Arm

Stick Arm may sound like a new concept. It is used only by the very best defenders at the highest levels of basketball. Stick Arm is an advanced defensive technique used to disrupt the shooting rhythm of an offensive player. To use Stick Arm, put one arm forward to touch the area of the offensive player's shooting arm near the basketball (see Figure 7.25). Which arm you use to reach forward (*not* reach in) is critical.

If you are defending a right-handed shooter, for example, place your left arm into your opponent's right-shoulder area. This will force the shooter to bring the

PALM FACING UP

PALM FACING DOWN

FIGURE 7.25   Two Forms of Stick Arm

ball around and over your arm to make a shot. This offsets the usual technique of rising straight up with the ball. If you try to use your right arm on a right-handed shooter, you will turn your body off balance. Stick Arm will also allow you to stay low on defense (using Chin Level) and not worry about trying to block a perimeter shot. Never try to block a perimeter shot. Stay down and prepare to move your feet in order to contain your opponent at all times.

In Stick Arm, your hand should assume one of two positions: palm facing up or palm facing down. When a shooter is facing the basket with the ball above the chest area, use Stick Arm with the palm facing up. Your left hand should almost be touching the offensive player's right shoulder. This position will frustrate opponents and make it very difficult to take a normal shot in rhythm. When an offensive player has the ball above the shoulder pad, this Stick Arm position impedes the ability to bring the ball down to drive.

Conversely, if the offensive player is holding the ball either below the shoulder pad or below the waist, use Stick Arm *above the ball,* with the palm of the hand facing down. This will allow you to tap at the ball without leaning forward and getting off balance. Actually, Stick Arm has the same effect when the ball is below the opponent's waist area by impeding shot movement. It takes discipline to use this technique effectively. Stick Arm is a weapon for frustrating the opponent, not for reaching in. Use the principle correctly, and it will make you a better defensive player.

In conclusion, remember that you play defense with your head (intelligence), your heart (desire), and your feet (footwork). Your goal should be to disrupt the rhythm of your opponent's play. If you still need a motivation to play defense, consider what you will get out of it—pride and confidence, better physical conditioning, and the respect of your coaches and peers. Defense will add another dimension to your game and help you to be a better all-round player. Most important, it will keep you in the game rather than on the bench. Most players can shoot a basketball; very few can play great defense. A player can always have an off night in shooting, but defense is simply a matter of desire, and you should never have an off night playing defense.

Defense will also help you jump-start your offensive game if you feel a little out of synch. When you dig in and play good defense, your intensity and concentration increase. As you frustrate your opponents, they'll end up on the defensive end of the court. While they worry about their offense, they will forget to concentrate on their own defense, which makes it easier for you to score. Defense creates better offense. It really does work.

The Five Laws of Defense
1. *Never* give up an uncontested layup.
2. *Never* give up an offensive rebound.
3. *Never* give up an open three-point shot.
4. *Never* give up an offensive drive to the basket.
5. *Never* give up an uncontested open cut through the lane.

COACHES DON'T DECIDE WHO WILL DECIDE WHO WILL PLAY;

PLAYERS DECIDE.

JIM VALVANO
FORMER HEAD COACH,
NORTH CAROLINA STATE UNIVERSITY
NCAA NATIONAL CHAMPIONSHIP COACH

▌ COACHES' CHALK TALK: TEAM DEFENSE DRILLS

Although defense is 50 percent of the game, don't use 50 percent of practice time to work on defense. However, the time spent on defensive drills really has to count. As a coach, you should not merely blow your whistle, look at your clipboard, or shoot the breeze while your players do defensive drills.

Defense, like any other skill, requires confidence, which can come only from practicing a skill correctly every day. If your team does not practice playing defense correctly every day, it will play poor defense. An effective coach must pay attention to the details. When your players practice defense, teach them how to do it correctly—step by step, in slow motion if necessary, until they all do it right. As they learn the correct positions and habits they will, with daily rehearsals, develop the quickness, confidence, pride, and desire required to play good defense.

Team defense can be divided into three general areas: presses, zone defenses, and man-to-man defenses. This book does not discuss presses. Not all coaches use them, and the many different philosophies about presses would require an entire text of its own. However, all coaches at one time or another will use man-to-man and zone defenses.

Zone Defense

A zone defense is a situation when each player is assigned a specific area and role to play instead of covering an individual opponent. There are at least four situations that call for a zone defense: (1) when a team wants to disrupt an opponent's rhythm because the opponent is scoring well, (2) when a team gets in foul trouble, (3) when there is a size difference between the teams, and (4) when competing against a much quicker and faster team. If you decide to play a zone defense, keep these four objectives in mind:

1. Force a team to throw long, cross-court passes and to take long shots that are less likely to be successful.
2. Double-team taller players.
3. Fill the open spaces in passing lanes and in the middle of the three-second lane area by having the defenders keep their hands up at all times.
4. Stop players who drive or slash from being effective.

You can accomplish all these objectives by having your players fully extend their arms and hands to fill the passing lanes and by having players shift quickly into correct positions with each pass of the ball to prevent opponents from receiving passes, making shots, and making passes in the lane. Many coaches have their team practice a zone defense, showing the correct positions and so on, but little time is provided to work on a zone properly. Players may have a basic understanding of how to play a zone but lack the discipline to keep doing it correctly and consistently with movement, communication, boxing out in a zone, double-teaming, and so on.

Most zone defenses break down after the first few minutes of a game, once the first spurt of adrenaline wears off. Often the reason is lack of defensive discipline. Players get tired or lazy and think they can rest because they are in a zone defense. They know the correct way to play a zone defense, but they have not practiced maintaining discipline every time they go downcourt. If you plan to play a zone defense, your team should practice a few minutes each day to develop correct habits. Habit is the greatest discipline of all. Once your players get in the habit of playing a zone defense correctly, they will perform well in games and play with more confidence and desire because they will see their efforts bringing immediate success.

Zone Defense Drills. An excellent practice drill is to put five players in a zone defense and five players on offense. Put them through a nonstop sixty-second drill. Have the offense quickly try to score layups or other shots in the three-second area only. Instruct your defensive players to (1) keep moving quickly and (2) keep the hands up and their arms fully extended for the entire sixty seconds, working hard. If a defensive player stops doing either of these, start the sixty seconds over again until all do the drill correctly. Have the offensive and defensive players change positions after the drill has been done correctly. Repeat the drill two or three times for each group. It will build discipline and correct defensive habits. Also, your players will learn to pass better against zone defenses and become more united as they work, talk, and encourage one another toward a common goal—playing the whole sixty seconds without having to start over. Finally, this is an excellent drill for defensive stamina and conditioning. Once your players develop the habit of using the tools of a zone defense through daily practice, they will use them in games from start to finish.

Man-to-Man Defense

Man-to-man defense is the most common defensive strategy used in basketball. Even in pick-up games played on playgrounds, driveways, streets, and schoolyards around the world, you will find players using man-to-man defense.

In a team setting with organized practices and games, playing a man-to-man defense is definitely a conscious decision. A man-to-man defense is typically more aggressive than a zone defense. It creates numerous isolation situations for both offensive and defensive players. Man-to-man defense would not be the best choice if your players are less athletic and slower than your opponents. Following are situations in which it is good to employ man-to-man defense:

1. When you have a deep bench
2. When you have better and faster athletes
3. When you want to change the tempo of the game
4. When you want to play a more attacking, aggressive defense
5. When you are behind and want to pressure and deny the ball

Correct fundamentals when playing defense can help you to be up to a full second quicker on each pass, play, and move. Master defensive fundamentals and playing defense will become more fun.

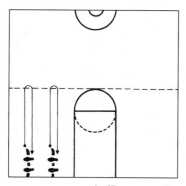

FIGURE 7.26   Shuffle-Step Drill

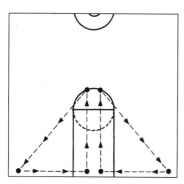

FIGURE 7.27   Triangle Drill

FIGURE 7.28   Pointer Help-Defense Drill

Man-to-Man Defense Drills

   1. *Shuffle-step drill:* Have all your players line up on the baseline and face the sidelines in a defensive position. Have them quickly shuffle-step to the top of the key and back to the end line four times (see Figure 7.26).

   2. *Triangle drill:* Arrange players in two lines at the top of the key, with three to four players in each line. Have each player shuffle-step in a defensive slide to the corner of the court. When the first player in line reaches the corner, the second player in line should start the slide. Each should quickly drop-step and shuffle-step to the middle of the foul-lane area and then jog forward to the top of the key (see Figure 7.27). Have them repeat this drill two more times, concentrating on correct footwork and making sure that the heels do not touch.

   3. *Drop-step drills:*

   A. *End-to-end:* Arrange your players in no more than two lines on the baseline, with their backs to the court in a defensive position. Have them do the drop-step drill explained earlier in this chapter. Each player does it two times to the opposite baseline and back; then rotate players, so that each does two repetitions of the drill (four times in total).

   B. *Defend-the-dribble:* Have your players line up as in the end-to-end drill. The first player in each line will defend the second player in line. Have the second player dribble down the court and back in a zigzag motion; the defensive player uses a drop step to change directions. Then rotate the players, having the defensive player go to the end of the line. The dribbler becomes the defender, and the next player in line becomes the dribbler. Have each player do the drill two times to the opposite baseline and back.

   4. *Pointer help-defense drill:* Place five offensive players in position on the court (see Figure 7.28). Then have five defensive players use their Pointers to follow the ball as it is passed. Unless defensive players have the ball, they should play one or two steps off the offensive players, depending on where the ball is. Have the players on offense pass the ball to all five spots on the perimeter; This drill will develop players' peripheral vision and their ability to use their Pointers. It also teaches good defensive help position and team defense. This is also a full-speed drill. Do it for one minute, then rotate positions: offense plays defense and vice versa.

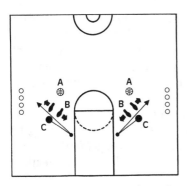

FIGURE 7.29   Denying-the-Ball Drill

FIGURE 7.30   Denying-the-Cut Drill

5. *Denying-the-ball drill:* Put your players in two lines, one on each side of the court (see Figure 7.29). Set up a passer (A), a defensive player (B), and an offensive player (C). Have C try to get open, but only by cutting in at an angle back and forth. The drill is completed after ten seconds or when B blocks the pass. If C receives the pass, have the players start over. The emphasis is to complete the drill correctly. After completion, A goes to the end of the line, B becomes the passer, C becomes the defensive player, and the next person in line becomes the new offensive player. Continue until each player has done two repetitions at each position at full speed. (This is an excellent drill for developing good defensive denial, passing, and getting open to receive the ball.)

6. *Denying-the-cut drill:* Put your players in two lines, one at each end of the court. Set up three players as shown in Figure 7.30 (A, B, and C). Have the defensive player deny the cut to the heart of the lane by using the body, not the arm. Have the offensive player cut up or down as the defensive player continues to deny the ball. Repeat the drill two or three times correctly, then rotate players. Do the drill at full speed. (Back-door passes are not allowed in this drill. The offensive player must try to receive the ball by getting by the defensive player on the cut.)

All of these defensive drills are excellent for building players' physical endurance and conditioning. However, it is nearly impossible to fit them all into one team practice! Alternate the drills every other day, using half of the drills each time. Here is a sample schedule:

Monday
1. Shuffle-step and drop-step drills
2. Pointer help-defense drill, sixty-second zone-defense drills
3. Team defensive preparation for game

Tuesday
1. Triangle drill and drop-step drills
2. Denying-the-ball and denying-the-cut drills
3. Team defensive preparation for game

Wednesday
Same as Monday's drills

Thursday
Same as Tuesday's drills

Drills build and maintain proper habits; that is why all skills must be practiced correctly. Some defensive skills are habit skills (using the Pointers, using the hands in a zone defense, denying the ball, denying the cut) and can be practiced every other day. Defensive skills that involve a lot of movement, choreography, and stamina (the shuffle step and the drop step) should be practiced daily, varying the drill so the players can develop more quickness, confidence, endurance, and proficiency. Also, these defensive drills will be extremely effective in physically conditioning the team—they accomplish two things in one.

As you practice these drills correctly in team practice, you will see results in games. Being a good coach means taking the time to be a good teacher. Your players will respect you more as they see themselves improve. You will get farther ahead with two steps in the right direction than with twenty steps in the wrong direction; practice drills correctly.

CHAPTER QUESTIONS

1. Explain the value of playing good defense, and define what good defense means to you.

2. Describe the two levels of defense and the goals of each level.

3. List the three elements of defense, and give a brief description of each.

4. Explain Chin Level and why it is important.

5. What is the purpose of using Pointers when playing defense?

6. What are the four major objectives of Level 1 defense?

7. Explain the difference between strong-side and weak-side defense.

8. Why is communication on defense important?

9. What are two premises for using denial principles in defensive play?

10. List three ways in which denial principles can be used in a game situation.

11. Name three ways in which a defender can disrupt a low-post player's scoring.

12. What are the five laws of defense?

13. Name three situations appropriate for a zone defense.

14. What four objectives should a team try to achieve when playing a zone defense?

Dribbling Fundamentals

IN THIS CHAPTER YOU WILL LEARN:

- That good dribbling is an essential skill for great players
- Twenty-five drills to develop exceptional dribbling skills
- Warm-up dribbling drills for skill development
- Dozens of drills for both half-court and full-court game situations
- Closet dribbling drills for quickness

WHY PRACTICE DRIBBLING?

A seriously neglected skill area in the game of basketball is dribbling. Most turnovers and mistakes, such as double dribbling, traveling, palming, or even making bad passes off the dribble, result from poor dribbling skills. A player who dribbles with eyes down or who has to glance down at the ball often commits a charging foul or even misses an open pass to a teammate or an easy layup. Good dribbling skills add a dimension to any player and team and cause additional problems for the opposing team.

If you do not believe dribbling is important, ask yourself these questions:

- How many players can dribble equally well left-handed and right-handed?
- How many players can dribble at full speed without ever having to look down at the ball?
- How many can use a jab-step dribble to drive through an open lane?
- At full speed, how many players can, without losing pace or looking down at the ball, change direction with a reverse pivot, a between-the-legs move, or a behind-the-back dribble, while protecting the ball?
- How many players have a weak dribbling hand that makes them ineffective and uncomfortable?

All of these questions involve fundamental dribbling skills. Every coach loves players who have the ability to break a press on their own or control a fast break quickly and effectively. All coaches love a player who can see the whole court and give soft, timely, accurate passes. However, sometimes players who make a dribbling-control error get the blame for lacking something they were never taught—correct dribbling fundamentals.

How many fast breaks do you see run only by passes? How many teams win without an effective fast break? The game is changing. Players today are bigger, stronger, and faster. Shot clocks are being used at every level—professional, international, and collegiate. It makes basketball a faster, more exciting game. Dribbling is a key element for success in the modern game.

Practice the dribbling skills related to the other skills you use or need on the basketball court. Developing specific dribbling moves, especially for guards, is vitally important to being a complete player. Reverse pivots, jab steps, dribbling behind the back, dribbling between the legs, changing directions, changing pace—all of these (and more) are directly applicable to games. They are choreographic moves that, rehearsed over and over, become second nature and can be used effectively and artistically in games.

Becoming a good dribbler develops important game skills, builds confidence, and makes a player more valuable to a team. A coach loves a great shooter, but a great shooter who can dribble and pass the ball well has triple value to the coach and to the team. The player also has multiplied his or her chances of playing by three, which is especially significant if there are other good shooters on the team.

Dribbling skills are difficult to master. They require great exertion and energy to practice. It is better to practice fifteen minutes to half an hour every day than to practice two hours one day and none the rest of the week. Do not burn yourself out. Be consistent. Decide on which drills you want to practice, and then consistently strive to build those skills every day. Think about these objectives as you practice: by doing a little each day, your talent and confidence will consistently grow.

Three Objectives for Dribbling Practice

1. *Dribble with your head and eyes up:* This will enable you to see the whole court and keep you from committing fouls and turnovers. You can also spot open teammates more easily. You should never have to look down to see the ball.
2. *Develop a "feel" for the ball:* Work and work at these drills until the ball feels like part of your hand and fits your hand like a glove. Once you develop a feel for the basketball, you will never need to look down while dribbling. The ball will be like a magnet always drawn back to its proper place—your hand.
3. *Use your fingertips:* Use your fingertips, or "finger pads," to dribble and control the ball. Never let the ball touch your palms; if you do, it will make controlling the basketball more difficult.

In the next sections you will find a variety of drills to use in improving your dribbling. These skills will come in handy in a variety of game situations. Your practice will not be in vain!

WARM-UP DRIBBLING DRILLS

The warm-up dribbling drills should be done before practicing any other dribbling drills. You can also call these in-place dribbling drills. They are designed to develop a better touch and feel on the ball. Always practice these drills with your feet stationary.

The Left-Hand Dribble

Follow these steps to execute the left-hand dribble:

1. Stand low, knees bent and right hand extended to the side.
2. Dribble the ball straight up and down, without looking down at the ball.
3. Complete twenty-five repetitions, or dribbles, of this drill.
4. If the left hand is your weak hand, do the drill twice, practicing with the right hand between the two sets for your left hand.

The Right-Hand Dribble

Follow the procedure for the left-hand dribble, but use the right hand.

▌TRAINING TIP _____

Once you become proficient at these first two drills, go directly to the three-point-bounce dribbling drills.

The Three-Point Bounce with the Left Hand

If the left hand is your weak hand, do this drill twice, practicing with the right hand between the two sets for the left hand. Follow these steps to execute the three-point bounce for the left hand:

THREE-POINT BOUNCE WITH THE LEFT HAND

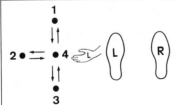

Stand low, knees bent and right hand extended to the side. Dribble the ball in a "four-spot" half-circle motion. Complete twenty repetitions of these half-circles. Each rotation should involve dribbling to each of the four spots to complete one repetition.

The Three-Point Bounce with the Right Hand

Follow the procedure for the left-hand three-point bounce, but use the right hand instead.

The Stationary Two-Bounce Figure-Eight Drill

As you work on this drill, keep your feet stationary. Follow these steps to do the two-bounce figure-eight drill:

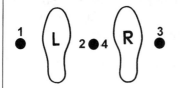

THE STATIONARY TWO-BOUNCE FIGURE-EIGHT DRILL

1. One bounce with the left hand
2. One bounce through front of the legs from left hand to right hand
3. One bounce with the right hand
4. One bounce through front of the legs from right hand to left hand

Repeat the sequence quickly. Complete twenty repetitions.

The Stationary One-Bounce Figure-Eight Drill

Do as in the stationary two-bounce drill, but use only one bounce to dribble through your legs. Do not dribble the ball any higher than knee height. Keep your head and eyes up at all times. Pick a spot or target to keep your eyes focused on and up. Do not look down at the ball. Follow these steps:

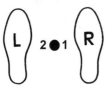

THE STATIONARY ONE-BOUNCE FIGURE-EIGHT DRILL

First, dribble the ball one bounce with your left hand on the left side of your body. Without picking up the ball, dribble through your legs. (Ball always moves front to back of legs.) Next, dribble through your legs using one bounce. This is one repetition. Repeat. Complete twenty repetitions.

▚▎ TRAINING TIP

The warm-up dribbling drills are excellent for practice in the locker room or hall as a pregame preparation. They will help you to warm up your touch on the ball without getting tired and will only take five minutes.

▟ FULL-COURT DRIBBLING DRILLS

Although the best place to practice full-court dribbling drills is a full-length court or gym, you may also use school hallways after school or an empty street (pretend the distance between two telephone poles is your court). You can use tennis or racquetball courts, pretending to dribble to half court and then back to the baseline. All you need is some room, a basketball, and some imagination.

The next two drills—"walking" drills—are not directly applicable to games, but the benefits from practicing them are. The walking drills will help you to do the following:

1. Concentrate on keeping your head and eyes up (pick a spot on the wall).
2. Develop a better "feel" for handling the ball.
3. Rapidly develop choreography and movement for the between-the-legs speed dribble.

The Two-Bounce Walk

For this drill, dribble the ball at hip height. Do this move as you walk up the court and back. Complete two to three repetitions of the drill. Follow these steps to execute the two-bounce walk:

THE TWO-BOUNCE WALK

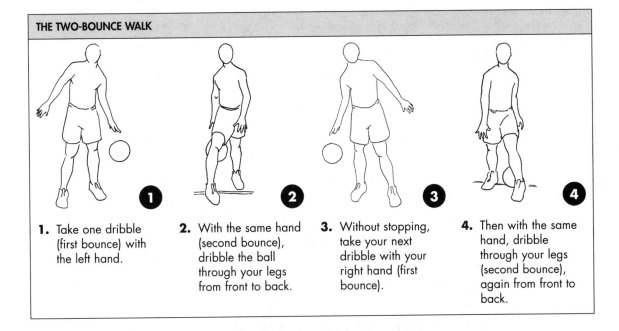

1. Take one dribble (first bounce) with the left hand.

2. With the same hand (second bounce), dribble the ball through your legs from front to back.

3. Without stopping, take your next dribble with your right hand (first bounce).

4. Then with the same hand, dribble through your legs (second bounce), again from front to back.

▌ TRAINING TIP _____

Do You Know What Four Good Reasons to Dribble a Ball Are?

1. To advance the ball up the court
2. To relieve defensive pressure
3. To improve a passing angle to a teammate
4. To drive to the basket

The One-Bounce Walk

This drill is done with both legs moving in a scissor motion as you walk forward. It is the same as the two-bounce drill except that you use only one bounce when dribbling the ball from side to side between your legs.

Alternate hands with every dribble. Each dribble goes in a front-to-back scissor motion between your legs. Do not pick up your dribble. Complete two to three repetitions of the drill. Traveling one length of the court and back, without stopping, makes one repetition. Follow these steps:

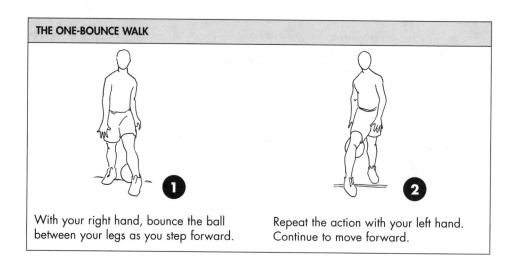

THE ONE-BOUNCE WALK

1 With your right hand, bounce the ball between your legs as you step forward.

2 Repeat the action with your left hand. Continue to move forward.

▌ TRAINING TIP

The two walking drills are excellent for practice between full-court speed drills. You can also practice taking ten free throws or trying to make five free throws in a row between sets of speed drills. Either option will provide adequate rest between periods of full-speed practice.

Guidelines for Full-Court Dribbling Drills

Follow these guidelines as you practice full-court dribbling:

1. *Eyes up:* Pick a spot on the wall at the opposite end of the court. Keep your eyes on this spot as you dribble. This will train you to see the whole court as you advance the ball.
2. *Full speed:* Do all drills as fast as you can, but under control. Your dribbling speed may be slow at first, but you will improve as you practice. To begin, get your footwork down properly. Speed will come as you work hard.

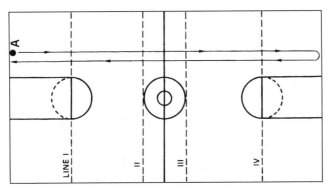

FIGURE 8.1   Lines on the Full Court

3. *Hip height:* Never dribble the ball higher than your hips. (Your hips are not your waist; your waist is higher.) This provides much better control of the ball than dribbling the ball at waist height.
4. *One set:* In these drills, go to the opposite end line and return. Do each drill a minimum of two repetitions, up to a maximum of five repetitions. This is one set.
5. *Repeat moves:* As you go past each foul line and half-court line, make a dribbling move at each line on the full court (see Figure 8.1).

The Right-Hand Speed Dribble

For this drill, dribble at full speed, pushing the ball ahead of you while keeping it to the right side of your body. Follow these steps:

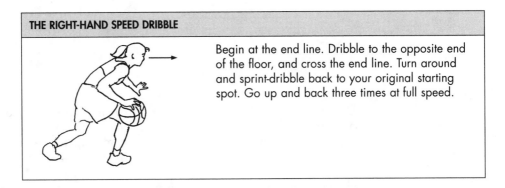

THE RIGHT-HAND SPEED DRIBBLE

Begin at the end line. Dribble to the opposite end of the floor, and cross the end line. Turn around and sprint-dribble back to your original starting spot. Go up and back three times at full speed.

The Left-Hand Speed Dribble

Follow the procedure for the right-hand speed dribble, this time using the left hand. If you are right-handed, work hard to develop your left hand, and vice versa. If the left hand is your weak hand, practice the left-hand speed dribble twice, before and after you do the right-hand speed drill.

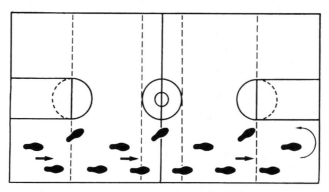

FIGURE 8.2 Footwork for the Jab-Step Dribble

The Jab-Step Dribble

The jab step allows you to fake out a defender without changing dribbling hands or direction (see Figure 8.2).

Practice the drill using both hands. Do not overextend yourself by jabbing too far; you may lose your balance. You need to jab only about 12 inches to the side to fake out the defender. Follow these steps:

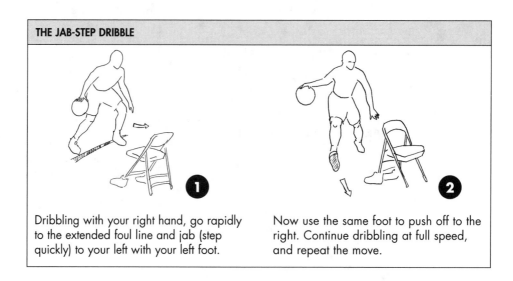

THE JAB-STEP DRIBBLE

1 Dribbling with your right hand, go rapidly to the extended foul line and jab (step quickly) to your left with your left foot.

2 Now use the same foot to push off to the right. Continue dribbling at full speed, and repeat the move.

▍TRAINING TIP

Stay low. When you are executing controlled dribbling moves, bend your knees and get lower to achieve greater balance, control, and quickness. You should dribble no higher than knee height when you execute a move and no higher than hip height in a full-speed open-court dribble.

The Crossover Dribble

The crossover dribble is a manuever used to change direction while advancing the ball forward. It can be used in an open court (full-speed) situation or in a controlled dribble setting. To perform the crossover dribble begin by dribbling with your right hand no higher than above knee level and to the right side of your body. Quickly push the ball down below your knees in front of your body as you change direction, with the ball moving from your right side to your left side. Then quickly advance, pushing the ball up the court with the left hand. This is a change-of-direction move, so at each line change directions going from right to left, then left to right and so on. Complete three to five repetitions of the drill.

▌ TRAINING TIP

The crossover move is best used when you have a great deal of room between you and the defender (at least two arm's lengths away). If the defender is closer than this, they may be able to reach down and sweep the ball away. The crossover is a faster change-of-direction move than the between-the-legs dribble, but it is also more dangerous because it exposes the ball to the defender. Know how far away the defense is when you decide which change-of-direction move to use. This move is most effective when a dribbler attacks the side of the defender's lead foot and moves in that direction.

The Between-the-Legs Dribble

The between-the-legs dribble enables players to change direction without having to dribble the ball in front of them or turn their back to the basket. It is effective and quick and allows the dribbler to protect the ball. Follow these directions to execute the between-the-legs dribble:

THE BETWEEN-THE-LEGS DRIBBLE

1 Dribble at full speed with your right hand from end line to end line. At each foul line and half-court line, make a dribble-between-the-legs move.

2 The ball should always move in a front-to-back motion when going between the legs.

3 As the ball touches the receiving hand, immediately push the ball forward and continue down the court, exploding ahead with your body. This is a change-of-direction move, so at each line, change directions, going from left to right, then right to left. Complete three to five repetitions of the drill.

The Reverse-Pivot Dribble

This dribbling move is especially effective when a defensive player is overplaying you to one side of the court or when you are heading toward a sideline or baseline while being defended. Do exactly what the name says—pivot to the reverse, or opposite, side. At each foul line and half-court line, change direction, using a reverse-pivot dribble. Here's the sequence: right-hand dribble, reverse pivot into a left-hand dribble, explode ahead, and change direction with a reverse pivot; dribble ahead with a right-hand dribble again. Follow these directions to practice the reverse-pivot dribble:

THE REVERSE-PIVOT DRIBBLE

1

2

Plant your left foot, and pivot your body backward, three-quarters of the way to the left. Keep the ball at your right hand and no higher than your knees. Your last dribble before pivoting should be a hard, low dribble, with your right hand meeting the ball at knee level and keeping contact with it until you complete the pivot. A hard dribble will make the ball hug your hand on the pivot movement.

As you pivot, allow the ball to drop from your hand. Your left hand should then dribble the ball as you go in the other direction, pushing the ball ahead with your left hand.

Repeat the process, this time making the pivot move from left to right using your right foot to pivot and your right hand to control the ball. Complete three to five repetitions of the drill.

The Behind-the-Back Dribble

This dribbling move allows you to laterally change direction with the ball and avoid a defensive player in the open court, without losing forward momentum and speed. It can be very useful in a fast-break situation. To practice this move, follow these steps:

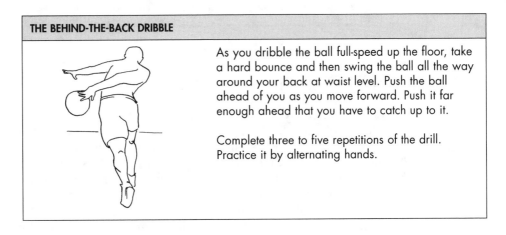

THE BEHIND-THE-BACK DRIBBLE

As you dribble the ball full-speed up the floor, take a hard bounce and then swing the ball all the way around your back at waist level. Push the ball ahead of you as you move forward. Push it far enough ahead that you have to catch up to it.

Complete three to five repetitions of the drill. Practice it by alternating hands.

The Change of Pace

This dribbling move allows you to catch a defender off guard by keeping your dribble at half speed, then instantly changing pace by accelerating to full speed. It is excellent for keeping off a defender who is applying tight full-court pressure up the floor and trying to reach in. To practice this move, follow these steps:

1. As you dribble, move up the floor at half speed, keeping the same pace for at least three to five dribbles.
2. Next, instantly explode to full speed, changing the pace of your dribble. This will catch a defender off guard. Take three to four steps at full speed, then repeat the move again by slowing down to half speed for another three to four steps.
3. Complete two to three repetitions of this drill, full court.

The Stop-and-Go Dribble

This is another dribbling move used to keep off a tight defender. The constant stop-and-go movement will set the defender off balance, tire the defender's legs, and prevent them from reaching in. Follow these steps to practice the stop-and-go dribble:

1. As you dribble up the floor at full speed, stop and hold your position for one full second while continuing to dribble.
2. Next, instantly explode to full speed, changing the speed of your dribble.
3. Complete two to three repetitions of the drill, full court. Practice with both hands.

▌▌▌ TRAINING TIP _____

Never allow a defender to get closer than two arm's lengths away from you when you are dribbling. A defender who is one arm's length away from you is also one arm's length away from the ball and has a chance to steal it. Use various dribbling moves to keep the defender at a distance of two arm's lengths at all times. You should not be dribbling in a stationary spot. Always stay on the move. This will keep the defender on the move also.

▌ CLOSET DRIBBLING DRILLS

If you do not have access to a gym but still want to improve your dribbling skills, closet dribbling drills are designed for you. You need very little room to do these drills, which is why they are called closet drills. They are perfect for the player who does not have a full- or even half-court gym but does have the will to work. These drills can be done in basements, on driveways, in garages, on sidewalks, on patios, on roof terraces, in closets, and even in gyms. They can be done in any weather: sun, rain, wind, or snow. All you need is desire and a basketball. Closet drills are excellent practice for half-court situations in a game running down the clock, such as directing and controlling offenses, playing a delay game, and for improving over-all dribbling skills. You need to work on these dribbling skills. If you do not want to sit on the bench during the season, do not sit in the off-season. Work—it's that simple.

Follow these guidelines to make the most of practicing closet dribbling drills:

Practicing Closet Drills

1. *Maintain knee height:* Never dribble above knee height (except for the walk dribbling drills, which are done at hip height for a rest period). This height will give you quicker reactions and better ball control. Bend your knees, but not your back—you have to keep your head and eyes up at all times.
2. *Pick a spot:* Pick a spot to look at: a spot on the wall, a tree, a pole, a house, or whatever. Keep your eyes up as you practice. Never look down at the ball. You can even find a dark room or garage and dribble with the lights off.
3. *Work hard:* Concentrate and develop speed in these drills. If you are lazy in practice, you will not react quickly in a game.

▌▌▌ TRAINING TIP _____

For an extra challenge, practice each closet dribbling drill by completing five repetitions in a row, without a miss or mistake, and at full speed and intensity. As your skills improve, move the number up to ten, fifteen, or even twenty in a row.

IF YOU THINK PRACTICE IS BORING,

TRY SITTING ON THE BENCH.

SCOTISM

The Between-the-Legs Two-Bounce Dribble with In-Place Walk

For this drill, stand erect, keeping your head and eyes up. Dribble no higher than your hip, and don't look down at the ball. Follow these steps:

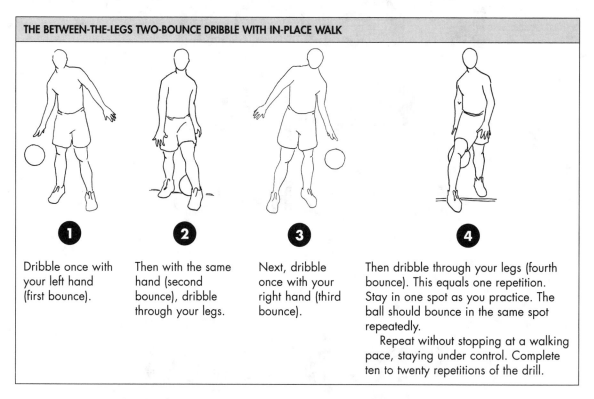

THE BETWEEN-THE-LEGS TWO-BOUNCE DRIBBLE WITH IN-PLACE WALK

❶ Dribble once with your left hand (first bounce).

❷ Then with the same hand (second bounce), dribble through your legs.

❸ Next, dribble once with your right hand (third bounce).

❹ Then dribble through your legs (fourth bounce). This equals one repetition. Stay in one spot as you practice. The ball should bounce in the same spot repeatedly.
    Repeat without stopping at a walking pace, staying under control. Complete ten to twenty repetitions of the drill.

The Between-the-Legs One-Bounce Dribble with In-Place Walk

Follow the procedure for the two-bounce drill, but use only one bounce before moving the ball side to side. Move your legs in a scissor motion. Repeat without stopping at a walking pace, staying under control. Complete twenty repetitions without looking down at the ball.

> ◾| **TRAINING TIP** _____
>
> Practice the two walking drills between the other closet speed drills. They will provide an adequate rest period between full-speed drills.

The Jab-Step Speed Drill

Follow the procedure for the full-court jab-step drill, but stay in one spot. Jab, stay low, and take a few dribbles. Then jab again, keeping the ball on the same side with the same hand. One jab equals one repetition. Complete twenty repetitions of the drill with each hand.

The Between-the-Legs Two-Bounce Speed Dribble

Stay low, keeping your head up. Dribble no higher than your knees. Dribble once with your left hand (first bounce), on the outside of your left leg. Then with the same hand (second bounce), dribble through your legs. Next, dribble once with your right hand (third bounce) on the outside of your right leg, and then dribble through your legs (fourth bounce). This equals one repetition. Repeat this drill without stopping, dribbling as fast as you can. Complete twenty repetitions of the drill.

The Between-the-Legs One-Bounce Speed Dribble

Follow the procedure for the two-bounce drill, but use only one bounce when moving the ball from side to side as you dribble through your legs. Move your legs in a scissor motion to do the drill. Repeat without stopping, working as fast as you can. Complete twenty repetitions of the drill.

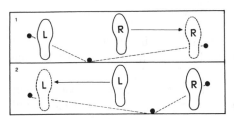

FIGURE 8.3   Footwork for the Lateral-Shuffle Dribble

The Lateral-Shuffle Dribble

This is an excellent drill for developing coordination, quickness, lateral speed, and agility with the ball. Follow the procedure for the two-bounce drill, but instead of moving your legs in a front-to-back scissor motion, move them laterally (from side to side), right to left and then left to right (see Figure 8.3). Imagine a box around you that is 6 feet from side to side and 3 feet from front to back. Try to stay in this box during the drill. Follow these steps:

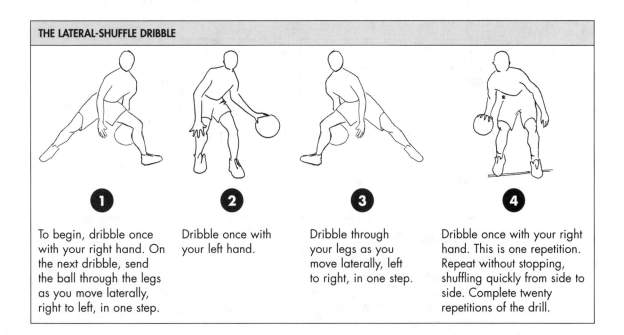

THE LATERAL-SHUFFLE DRIBBLE

1 To begin, dribble once with your right hand. On the next dribble, send the ball through the legs as you move laterally, right to left, in one step.

2 Dribble once with your left hand.

3 Dribble through your legs as you move laterally, left to right, in one step.

4 Dribble once with your right hand. This is one repetition. Repeat without stopping, shuffling quickly from side to side. Complete twenty repetitions of the drill.

TRAINING TIP _____

Once you get good at these drills, for an added challenge, try doing the drills while dribbling with gloves on. If you don't have gloves, practice with your eyes closed. Both will help to increase your feel and control with the ball.

The next two drills can be done in a foul-lane area, dribbling from the baseline to the foul line and back. *Always keep the ball in the lane area.* This will help you remember to practice each dribbling move with both hands. If you do not have a foul lane, use an equivalent distance on your driveway, in your basement, or on a sidewalk.

Left-Hand/Right-Hand Foul-Lane Dribbling Drill

Follow these steps to execute the left-hand and right-hand foul-lane dribbling drill. See Figure 8.4 for details.

1. Begin below the baseline, with both feet behind the line. Dribble at full speed with your left hand at hip height to the foul line, making sure both feet come above the foul line.
2. Without picking up your dribble, change directions by pivoting back toward the lane and dribbling at full speed back toward the baseline. Make sure both feet cross behind the baseline. This is one repetition.
3. Without picking up your dribble, again pivot back toward the lane by spinning to your left and exploding with a dribble back toward the foul line.
4. Do as many dribbling repetitions as you can in thirty seconds or sixty seconds.

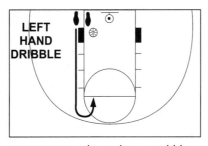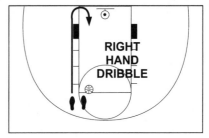

FIGURE 8.4   The Foul-Lane Dribbling Drill

TRAINING TIP _____

You can also use the lane-dribbling concept to practice jab-step moves, stop-and-go moves, and reverse-pivot moves. Simply work on the jab-step and stop-and-go moves halfway up the lane area; work on the reverse-pivot moves at each end of the foul lane, using the foul lines as your pivot point for changing directions.

The Between-the-Legs Foul-Lane Dribbling Drill

1. Begin below the baseline, with both feet behind the line as in the previous drill. Dribble at full speed to the foul line, with your left hand at hip height. Make sure both feet come above the foul line into a jump stop.
2. Without picking up your dribble, change directions by dribbling through your legs at hip height from left to right. Then quickly pivot back toward the lane and dribble at full speed back toward the baseline. Make sure both feet cross behind the baseline, making a jump stop as you dribble right to left and pivot back toward the lane area again.
3. You have just completed one repetition of the drill. Without picking up your dribble, again pivot back toward the lane by spinning to your left and exploding with the dribble back toward the foul line. Do as many repetitions or lengths as you can in thirty or sixty seconds.

COACHES' CHALK TALK: TEAM DRIBBLING SKILLS

A team can cut down on its turnovers by 30 to 50 percent if players develop good dribbling skills and can learn to dribble with eyes up, watching the entire court. Take only five minutes of daily practice time to improve players' dribbling skills. You can use the following drills to replace some conditioning drills you use now, whether to warm up your players or to improve their physical strength and stamina. Full-court dribbling drills are excellent for conditioning and can be used in place of sprints or running. Here's how to use both full-court and closet dribbling drills in practice.

Around-the-Court Dribbling Drills

In this drill, start all players at half court on the sideline. Each player must dribble down the sideline to the baseline corner, then to the other baseline corner, the opposite sideline, the opposite baseline, and back to the original spot. Have the players practice a variation of moves in the following manner:

- At each corner of the court, perform a reverse-pivot dribble.
- Under each main basket and at half court, perform a between-the-legs dribble.
- At the four side baskets, practice a jab-step dribble, a change of pace, or a stop-and-go dribble.
- To begin, space the players 15 to 20 feet apart. Have them work clockwise around the court for two minutes, then reverse direction, doing the same moves with the opposite hand for two more minutes.

Full-Court Dribbling Drills

Depending on the number of players you have, put them in either four or five lines (no more than five) across the end line (unless you have more space to the side) (see Figure 8.5). Each line should have a minimum of two players and a maximum

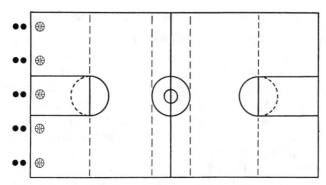

FIGURE 8.5   Setup for Full-Court Dribbling Drills

of three. Have the players do all the full-court dribbling drills explained in this chapter. They should do each drill three or four times in a row, to the opposite end line and back. Head and eyes should be kept up.

Closet Dribbling Drills

These make excellent warm-up drills. Line up the players as for the full-court drills. Have the first player in each line step to the extended foul line and do twenty repetitions, with the head and eyes up. Repeat with the remaining players in each line. Rotate players after each drill has been completed. These closet drills, when done rapidly, condition the legs and improve players' ball handling, quickness, and coordination. Team practice time is valuable, and it may not always be feasible to use closet drills. But if you can, they will bring great benefits. Your first priority should be to do the full-court dribbling drills every day; if you have extra time, do the closet drills.

Solo Dribbling Drills

Another variation is to have each player practice with his or her own ball. Do one drill for thirty to sixty seconds on the score clock, then change the drill for the entire team. Have all players line up around the half-court square or volleyball court lines, facing each other.

CHAPTER QUESTIONS

1. What are three objectives for practicing dribbling drills?

2. Why is it important to be able to dribble with either hand equally well?

3. Give at least two reasons for the importance of dribbling with the head and eyes up.

4. What are the four reasons to use a dribble in a game situation?

5. When you are dribbling the ball, how close should you allow a defender to get to you and why?

6. As a coach, what is the advantage of having a team with good fundamental skills? How will this help win more games?

Rebounding Fundamentals

IN THIS CHAPTER YOU WILL LEARN:
- Rebounding as a defensive tool
- How to score eight or more points per game simply by rebounding
- Ways to get the winning rebound position every time
- How to improve defensive productivity and value

REBOUNDING BASICS

Rebounding is one of the most important skills and statistics in the game because the team that controls "the boards," or gets the most rebounds, also controls the amount of second-shot opportunities the opposing team will get on offense. Every second-shot opportunity leads to another ball position for a team. How important are second-shot opportunities? Most offensive rebounds lead to layups, fouls that lead to free throws, or both: easy points for any team.

Rebounding, like defense, is simply a matter of hard work. Although being tall or a good jumper is always helpful in rebounding, neither is a requirement. Both jumping and height can be neutralized by an intelligent player who works hard and uses good rebounding skills and fundamentals. To rebound intelligently at both ends of the floor, a player must follow these guidelines:

The Four Rules of Rebounding
1. Obtain a good rebounding position.
2. Box out after obtaining a good position.
3. Use body leverage to gain strength and hold a good rebounding position.
4. *Always* assume that the shot will be missed (more than half of them will be!).

Rebounding is a "habit skill," which means that once you have developed the technique, you will not need daily practice and repetition (as shooting, dribbling, and foul-shooting skills do) to maintain a high level of skill.

Let's take a look at both offensive and defensive rebounding drills and skills.

DEFENSIVE REBOUNDING SKILLS

When you control the defensive boards and prevent offensive rebounds, you reduce the number of possessions and shot attempts the other team will get in a game. An offensive rebound is as good as a possession or a steal for another shot opportunity. Here are ways to stop offensive rebounds.

Boxing Out

Although "boxing out," or "screening off," your opponent from the rebound is often considered a defensive skill, it actually is just as it important in offensive rebounding. One benefit of playing defense is its advantageous rebounding position. When you play defense, you should already be between your opponent and the basket unless you forfeit this position by failing to block out your opponent. Attaining a good rebounding position is the first step to intelligent rebounding, and boxing out is the second step.

To box out means to block or impede the opponent's path to the basket and the rebound once a shot is taken. Sometimes a great jumper or a tall player neglects to think about boxing out. But one failure to box out may allow the opponent to get a key rebound at a critical moment during the game. In truth, any time an opponent gets an offensive rebound it is a critical moment. That is why it is better to use all available basketball tools, and boxing out is one of them.

To box out effectively, follow these steps:

BOXING OUT

Get position.

Get the best rebounding position possible. Put yourself between the opponent and the basket, then go after your opponent.

"Hit" your opponent.

Make contact by pivoting into the opposing player and his or her path to the basket. This will also help you face the basket to watch the flight of the ball. Try to make contact with your butt into their knee area, which is lower than the position typically taught. Being this low will limit the opponent's progress and jumping ability, and lower your center of gravity, making you stronger while allowing you to also jump quicker.

Get the ball.

After stopping the opposing player's advance, go after the ball. You can even let it drop to the floor—just do not let your opponent go by you to get it. Since your eyes will be on the ball, you must be able to feel your opponent's movement and location after you have boxed out. Use your butt, back, and one arm if you need to. When the ball comes off the rim, explode upward, springing off both feet and trying to grab the ball with both hands.

Using Leverage

The second important step to intelligent rebounding is to use leverage. Do this by bending your knees and dropping low after you have gotten a good rebounding position and boxed out your opponent. Ideally, you want to be "sitting" on your opponent's knees (see Figure 9.1).

FIGURE 9.1
Using Leverage

First, this will allow you to jump more quickly because your legs will already be bent, or "cocked," and ready to jump. Second, it will keep your opponent from moving around you; you will have "anchored" that player's center of gravity by impeding movement of the knees. Third, you can avoid being pushed out of your rebounding position.

Even if you are skinny or short, you can compensate by using leverage. The lower you get as you box out, the harder it will be to move you, and the harder it will be for your opponent to jump quickly, if at all.

Try boxing out a friend or teammate while standing straight up. Then try boxing out by using leverage and crouching low, back toward the player's knees. Feel the difference. On average this technique can make you 20 to 40 pounds stronger and one second quicker when you jump.

▌▌ TRAINING TIP _____

How Important Is Defensive Rebounding?

If you wonder whether it's worth practicing defensive rebound skills, consider these facts:

1. Offensive rebounds translate into layups 90 percent of the time.
2. Giving up offensive rebounds is the easiest way to lose a game.
3. Offensive rebounds for your opponent provide motivation and momentum.

▌ OFFENSIVE REBOUNDING SKILLS

Being a good offensive rebounder will take more work than defensive rebounding because, first, you must obtain a better rebounding position, and second, you must box out your opponent. To obtain good offensive rebounding position, always try to establish a position between the opposing player and the basket. If an opposing player is between you and the basket, you have two to three full seconds to get around your opponent to improve your rebounding position. The closer a shot is taken to the basket, the less time you will have to do this. Do not be lazy; work to get the best position possible every time a shot goes up. Don't try to jump over a defender's back to get an offensive rebound—that is not hustle and will only cause you to pick up needless fouls. Working to get better position than your opponent is real hustle. Real hustle involves getting better rebounding position and *then* finding the ball.

Wanting to rebound offensively requires mental toughness, and this can pay huge dividends. Good offensive rebounders can improve their scoring average by up to eight points per game just through hustling to get position.

Here are a few moves and ideas that will help you to obtain better offensive rebounding position.

FIGURE 9.2 The Three Phases of the Step-and-Cut Move

The Step-and-Cut Move

Cut to one side to fake out your opponent. Then, before the defensive player can box you out, step to the other side and get in front (see Figure 9.2). This works very effectively in offensive rebounding. Most defenders are too passive to effectively screen off an offensive player from the shot.

The Roll-and-Duck-Under Move

If an opposing player has good position and has blocked you out, don't try to jump over the person's back or push into the player for the rebound. Simply step around your opponent to one side or the other by lifting your leg and arm in front of him or her and ducking underneath the opponent's arm to get into a better rebounding position (see Figure 9.3).

FIGURE 9.3 The Roll-and-Duck-Under Move

FIGURE 9.4 The Spin Move

The Spin Move

If an opponent is boxing you out, quickly spin to one side or the other to avoid being pinned or moved back. Try to get at least a half or side position for the rebound (see Figure 9.4). This is a physically active, aggressive move. Keep moving, and don't let yourself get sealed off.

▌ TRAINING TIP

When working on being a better offensive rebounder, try to anticipate, or predict, when a shot will be taken by one of your teammates. Then move into a good rebounding position right before the shot is taken. These two steps will set you up to focus on offensive boards and to pick up easy baskets.

PRACTICE TIME

=

PLAYING TIME

SCOTISM

The Tip Drill

This is an excellent drill for low-post players and, of course, for all players. It will help you be a better offensive rebounder and develop control of the ball with one hand when rebounding. Many rebounds cannot be reached with two hands because of player traffic. This drill will teach you to tap the ball backward to a place where you can get better control of it—or tap it forward into the basket.

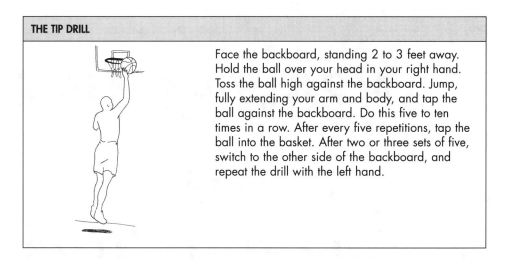

THE TIP DRILL

Face the backboard, standing 2 to 3 feet away. Hold the ball over your head in your right hand. Toss the ball high against the backboard. Jump, fully extending your arm and body, and tap the ball against the backboard. Do this five to ten times in a row. After every five repetitions, tap the ball into the basket. After two or three sets of five, switch to the other side of the backboard, and repeat the drill with the left hand.

▌▌ TRAINING TIP

Use your fingertips to control the ball. Do not let the ball touch the palms of your hands. If your hand is too small to control the ball while tipping it into the basket with one hand, tip it in with two hands.

▌▌ MORE TIPS FOR BETTER REBOUNDING

Use these ideas for rebounding, at either end of the court:

1. Follow the flight of the ball after it has been shot. Four out of five rebounds go to the side of the rim opposite from where the shot was taken from. Knowing this will help you to be in the right place at the right time.
2. If you cannot pull the ball down with both hands, tip it to an area where you can use one fully extended arm to retrieve the ball.
3. Rebounding is difficult to practice alone, but not impossible. Put the correct rebounding methods into your mental preparation sheet, and read it before you go to bed, picturing yourself doing rebounding skills and moves correctly. This is a mental exercise.

4. If you are a guard or a smaller player, you can still improve your rebounding. Once a shot is taken, always go to the top of the three-second lane area, just below the foul line. This is known as the "garbage pit" of rebounds, because long rebounds always end up here—especially rebounds from three-point shots.
5. The farther the shot is taken from the basket, the longer the rebound will be. Get in the right position.

▌▌ TRAINING TIP _____

You have up to three full seconds to execute a rebound. First, find your opponent. Second, "hit," or make contact with, your opponent. Third, get the ball. There is plenty of time to do all three!

For quick reference, here is a summary of rebound objectives at both ends of the court.

Defensive Rebounding
1. Box out and make contact with your opponent on every shot.
2. Never give up a single offensive rebound to your opponent in a game.

Offensive Rebounding
1. Never worry about the ball first. Concern yourself with rebounding position first. If you do this, the ball will be there when you turn to look for it.
2. When a shot is attempted, never stand and watch. Make an aggressive cutting move toward the basket if you are a center or a forward. If you are a guard, you must consider being a defensive safety to impede fast breaks. Do not go all the way to the basket for a rebound. Go to the foul-line area, to find an open gap just below the foul-line area and be prepared for long rebounds.

Zone Boxing Out versus Man-to-Man Boxing Out

In a man-to-man defense, a defensive player's job is much easier because the defender always knows whom to box out and the location of that person. In a zone, however, a single defender may have two offensive players close by when a shot goes up. The standard rule in a zone is to find an opponent to box out.

If you anticipate that a shot is pending, communicate to a teammate to box out the defender farthest from you in your area. When in doubt, box out the player closest to the basket. If two have a chance to retrieve the offensive rebound, take the bigger one! Your main objective, however, is find someone to box out. Never just turn and look for the ball—if you do, anyone can get it.

▮▮▮▮▮▮ COACHES' CHALK TALK: TEAM REBOUNDING

If you want to see some interesting statistics, look at your rebounding statistics (or any other team's) from last season. You will find a close relationship between rebounds and wins. In most, if not all, of the games you won, your team had more rebounds. In the games you lost, you were probably outrebounded. Many games are lost simply because players lack fundamental rebounding skills.

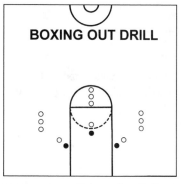

FIGURE 9.5   Rebounding Drill
(Boxing Out)

Good rebounding does not require talent, only interest. It is also a habit skill and should be practiced correctly. For a simple drill, put players in three lines at one basket (see Figure 9.5). The first player is on defense and must box out correctly. The second in line is the offensive player and must use a cut and step or a roll move to get a good rebounding position.

You can also use this team formation to practice offensive rebounding drills and moves shown earlier in this chapter. Have all players "walk" at half speed through all three rebounding moves one time to learn the correct steps and movements. Then have them practice at full speed. Have a player or coach take three to five shots, then rotate in two new players. Each player can do each drill three to five times.

Make sure your players are boxing out correctly and effectively. Otherwise you are just killing time. Finally, make sure to teach these simple rules for offensive rebounding:

1. When a player drives to the basket or receives the ball on the blocks in the low post, the center and forwards (who do not have the ball) should go to the basket immediately for an offensive rebound. They should not wait for the shot to go up; it will be too late. Teammates must be smart enough not to impede the path of the player with the ball to the basket.
2. Teach your players on offense *not* to get offensive rebounds. Teach them to get offensive position to rebound offensively. There is a difference. What does it mean to get an offensive rebound? To get offensive position. If your players get in the habit of anticipating the shots of teammates and getting offensive position, they will get offensive rebounds. Coaches must teach players this concept.
3. If some of your players are not good shooters or do not like to shoot, teach them to be role players—to set screens, go to the boards, and so on. This is what Red Auerbach did with Bill Russell. Auerbach had way too many great shooters on his Boston Celtics team, so to Russell, his 6-foot, 9-inch center, he said, "With you, we will count rebounds as points." The psychology worked. The Celtics won eleven championships with Russell, and Russell had a NBA record career, making an average of 22.5 rebounds per game *for his entire career!*
4. Give a player a game goal such as this one: "If you will get us five offensive rebounds, we will have a great chance to win this game." It will allow players to take pride in their role, give them a chance to score more on put backs, and be a great benefit to your team.

CHAPTER QUESTIONS

1. Why is it important for a team to control defensive rebounds?

2. What are the four rules of rebounding?

3. What is a box out, and how is it helpful in rebounding?

4. Why is tipping the ball on a rebound a good idea?

5. How much time do you have to obtain rebounding position and retrieve the rebound?

6. What are the benefits of using good body leverage or balance when boxing out?

7. What should be your primary objective when trying to get offensive rebounds?

8. As a coach, why is outrebounding the opposing team in a game important?

Ball-Handling Fundamentals

IN THIS CHAPTER YOU WILL LEARN:
- That good ball handling is an essential skill for great players
- Twenty drills to develop exceptional dribbling skills
- Extremely effective team drills for dribbling
- Fifteen advanced drills to build dexterity and coordination
- Ball handling you can practice *while* you watch television

THE MARAVICH LEGACY

Although shooting comes first in basketball, another game skill that is truly artistic is ball handling. A player who knows how to handle a basketball properly can be graceful, creative, and entertaining to watch. The Harlem Globetrotters are great examples of the art of ball handling. They are world renowned for their ball handling, not their shooting. Their ball-handling feats amaze and captivate millions of people each year. They have rehearsed ball-handling skills hundreds of thousands of times, practice the same moves and footwork over and over every day, and make everything look easy.

"Press" Maravich, the former LSU coach, and his son, "Pistol" Pete Maravich, the all-time NCAA scoring leader in history (44.1 points per game career scoring average) and former NBA all-star, developed and popularized many of these drills. Practicing them will improve ball-handling skills, coordination, and quickness while building strength and endurance in the arms and hands.

If you lack sufficient quickness, coordination, hand strength, agility, reaction time, or even ball control when catching or dribbling, ball-handling drills can form an excellent bridge to these important skills. Ball-handling drills don't simply improve work with the ball; they can also develop athletic skills. If you are coaching a team that lacks excellent physical skills, use ball-handling drills as a prepractice warm-up for five to ten minutes each day, or after practice. In only a few short weeks you will see dramatic improvement.

Ball-handling drills also can provide extra practice or fill up extra time. They can be done anywhere. In your individual practice, do not do these drills until after you practice dribbling and shooting drills first. Shooting and dribbling drills are directly applicable to game situations. Ball-handling drills are helpful as a secondary workout. The benefits, however, are universal. Consider using these as a warm-up program before starting your normal training or practice. Do the drills rapidly for a minimum of ten repetitions each.

▌▌ TRAINING TIP _____

Ball-handling drills *without* a dribble are more helpful in developing hand and body coordination, agility, and reaction time. Ball-handling drills *with* a dribble help develop feel for the ball, quickness, and ball control. Plan your practice program based on what you need.

Literally hundreds of ball-handling drills are available to you. This chapter avoids most "trick" ball-handling drills because they are not as broadly beneficial as those listed here. Trick ball-handling drills are less useful in game situations. The more than three dozen drills and tips provided will give you more than enough skill-building options. They fall into three categories:

1. Maravich ball-handling drills (both with and without a dribble)
2. TV drills
3. Tips for improving your ball-handling skills

▌ BALL-HANDLING DRILLS WITHOUT A DRIBBLE (MARAVICH DRILLS)

Learning these three types of ball-handling drills will prepare you for many game situations and give you a better feel for the ball.

1. *Slaps:* Holding the ball in front of your chest, slap the ball as hard as you can from hand to hand, moving it back and forth between your hands. Complete ten repetitions. Each back-and-forth motion equals one repetition.
2. *Pinches:* Holding the ball in your right hand, "pinch" it toward your left hand, using all five fingers. Then with the left hand, pinch it toward your right hand. Go back and forth. Complete ten repetitions.
3. *Taps:* Hold the ball over your head, with your arms fully extended. Tap the ball back and forth between your fingertips. Your arms should be up over your head and fully extended vertically. Complete ten repetitions.

The following drills will also build ball-handling abilities.

Circles

The circles drill is good for improving arm strength, ball-handling speed, hand–eye coordination, and passing skills.

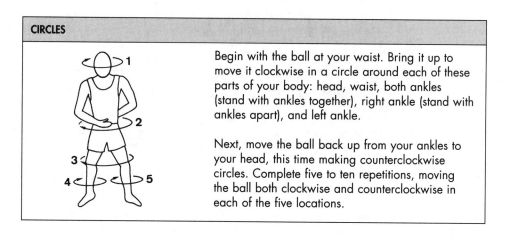

CIRCLES

Begin with the ball at your waist. Bring it up to move it clockwise in a circle around each of these parts of your body: head, waist, both ankles (stand with ankles together), right ankle (stand with ankles apart), and left ankle.

Next, move the ball back up from your ankles to your head, this time making counterclockwise circles. Complete five to ten repetitions, moving the ball both clockwise and counterclockwise in each of the five locations.

Figure Eights

This drill will develop hand coordination, quickness, hand–eye coordination, arm strength and endurance, and passing and ball-handling skills. Follow these steps:

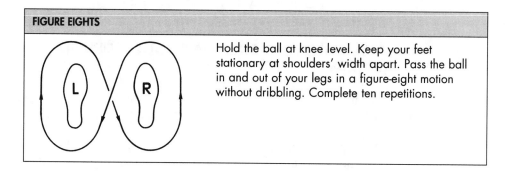

FIGURE EIGHTS

Hold the ball at knee level. Keep your feet stationary at shoulders' width apart. Pass the ball in and out of your legs in a figure-eight motion without dribbling. Complete ten repetitions.

Reverse Figure Eights

This drill is the same as the figure-eights drill, except the ball is moved in a back-to-front motion. Complete ten repetitions.

The Scissors Drill

This drill will improve conditioning, hand coordination, foot speed, and agility.

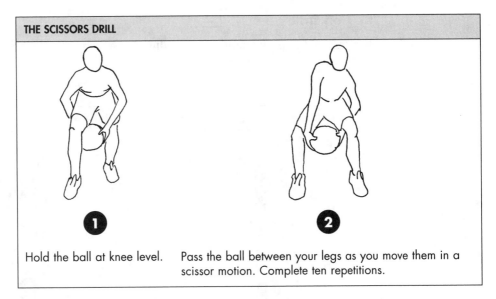

THE SCISSORS DRILL

1 Hold the ball at knee level.   **2** Pass the ball between your legs as you move them in a scissor motion. Complete ten repetitions.

The Reverse Scissors Drill

This drill is the same as the scissors drill, except the ball is moved in the opposite direction, going back to front between the legs. Complete ten repetitions.

The Rhythm Drill

This drill will develop hand–eye coordination and hand and foot quickness.

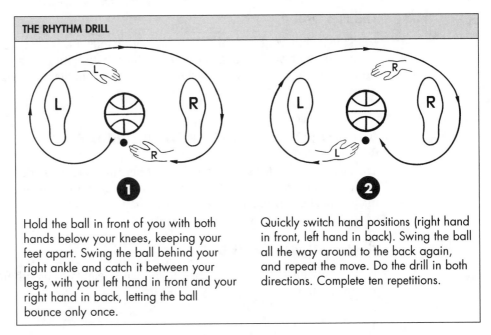

THE RHYTHM DRILL

1 Hold the ball in front of you with both hands below your knees, keeping your feet apart. Swing the ball behind your right ankle and catch it between your legs, with your left hand in front and your right hand in back, letting the ball bounce only once.

2 Quickly switch hand positions (right hand in front, left hand in back). Swing the ball all the way around to the back again, and repeat the move. Do the drill in both directions. Complete ten repetitions.

The Flop Drill

This drill will improve hand–eye coordination and hand quickness.

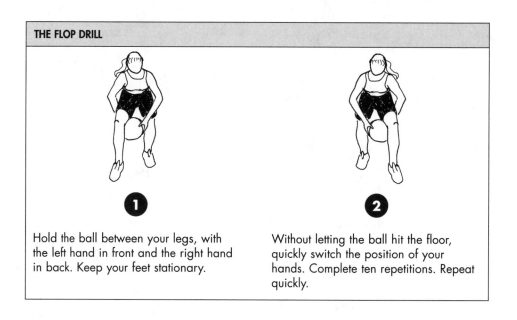

THE FLOP DRILL

1 Hold the ball between your legs, with the left hand in front and the right hand in back. Keep your feet stationary.

2 Without letting the ball hit the floor, quickly switch the position of your hands. Complete ten repetitions. Repeat quickly.

The Flip Drill

Hold the ball in front of your legs, using both hands. Keep your feet stationary. Flip the ball through your legs, and catch it in back with both hands. Then flip it to the front again. Repeat again as quickly as you can. Complete ten repetitions.

BALL-HANDLING DRILLS WITH A DRIBBLE

The next series of drills are more difficult because each one adds a dribble. Always practice each drill at full speed, and do not worry about mistakes. It is better to make a mistake in practice than to make one in a game!

The Low-Figure-Eights Drill

This drill involves the motion used in the figure-eights drill without a dribble. Follow these steps:

THE LOW-FIGURE-EIGHTS DRILL

Keep the ball as low to the ground as possible while dribbling the ball as rapidly as you can around your legs, in a figure-eight motion. Keep your feet stationary. Practice the drill in both directions. Complete ten repetitions. Then, practice going in the reverse direction.

The Stationary Two-Bounce Drill

This drill is similar to the low-figure-eights drill, except that the dribble is done at knee height. Follow these steps:

THE STATIONARY TWO-BOUNCE DRILL

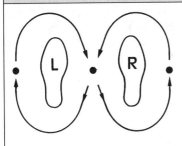

Begin by taking one dribble with the left hand, then bounce the ball through your legs, front to back, with your left hand, and receive the ball with your right hand. Quickly take one dribble on the right side of your right leg with your right hand, then again, dribble back through your legs (front to back) with your right hand. Do not pick up the ball or stop your dribble. This makes one repetition. Complete ten repetitions.

The following drills are useful for developing court vision, dribbling skills, hand-to-ball reaction time, and a feel for the ball.

The Stationary One-Bounce Drill

THE STATIONARY ONE-BOUNCE DRILL

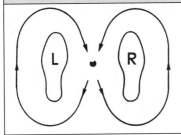

This is the same as the stationary figure eight with two dribbles, except the ball moves around the legs in a figure-eight motion. Take only one dribble with each hand to dribble the ball between your legs. One touch with each hand or one full rotation of a figure eight makes one repetition. Complete ten repetitions.

The One-Hand Circles Dribbling Drill

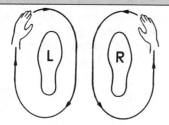

THE ONE-HAND CIRCLES DRIBBLING DRILL

L   R

Spread your feet apart, and keep them stationary. Dribble around the right ankle, using the right hand only. Switch to the left hand and the left ankle. Do this drill in a clockwise motion. Complete ten repetitions.

One-Hand Circles Roll Drill

ONE-HAND CIRCLES ROLL DRILL

Start by holding the ball in your right hand and rolling it around your entire hand without letting it lose touch with your hand or drop. Now roll the ball back in the other direction, touching the whole hand. Roll the ball as quickly as possible. Complete ten repetitions. Practice with both hands.

Reverse One-Hand Circles

This drill is done in the same way as one-hand circles but in a counterclockwise motion. Practice the drill with both hands. Complete ten repetitions.

The Reaction Drill

THE REACTION DRILL	
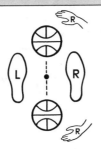	Keep the feet stationary, shoulders' width apart. Bounce the ball back and forth between your legs, using only your right hand. Let the ball bounce only once. Complete ten repetitions. Next, complete ten repetitions with your left hand.

The Three-Point-Bounce Drill

THE THREE-POINT-BOUNCE DRILL	
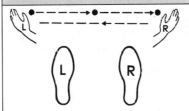	Stand stationary, with the feet shoulders' width apart. Dribble on your left side, then again, dribbling with your left hand, dribble once in front of you toward the middle of your feet, so that the ball is received on the right side with the right hand.

Next, without picking up the ball, dribble once with your right hand, then once again, pushing the ball back in front of you in the middle of your feet with the right hand, so that your left hand catches the ball after the dribble on the left side. This is one repetition. Do not stop your dribble when you repeat the drill. Complete ten repetitions.

The Reverse Three-Point-Bounce Drill

THE REVERSE THREE-POINT-BOUNCE DRILL	
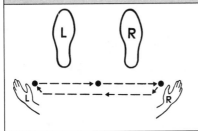	Stand stationary, with your feet apart. Dribbling behind you, bounce the ball once to your right, once behind your back, once to your left side, and once behind your back. Repeat quickly. Always bring the ball back to the middle starting point after taking a directional bounce dribble. Complete ten repetitions.

The Four-Point-Bounce Spider Drill

THE FOUR-POINT-BOUNCE SPIDER DRILL

Stand stationary, with the feet shoulders' width apart. Tap the ball once in front of your legs with the left hand, once with the right hand, then from behind once in back with the left hand, and once with the right hand, then from the front again. Repeat this quickly. Keep the ball low and in the middle of your legs. Complete ten repetitions.

TV BALL-HANDLING DRILLS

Although I do not advocate watching a lot of TV, I do know that players will do so. For that reason I have developed a series of drills that will allow you to work on basketball skills without having to break a sweat. It will also keep you from sitting and doing nothing.

These drills let you watch TV while keeping your mind on your goal—becoming a better basketball player. Keep a ball in your hands whenever you watch TV; it will help you develop a better feel for and confidence with the ball. Do the Maravich or the TV drills during breaks in the program. Practice a different drill during every break. If you watch TV for two hours and do nothing during commercials, you have wasted twenty minutes of potential practice time. If you do not keep a ball in your hand during the other hour and forty minutes, you have wasted that time as well.

The TV drills are broken up into two sections: TV show drills, and TV commercial drills. The TV show drills are simple and can be done while you are still watching a program. TV commercial drills require more activity, and are the perfect length to be done during a commercial break.

TV Show Drills

The Floor-Shooting Drill.   This drill will improve your follow-through and build endurance and strength in your arms. Follow these steps:

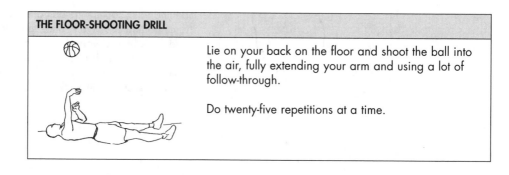

THE FLOOR-SHOOTING DRILL

Lie on your back on the floor and shoot the ball into the air, fully extending your arm and using a lot of follow-through.

Do twenty-five repetitions at a time.

The Chair-Drop Drill

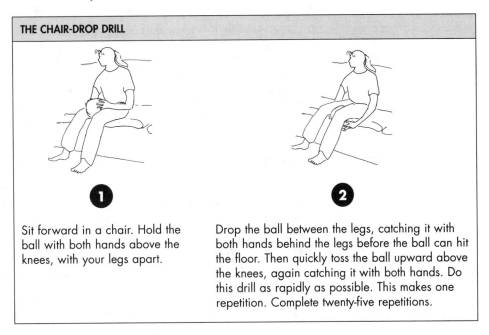

THE CHAIR-DROP DRILL

1 Sit forward in a chair. Hold the ball with both hands above the knees, with your legs apart.

2 Drop the ball between the legs, catching it with both hands behind the legs before the ball can hit the floor. Then quickly toss the ball upward above the knees, again catching it with both hands. Do this drill as rapidly as possible. This makes one repetition. Complete twenty-five repetitions.

The Hand-Roll Drill

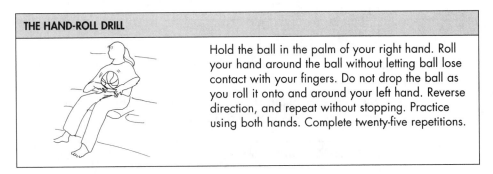

THE HAND-ROLL DRILL

Hold the ball in the palm of your right hand. Roll your hand around the ball without letting ball lose contact with your fingers. Do not drop the ball as you roll it onto and around your left hand. Reverse direction, and repeat without stopping. Practice using both hands. Complete twenty-five repetitions.

The Ball-Cuddle Drill.   This one is easy. Simply hold the ball in your hands while moving it around on your finger pads. You don't have to move it fast—just keep moving the ball around in your lap and from side to side. This requires no effort at all but is greatly beneficial for developing a better feel for the ball.

Ball Pinches.   Here's another no-brainer. As you sit and watch your favorite TV program(s), simply hold the ball and pinch it back and forth between your hands with your fingertips.

TV Commercial Drills

These drills can be performed during commercial breaks of three to five minutes. They are active and intense drills and will usually require you to get up off your . . . couch. They can be completed in short periods of time while providing long-term benefits.

The Triple-Threat Mirror Drill

THE TRIPLE-THREAT MIRROR DRILL

Stand in front of a mirror and slap your hands together to simulate catching the ball. As you clap your hands, go into a correct triple-threat position. The reason to practice this in front of the mirror is to make sure you are in the right position. Complete twenty-five repetitions of this drill.

The Mirror Shooting Drill.   This drill will help you make sure to finish your shot with the correct shooting form and follow-through. Follow these steps:

THE MIRROR SHOOTING DRILL

Stand in front of a mirror in a correct triple-threat position. Now, without a ball in your hand, simulate shooting the ball, making sure to use full arm extension and good follow-through. Complete twenty-five repetitions.

The One-Bounce Chair Dribble.   This is a little easier than the three-bounce chair dribble but still fun. Follow these steps:

THE ONE-BOUNCE CHAIR DRIBBLE

Take one dribble with each hand while pushing the ball back and forth from left to right, then right to left. Take only a single dribble for each hand. One back-and-forth motion makes one repetition. Complete twenty-five repetitions.

The Three-Bounce Chair Dribble.   A little more difficult than the one-bounce chair dribble, this simple drill will improve your ball handling, dribbling, and touch for the ball.

Sit on the edge of a chair so that you have room to dribble underneath your legs. Simply start with the ball on the left side of the chair, take one dribble with the left hand, then bounce the ball under your legs using only one bounce. Then take a dribble with your right hand on the right side of the chair, then bounce the ball back toward your left side with the right hand. This makes one repetition. Complete twenty-five repetitions. Do not look down at the ball; keep your head and eyes up.

Jump-Stop Pivot Drill.   You will find this drill in Chapter 2, on shooting. Practice it without a ball in front of the TV during commercials. Practiced daily, it will build tremendous game habits of facing the basket. The TV is just like a backboard—made of glass and rectangular—so pivot toward the TV and pretend you are facing the basket. Always pivot on your left foot if you are right-handed. Pivot on the correct pivot foot. Take two or three steps to your right, make a jump stop, and pivot, again facing the basket (TV) in a triple-threat position. Now go back to your left and do the same thing. This makes one full repetition. Complete twenty-five repetitions.

▌ TRAINING TIP _____

Use your imagination to make up additional drills to practice while watching television. You will be amazed at how much practice time you can get in. Get "tuned in" to working out with a prime-time TV program.

ADDITIONAL TIPS TO IMPROVE BALL HANDLING

Even when you've finished a practice session, there is more you can do to work on ball handling. These ideas will help you build skills during other daily activities:

1. *Walk with your head and eyes up:* Wherever you go, keep your head and eyes up as you walk. This is excellent training for developing peripheral vision and ability to see the whole court.
2. *Use your weak hand:* Try accomplishing a variety of tasks with your weak hand (if you are right-handed, for example, use your left hand). You can eat meals, brush your teeth, open doors, flush the toilet, or even write letters in this way. This will build your ability and confidence in using both hands on the court, and it will take very little extra time.
3. *Be prepared mentally:* Write a list of things you want to accomplish when you play. Read it, focusing on each item, and close your eyes as you picture yourself doing each one correctly. Do this before you go to bed at night.
4. *Carry a ball:* Everywhere you go (except to a house of worship), carry a ball. This includes visiting your friends, going to school, going to the movies, and so on.
5. *Walk/run and dribble:* Dribble the ball with your weak hand as you jog or even walk to school or other places. Keep your head and eyes up, and never look down at the ball.

COACHES' CHALK TALK: TEAM BALL HANDLING

Ball-handling drills can improve players' coordination, dexterity, and hand–eye coordination. But speaking realistically, team practices have time restraints, and it is not possible to cover everything. Think about including ball-handling drills on occasions like these:

1. Teach the drills at camps or as an off-season workout.
2. Teach them in a PE class as a five-minute warm-up for participants (who oftentimes are also players).
3. Have players practice the drills in the locker room while they wait for an earlier game to finish.
4. Do them as a prepractice warm-up in the hallways, if you share gym time with another team. Never waste time together as a team; when waiting for a gym or a game, ball handling can be a great warm-up.

CHAPTER QUESTIONS

1. What world-famous team has made ball handling popular? Who is considered to be the best ball handler of all time?

2. How can ball handling help in the development of a player's athletic skills?

3. In what ways can TV ball-handling drills improve a player's game skills?

4. List five tips a player can use to improve ball-handling skills.

5. When is a good time for coaches to have players practice ball-handling drills?

Cutting, Screening, and Pivoting Fundamentals

IN THIS CHAPTER YOU WILL LEARN:

- Sound concepts for cutting, pivoting, and setting screens
- That the better the cut and screen, the more you will score
- Drills for developing cutting, screening, and pivoting
- Additional insights and tips for improving your skills

OFFENSIVE BASICS

To be a complete offensive player, you must be able to pivot, cut, and screen effectively. You must cut to open spots on the court to receive the ball, as well as set and use screens effectively to get open shots. The most difficult players to defend are those who are always cutting, moving, and using screens, or "picks," so that they can receive the ball in a good scoring position. No one can get the basketball by standing in one spot, waiting for a pass from a teammate. Through cutting and using screens, you can more easily position yourself to score or to receive the ball in a good location within your perimeter.

CUTTING FUNDAMENTALS AND DRILLS

Players can use two types of offensive cutting movement: (1) inside cuts, or cuts into and through the lane area of the court, and (2) outside cuts to the perimeter areas. The objective of cutting, whether to the inside or the outside of the lane, is to get the ball as quickly as possible to an advantageous position. Be sure to make precise cuts and straight angles toward the ball. The shortest distance between two points is a straight line. If you do not make precise cuts and straight angles to open spots on the court, you will allow the defense more time to recover. Use a sharp, precise cut and angle to do the following:

1. Shed a defender long enough to receive a pass.
2. Receive the ball more quickly and more often.
3. Take defensive pressure off a teammate who needs someone to pass to.

When executing cutting moves, pay close attention to timing, and read the defense as you decide when to make your cuts. A good time to begin your cut to the ball is when the passer looks in your direction. This signals that the person is looking for someone to pass to, whether it be an inside or an outside cut.

▌ TRAINING TIP

The sharper the cut and the tighter the angle or turn, the quicker the ball will come to you and the quicker you can get to a good spot to receive a pass or get off a shot.

The Change-of-Pace Cut

As with all cuts, the most important thing is to plant the foot with which you fake and step, so you can push off it quickly to get open.

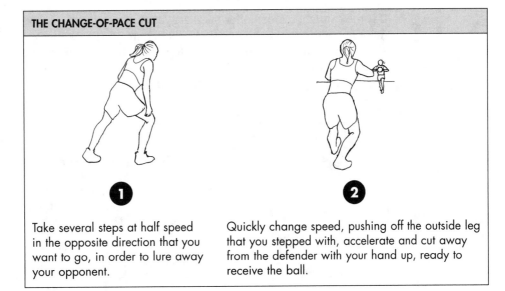

THE CHANGE-OF-PACE CUT

1 Take several steps at half speed in the opposite direction that you want to go, in order to lure away your opponent.

2 Quickly change speed, pushing off the outside leg that you stepped with, accelerate and cut away from the defender with your hand up, ready to receive the ball.

The Pivot Cut Move

The pivot cut is an inside cut.

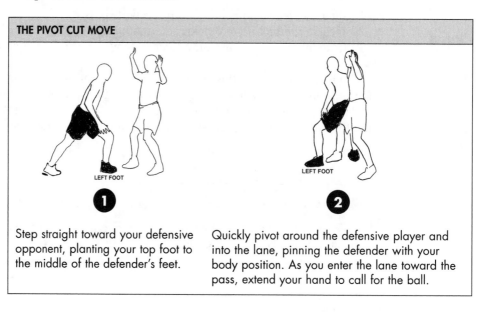

THE PIVOT CUT MOVE

1 Step straight toward your defensive opponent, planting your top foot to the middle of the defender's feet.

2 Quickly pivot around the defensive player and into the lane, pinning the defender with your body position. As you enter the lane toward the pass, extend your hand to call for the ball.

The Body Cut (or Crotch Cut)

Use this cut when a defender blankets you and gives you no room to move around. Its purpose is simply to make the defender step back. Do not cause injury or knee an opponent; this constitutes illegal foul play. This cut allows you to begin close to the lane or the defender and to conserve energy. Instead of running around to get open, you simply step into your defender, making the person move away, then cut to receive the pass.

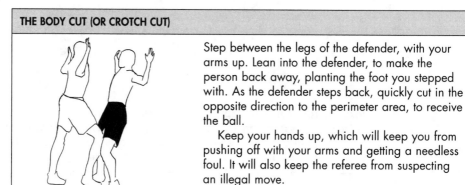

THE BODY CUT (OR CROTCH CUT)

Step between the legs of the defender, with your arms up. Lean into the defender, to make the person back away, planting the foot you stepped with. As the defender steps back, quickly cut in the opposite direction to the perimeter area, to receive the ball.

Keep your hands up, which will keep you from pushing off with your arms and getting a needless foul. It will also keep the referee from suspecting an illegal move.

The V-Cut Move

This cut gives a player quick, explosive, and efficient movements. To also divert or decoy the defender away from the direction you really wish to go in, plant your foot and push off quickly, making a sharp cut to the ball or basket. The V-cut move can also be used in all areas of the court, the low-post area, the perimeter, the lane, and even on the fast break.

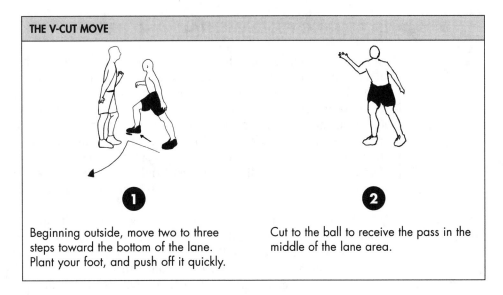

THE V-CUT MOVE

1 Beginning outside, move two to three steps toward the bottom of the lane. Plant your foot, and push off it quickly.

2 Cut to the ball to receive the pass in the middle of the lane area.

The Back-Door Cut

The back-door cut can be used in all areas of the court. It is useful whether defensive pressure is being applied in full-court, half-court, or quarter-court situations.

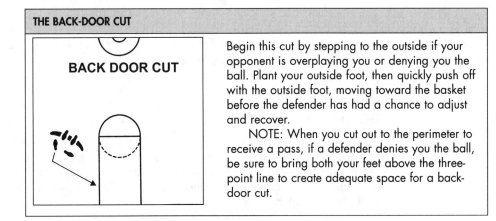

THE BACK-DOOR CUT

BACK DOOR CUT

Begin this cut by stepping to the outside if your opponent is overplaying you or denying you the ball. Plant your outside foot, then quickly push off with the outside foot, moving toward the basket before the defender has had a chance to adjust and recover.

NOTE: When you cut out to the perimeter to receive a pass, if a defender denies you the ball, be sure to bring both your feet above the three-point line to create adequate space for a back-door cut.

■■■■■■■SCREENING FUNDAMENTALS AND DRILLS

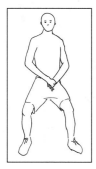

FIGURE 11.1
Setting a Screen

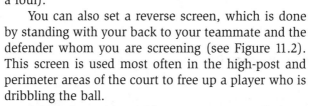

FIGURE 11.3   Making
Contact with a Teammate
during a Screen

What is a screen, or pick? It is a wall that is set up with your body to block a defender from following a teammate who needs to receive a pass or take an open shot. Screens and picks are an important part of offensive basketball. Coaches use them to free up the best shooters. Teams run plays employing screens to get players open shots in various spots on the court. Players use screens to open space to receive the ball, to pick and roll in a two-on-two half-court situation, and even to free dribblers or shooters from defensive pressure. Screens are vital to offensive effectiveness for both individual players and teams. Being able to set screens properly is as critical as having screens used to help you to get an open shot.

To set a screen correctly, stand with your feet a little wider than shoulders' width apart. Use your hands to cover your crotch area (see Figure 11.1). Do not lean into the defender with your knee or body (this is called a "moving screen" and is illegal; you will be called for a foul).

You can also set a reverse screen, which is done by standing with your back to your teammate and the defender whom you are screening (see Figure 11.2). This screen is used most often in the high-post and perimeter areas of the court to free up a player who is dribbling the ball.

FIGURE 11.2
A Reverse Screen

A key element in making a screen correctly is contact. You must make contact with your teammate who is setting the screen in order to rub the defender off (see Figure 11.3). If you do not make contact with the screener, you will give the defender space to get through and miss a chance for the shot or pass that had been intended.

YOU HAVE TO *DO* MORE THAN YOUR COMPETITION

IF YOU WANT TO *BE* MORE THAN YOUR COMPETITION.

SCOTISM

The Pivot Screen

With this screen you pivot into the path of the defensive player by creating a wider "gate," or area in which the defender must get through in order to follow a cutter to the ball. Be careful not to bang hard into a defender. You will be called for a foul.

THE PIVOT SCREEN

LEFT PIVOT FOOT

To execute a pivot pick or screen, let your teammate run past you. As this happens, pivot your back into the path of the defender. This will keep you from leaning into the defender with your knee or leg.

Do not use this move when setting a pick for a dribbler—it is too obvious!

◼◼ TRAINING TIP

The offensive player who sets the screen cannot move. It is the responsibility of the teammate using the screen or pick to rub shoulders and make contact with the screener. Moving when setting a screen for a teammate can cause you to pick up needless fouls.

◼ PIVOTING FUNDAMENTALS

Pivoting is another essential skill for the complete offensive player. Pivoting is a critical fundamental to master beacuse it helps prevent traveling violations. Pivoting is done with one foot, which must remain stationary on the ground during possession of the ball. Turn, or pivot, on the ball of the stationary foot in order to turn to the left or the right. A pivot can be used in several situations:

1. To turn, or pivot, away from defensive pressure in order to protect or pass the ball
2. To pivot to the outside of the lane on a defensive rebound in order to pass or dribble the ball up the floor
3. To make an offensive move in the low-post area with either pivot foot in order to get past a defensive player
4. To pivot toward and face the basket upon receiving the ball

Choice of pivot foot depends on where you are playing on the court. On the offensive end of the floor in the perimeter area, always pivot on the same foot to be as effective as possible offensively. (Review the pivot foot information in Chapter 2.) If you are playing in the low-post area on offense down in the blocks, either make a jump stop or keep both feet stationary in order to receive the ball. Then you can use *either* pivot foot after receiving the ball and go in either direction toward the basket against a defender. This is true for jump shots coming off screens and on defensive rebounds as well. You need the ability to pivot with either foot to the outside, away from the lane, where most player traffic is.

▌ TRAINING TIP

You can practice the fundamentals of cutting, screening, and pivoting skills without a ball, partner, basket, or gym. Practice each cut five times a day for a month to develop greater offensive skills and productivity as a player. Cutting, screening, and pivoting skills are also "habit skills," which don't require regular practice once they are mastered. They become an instinct. Learning them correctly is therefore of the utmost importance. During the first week of practice, start slowly; emphasize the correct movements and mechanics so that you learn perfect moves.

▌ COACHES' CHALK TALK: TEAM DRILLS FOR CUTTING, SCREENING, AND PIVOTING

In a team practice, teach at least three of the five basic cuts illustrated in this chapter: an inside cut, an outside cut, and a back-door cut. Variations of these three cuts were demonstrated; decide which ones best suit your own thinking and needs. Or you may use all of the inside and outside cuts along with the back-door cuts.

A simple way to have your team practice these cuts is to put your players into two lines, one on each side of the court (see Figure 11.4). Have them practice each cut, doing it correctly three to five times. Then practice a different cut until you have practiced them all (at least one inside cut, at least one outside cut, and the back-door cut).

You can rotate cutting, screening, and pivoting drills daily, together with the other habit skills mentioned in earlier chapters. Practice a different drill each day. As your players become more proficient at cutting, screening, and pivoting, they will become more intelligent and sound offensive players.

FIGURE 11.4 The Pivot Cut and the Body Cut

Team Back-Door Cut–Jump Stop Conditioning Drill

Place eight players (four on each team) on the court. Have them play four-on-four for two minutes. The losing team has to run a sprint. Here are the rules:

- Each player must stay within 5 feet of their opponent.
- No player is allowed to dribble. A dribble will be treated as a turnover.
- Each offensive player must move in 10-foot patterns to get open and receive a pass. "Move ahead of the ball; come back to the ball."
- Offensive players must make a jump stop when receiving a pass (especially since there is no dribbling).
- Defense must try to deny the pass at all times or steal the ball. If a team scores, the opponent gets the ball and must advance the full length of the court to score without a dribble.
- Team with the highest score in two minutes wins.

CHAPTER QUESTIONS

1. What are the advantages of making sharp, precise cutting moves?

2. What rule can a player follow to be a better offensive player and a help to teammates without putting in extra practice time?

3. Describe game situations suitable for using a body cut, a back-door cut, and a V-cut.

4. How are screens useful to a team while playing offense?

5. What is the key element of a screen or pick?

6. How can cutting, screening, and pivoting fundamentals make coaches more successful?

Fast-Break
Fundamentals

IN THIS CHAPTER YOU WILL LEARN:
- How to convert fast breaks into baskets, not just run fast breaks
- To properly "read" defenders and when to attack them on the fast break
- Proper techniques and rules for running three-on-two, two-on-one, and one-on-one fast breaks
- Moves to beat a defender one-on-one in a fast-break situation
- Individual and team drills for improving fast-break skills
- Tips for improving fast-break skills during pregame warm-up drills

FAST BREAK BASICS: A GREAT WAY TO SCORE

Fast-break basketball is the perfect forum for displaying teamwork, individual passing, ball-handling and scoring skills, and of course, sheer athleticism. The intent and purpose of running a fast break is to score easy baskets. If you can create a mismatch against only one or two defenders, it will be easier to score baskets. Some teams and players are better suited to fast-break basketball. A fast break is when one team attempts to quickly advance the ball against their opponent. This creates a numerical player advantage, thus making it easier for your team to score. A fast break allows more open shots to be taken, which usually results in higher percentage shots. Fast break basketball is also the number one offense of playground and pick-up-game basketball. Everyone should want to learn more about and excel at fast-break basketball.

Most fast breaks begin because of (1) good defense in the form of a blocked shot, turnover, or steal, or (2) a team's defensive rebound. There are two distinct types of fast-break offenses. The first, of course, is the freelance type of fast break, without structured offense or play patterns. Its objective is simply to advance the ball up the floor quickly to create a numbers advantage and to score easily. The second type of fast-break offense is structured, designed around set patterns and plays, and may even be used as an early offense or preliminary format to get a team into regular offensive plays to score an easy basket.

For this reason, this chapter includes basics such as a correct left-handed lay-up before progressing to two-on-one fundamentals, three-on-two fundamentals, one-on-one fundamentals, and team and individual drills, as well as additional fast-break concepts. Fast-break philosophies for coaches and players alike will be discussed.

▮▮ TRAINING TIP _____

Making Correct Defensive Reads

It is not the number of fast breaks you get in the game that bring success, but rather the number of conversions (scores) that you make (or score) on those fast breaks. It does little good to enter a fast-break situation only to miss a layup when contested by a defender or to throw a pass away because of an incorrect defensive read. The trick is to learn to recognize which option is really open, and when. Increasing your ability to make correct reads of the defense will lead to good decisions and provide more opportunities to score.

▮ FAST-BREAK SITUATIONS AND DRILLS

The most common fast-break situations are the two-on-one (two offensive players versus one defensive player), three-on-two, and one-on-one situations. Other scenarios include four-on-two, four-on-three, five-on-two, five-on-three, and five-on-four situations.

The involvement of several players, as in four-on-two and even five-on-five fast-break situations, usually indicates that a team has very structured offensive patterns and actually uses set fast-break patterns, screens, and shots as part of the offensive game plan. These structured fast-break situations are dictated by coaches' game plans and fast-break offenses that they like to run.

This chapter will address the most common situations and how to best succeed at one-on-one, two-on-one, and three-on-two fast-break situations.

Two-on-One Fast-Break Situations

A two-on-one fast-break situation is the highest-percentage scoring opportunity apart from an uncontested layup. This situation requires that the defender defend the basket, the ball, and two offensive players. A good player or team will score 80 percent of the time in this situation.

In order to gain more baskets in fast-break opportunities, make a correct read of the defense. When player 1 comes down on a fast break, at the three-point-line area a decision must be made about the defender and what to do with the ball. Player 1 must either drive all the way to the basket or pass the ball to a teammate (see Figure 12.1). To decide any later than at the three-point circle will create problems: one second later and the defender will be within reach of the ball and both offen-

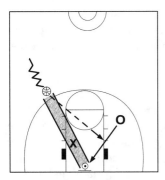

FIGURE 12.1 Making a Decision on the Fast Break

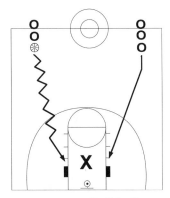

FIGURE 12.2 Drill for Two-on-One Fast Breaks

sive players, and it will be considerably easier for the defender to cover both offensive players at the same time.

Players should develop the habit of making a decision just as they reach or break the three-point-line area on the way to the basket. A player should never settle for a jump shot in a two-on-one situation; it's far better to score the basket or pass the ball to a teammate who can score. If you do attack the basket and the opponent defends you, make them foul you or back away.

For a simple drill for two-on-one fast-break situations, begin with two lines of offensive players on both sides of the half court (see Figure 12.2). One line will have a basketball in it. One defender will play in the foul-lane area. A dribbler from the ball line will drive to the basket, while a teammate from the other offensive line will fill in the fast-break lane and go to the basket, to receive a pass or get the rebound from a shot. The defender will try to defend the basket. If the offensive players score, the defender stays on defense. If the defender stops the fast break, the offensive player who either shot the ball or made a turnover goes to a defensive spot. The drill continues, lasting for three to four minutes.

▌▌ TRAINING TIP _____

Make the two-on-one drill more competitive by dividing players into groups of three. Then run the drill in sets of ten for each team. The team with the most made baskets is the winner. You can also do the drill as an entire team. The team must convert seven or eight out of ten opportunities to win.

Three-on-Two Fast-Break Situations

A three-on-two fast-break situation is also a high-percentage opportunity to score (see Figure 12.3). The objective is to penetrate the defenders as far as possible and to obtain the best open shot possible. In order to do so, the dribbler should pass the ball early to a wing, even when at half court, in order to turn the top defender out and spread out the defense (see Figure 12.4). This will open up driving and shooting lanes to the basket for the other two offensive players.

To practice a three-on-two fast-break situation, start with three offensive lines on the baseline. Place two defenders at the opposite end of the floor to defend the basket (see Figure 12.4). The two defenders will stay on defense until all the offensive players have gone through the drill, coming toward them. Start the wings a few steps ahead of the baseline or level with the foul line extended toward the sideline. The basketballs will be at the middle line on offense.

Player 1 will dribble the ball up the floor at full speed, looking for the best scoring opportunity for the team. Once all of the offensive players on the team have gone through the drill, pick two new defenders to play defense at the other end of the court. Repeat the drill, going in the opposite direction. Conduct the drill for

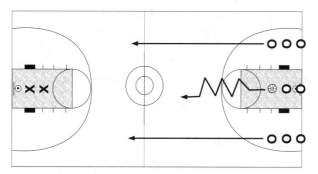

FIGURE 12.3   The Three-on-Two Fast Break

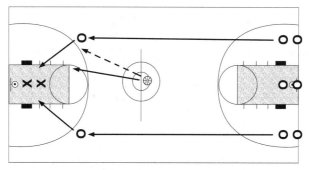

FIGURE 12.4   Drill for Three-on-Two Fast Breaks

three to four minutes so that all players have an opportunity to play in all spots of the drill.

A fundamental rule for advancing the ball with the dribble on the fast break is to give the ball up early to one of the wings. By the time a dribbler reaches half court, he or she should be deciding which side of the floor to go to and which teammate to pass to (see Figure 12.4). If a player dribbles all the way to the opposing three-point line or foul line on the fast break, it will be much easier for the two defenders to cover all three offensive players and the ball—all five players will be close together inside the three point arc and foul lane areas. Giving the ball up early actually turns the top defender to the ball side of the court, which will open up the top of the foul-line area.

Upon passing to a wing, the dribbler should trail the ball toward the foul-line corner and stop there (see Figure 12.4). The player should not overpenetrate the lane after giving up the ball. Stopping at the foul-line corner on the ball side maintains good spacing and forces the defense to move farther in order to cover the ball and all three offensive players.

This also can provide the setup to turn a three-on-two fast break into a two-on-one fast break. The wing with the ball will have a direct lane to the basket unless the bottom defender steps into the path. The opposite wing can cut to the basket, creating a two-on-one situation. If the top defender does drop down, it will leave the offensive guard at the foul line, wide open for an easy jump shot.

When run correctly, a three-on-two fast break should succeed 80 percent of the time. Success depends on giving up the ball early and making good defensive reads to obtain the highest percentage shot opportunities.

▮▮▮ TRAINING TIP

Both wings should run all the way to the basket and stop in front of the rim on their own side for offensive rebounding position or a pass back from the guard at the foul line. The wing receiving the ball from the guard at half court must go directly to the basket unless a defender blocks the path. If the defender has not committed and taken your path to the basket away, *go to the rim*. If the defender is in the way, two other options are available:

1. A pass to the other wing (if the top defender does not drop down)
2. A pass back to the guard at the foul-line corner

Making good decisions will increase scoring opportunities. Players who make good decisions will make successful plays. Teams should follow the same running patterns, locations, and passing rules so that all teammates will know when to expect a pass and where teammates will be.

Three-on-Two/Two-on-One Fast-Break Combination Drill

Next let's look at a universal three-on-two/two-on-one combination drill. Use the full length of the basketball court. At one end of the floor, set up three offensive lines, with the ball in the middle. At the other end of the court, put two defenders in the foul-lane area (see Figure 12.5). Three offensive players will attack the basket where the two defenders are located.

After the three offensive players score or miss, the offensive player (player 2 in the figure) who shoots the ball or turns the ball over will immediately retreat to the other end of the floor and become the sole defender. The original two defenders will, upon retrieving the ball (via rebound or out of bounds pass after the made basket or turnover) now become the offensive players and make a fast break to the opposite end of the floor, creating a two-on-one fast-break situation (see Figure 12.6).

The two original offensive players (players 1 and 3 in the figure) who did not shoot the ball or make a turnover will stay at the defensive end of the floor and become the defenders for the next three-on-two fast break. Once the two-on-one fast break is completed or successfully defended, the next three offensive players will make a fast break to the opposite side of the court, initiating a new three-on-two fast break. Then the drill simply repeats itself. The ball will go in one direction three-on-two, then back to the other end of the court with a two-on-one fast break. The drill takes four to six minutes.

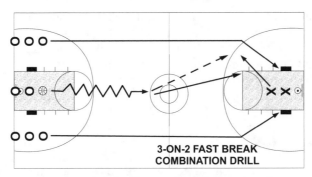

FIGURE 12.5   Drill for Three-on-Two/Two-on-One Fast-Break Combination Drill (Step 1)

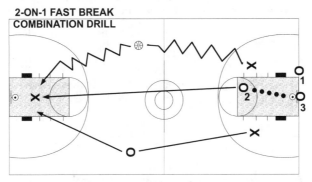

FIGURE 12.6   Drill for Three-on-Two/Two-on-One Fast-Break Combination Drill (Step 2)

▌▌ TRAINING TIP

The offensive wings should call out "trail right" or "trail left," depending on what side of the ball the players are on, so that the dribbler will know they are coming. If they are ahead of the ball, the dribbler will be more aware that they are prepared to receive the ball.

▌ FAST-BREAK FUNDAMENTALS

To be an effective player and team member when running a fast break, get into the habit of performing certain fundamentals. It is not enough just to have a numerical advantage when speeding to the offensive end of the floor. Without maintaining good court balance, running correct lanes, and making good decisions, you will not have consistent success. The following fundamentals will encourage more intelligent decisions and more efficient action when running a fast break.

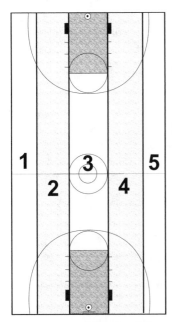

FIGURE 12.7 Fast-Break Lanes

Fundamental 1: Fast-Break Lanes

Whenever you run a fast break, spread out the defense to make them cover as much space as possible at the defensive end of the floor. The best way to do this is to execute a fast break in specific fast-break lanes (see Figure 12.7). These lanes are most easily designated by numbers 1 through 5. (Some coaches prefer a sideline dribbling fast break. No problem. In this case the ball will change from lane 3 to lane 1 or lane 5. The numbers assigned to the fast-break lanes, however, will stay the same.)

Lanes 1 and 5. These are typically designated as the "wing" areas of the fast break. The players on the wings (who are also referred to as wings) usually try to get ahead of the teammate dribbling the ball in order to accomplish these things:

1. Score more easily by filling the cutting lanes to the basket
2. Provide a teammate for the dribbler to pass the ball to which will turn the defense and create mismatches (Defenders typically defend the ball first, then protect the basket.)

Lanes 2 and 4. These are called the "trailer" lanes. In most situations players will trail the ball and should make a cut down the foul-lane sideline in order to accomplish these things:

1. Provide opportunity for a trailing jump shot or layup
2. Have the chance to get offensive rebounding position
3. Set a late screen so that the dribbler can execute a pick-and-roll maneuver
4. Begin the offense quickly by securing immediate position in the low post or setting a screen for a wing

Lane 3. This is known as the "ball lane," where most teams try to get the ball in order to run a fast break (unless it is a two-on-one situation). The purpose of having the ball in the middle is threefold:

1. Make the defense commit to the ball
2. Open up scoring lanes to the basket from both sides of the floor
3. Shorten the distance for passing the ball to a teammate by preventing cross-court passes

Fundamental 2: In-the-Lane/Out-of-the-Lane Rule

When you attack the basket with the ball in your hand, determine whether or not the defense is in your direct path to the basket or not. This is the in-the-lane/out-of-the-lane rule. It is simple to understand and takes the guesswork out of decision making in a fast break. No matter where you receive the ball on the

DEFENDER
IN YOUR LANE,
PASS THE BALL

(a) First option

DEFENDER
OUT OF YOUR LANE,
GO TO THE BASKET

(b) Second option

FIGURE 12.8   The In-the-Lane/Out-of-the-Lane Rule

offensive half of the court during a fast break, dribble and drive in a direct line to the rim. Upon penetrating the three-point arc, make one of two choices (see Figure 12.8):

1. *In the lane:* If a defender is in your direct path to the rim (in other words, you are chest to chest, facing each other), pass the basketball to a teammate. This will be easy because the defender is in the driving lane to the basket, not in the passing lane.

2. *Out of the lane:* If a defender is not directly in your lane to the basket, *go to the rim,* and do it with commitment. Show no fear. The result will be a scored basket or free throws, nine out of ten times.

When faced with this situation, most players typically try to avoid any chance of contact with a defender and pass the ball prematurely. Doing so often allows a defender to play the passing lane and obtain a tipped pass or a steal. A player must make a correct read of the defender's position and then make a correct decision.

Practicing this fundamental is easy. Simply integrate the concept into a regular fast-break drill. The in-the-lane/out-of-the-lane rule is applicable to all types of fast-break situations, including one-on-one, three-on-two, two-on-one fast breaks, and so on.

Fundamental 3: Going through the Gate to Score

FIGURE 12.9   The Gate

What is "the Gate"? It is the area between the block closest to the baseline and the third hash mark toward the free-throw line. The Gate is an imaginary door through which all offensive players should cut when making a move toward the basket from the wing sideline cut (see Figure 12.9).

This fundamental can be practiced when working on normal cutting drills and practicing in fast-break lanes in an individual or team practice setting. The lines of a basketball court assist in learning this fundamental concept. On either side of the foul lane are four hash marks used for lining up for a foul shot. All offensive cuts from the wing by an offensive player should come through these two hash marks for the following reasons:

1. The dribbler/passer will always know where to pass the ball.
2. You will have a better angle to the backboard and rim when attempting a shot.
3. The defender will not be able to force you under the backboard or "put you in jail" by using the backboard as a "second defender" that you must overcome in order to shoot.

MORE FAST-BREAK DRILLS

Drill 1: The One-Step Layup Drill (How to Finish a Fast Break)

This basic drill for developing correct fundamentals for layups can be practiced individually or in a team setting. In team practice, use two lines, one located on the block on the right side facing the backboard, and the second one on the block on the left side. Players from the two lines will alternate laying up the ball and time their starts off each other. Each will start with the ball on the correct shoulder pad. (The line on the left side of the court will have the ball on the left shoulder pad in a correct triple-threat position; the line on the right side of the court will have the ball on the right shoulder pad.) The ball should not be shot underhand; it should be shot off the shoulder pad and released above the head.

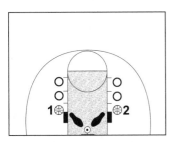

FIGURE 12.10 Positioning for the One-Step Layup Drill

Player 1 on the right side will step forward with the left foot and lay up the ball by shooting it off the shoulder pad. Player 2 on the left will wait until player 1 has begun to take a shot before beginning the step, lift, and shoot technique from the left side (refer to Chapter 2 for the exact mechanics). Each player will retrieve his or her own rebound and then alternate lines and alternate turns shooting from both the left and right sides of the basket. Players time the shots to follow one another (see Figure 12.10). This is an easy way to master both left-and right-handed layups.

It is important to get players to make a left-handed and right-handed layup on the correct side of the basket. When an offensive player drives to the basket and a defender contests the shot, if the ball is shot underhand or with the wrong hand, the defense will have a much greater opportunity to block or deflect a shot attempt (see Figure 12.11).

On the other hand, if the offensive player approaches the basket and holds the ball in a protected position in the shooting pocket, even if a defender contests the shot, the chances for a successful shot are much higher; also the defender may commit a foul because the defender will have to go through the body of the shooter in order to get to the ball (see Figure 12.12). An offensive player will also have a much better chance at a three-point play. That makes this an important drill. Players must learn to make a strong approach to the basket, especially when a shot is being contested by defenders. Using correct form can create extra scoring opportunities.

This drill can be done alone on alternate sides of the basket. Make a total of ten shots as part of your warm-up before you begin to play or practice each day.

(a) Shooting underhand

(b) Shooting with the wrong hand

FIGURE 12.11 Layup Errors

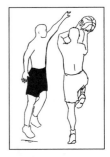

FIGURE 12.12 Protecting the Ball in the Shooting Pocket

Drill 2: The Eyes-Up Walk Drill

Many fast breaks never get completed because players are dribbling with their eyes down. They don't see what is happening and may completely miss open passes. This simple drill does not require a gym and will improve peripheral vision, broaden players' sense of the court as a whole, and build the ability to spot openings. It's a good prepractice warm-up drill because it moves the legs and gets the blood flowing. To perform the walk drill, simply walk across the court, then back, walking with the eyes up at all times. For an extra challenge, use peripheral vision to make sure you do not step on any lines on the court.

Drill 3: Fast-Break Cuts to the Basket

Fast-break cuts require precision and good execution. Knowing when to cut and where is essential to a successful fast break. Outbound cuts involve transition from the defensive end of the floor to offense, which usually occurs after a steal, a rebound, or a scored basket, and the ball is quickly advanced. In this cut, the first three players on a fast break will advance the ball by having one player fill the center lane while advancing the ball with a dribble. The other two players take a spot in one of the two wing lanes. Trailers follow in the rear positions.

Inbound cuts involve transition to the offensive end of the floor when attacking the basket. Between outbound cuts and inbound cuts (in the area between three-point arcs at both ends of the floor), players will run inside one of the fast-break lanes described earlier.

Lines on the basketball floor can assist players as they run in fast-break lanes and make fast-break cuts. The foul lane and the three-point-arc lines provide "targets" for players.

For example, wings should get outside the three-point-line area that parallels the sidelines (see Figure 12.13). Trailers should run down the court in a direct line

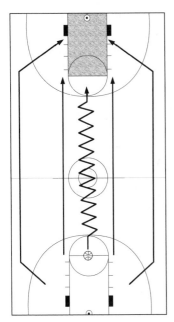

FIGURE 12.13   Using Floor Lines during Cuts to the Basket

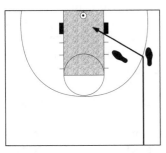

FIGURE 12.14   An Inside Cut to the Basket

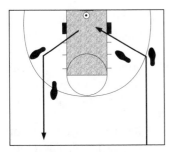

FIGURE 12.15   A V-Cut to the Other Side

with the sides of the foul lanes. The dribbler should push the ball to the middle of the court, using the middle of the foul lane as a target for the correct fast-break lane.

Drill 4: The Inbound Fast-Break Cutting Drill

This drill can be practiced individually or in a team setting. Begin at half court, and run down the sideline until reaching an imaginary line at the three-point arc. Make an inside cut to the basket by planting the outside foot closest to the sideline and then pushing off the outside foot while making a direct cut to the rim (see Figure 12.14).

Extend the lead hand (closest to the rim) to provide a target hand for a passer. Upon reaching a spot underneath the backboard, plant the foot closest to the baseline and make a V-cut to the other side of the half court (see Figure 12.15). Next, run down the sideline from the left side of the court and repeat the process. Two lines of players can perform this drill simultaneously or an individual player can work on it. It may be practiced only one time a week to maintain good fast-break cutting fundamentals.

In a variation of this drill, start with two lines underneath the backboard. Have the first player in each line jump up and touch the backboard, turn to the outside (toward the sideline), and follow the lane pattern shown in Figure 12.15. The drill should take two minutes.

Drill 5: The One-on-One Fast-Break Drill with a Defender

This drill actually accomplishes several things at once. First, it will provide practice in facing an open-court, one-on-one situation on a fast break. Second, it will simulate a half-court situation in which a point guard is being defended tightly and needs to break down a defender using a jab-step dribble, a reverse pivot, a between-the-legs move, a change of pace, or another move to get to the basket to create a scoring opportunity. To do this drill, begin with a line for dribblers at center court (see Figure 12.16). Follow these three rules:

1. A defender will begin no more than 10 feet away from the offensive player or at the bottom of the jump-ball circle.
2. The offensive player will begin at the back of the center jump-ball circle in the backcourt. The offensive player must attack the basket quickly and will only be allowed four seconds to take a shot.
3. The offensive player must shoot the ball inside the foul-lane area within 4 seconds. If a shot is taken outside the foul lane, or not shot within four seconds, the delay is treated as a turnover, and no score will be given.

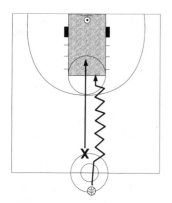

FIGURE 12.16 The One-on-One Fast-Break Drill with a Defender

The defender who stops the offensive player gets one point. A scoring player gets two points. This is an excellent breakdown drill, dribbling drill, and fast-break drill. Play to a score of no more than five or for a timed period. The drill will require three to four minutes.

▮▮ TRAINING TIP _____

Great conditioning is an important element of any fast-breaking team. Top physical condition is required to keep up the fast pace.

▮ FAST-BREAK DEFENSE

Playing defense against a fast break is never easy. Obviously, getting all five teammates back on defense to stop a fast break is the best solution, but this will not occur all of the time. When it does not happen, the best scenario is to build a defense from the inside out. This means that a lone defender should *never* try to stop the break at half court by stealing the ball. The best recourse is to turn around and sprint toward the opponents' basket. The defender should stop 3 feet in front of the rim, and face the attackers. This accomplishes three things:

1. The defender beats the ball down the court and can certainly stop an easy layup.
2. It may force the opponent to settle for a poorer shot or jump shot, or the offensive player may stop altogether and set up an offense.
3. It allows the defender's teammates time to catch up to the play and help defend the basket.

There will always be situations when a team may need a three-point shot, or an opposing team may like to take three-point shots off the break. A coach will prepare team members for such potential situations. But as a general rule, build a fast-break defense from the inside out. Too often players get frustrated or tired and will try to reach in after the other team has secured a defensive rebound or steal. Also, many players stop running when the ball is advancing toward half court, turn, and try to defend the ball against an opponent moving at full speed. Such reactions can be very costly and are a lazy, unintelligent way to play defense. Players do not shoot shots from three-fourths or half the court unless time is expiring. Therefore it is needless to play defense this far away from the basket, which, by the way, also leaves the basket area exposed. Players who make such moves may also pick up needless fouls, which may put the other team in a bonus situation with free throws. So be smart: get back to the paint on defense, find the ball, and then find the opponent you are guarding. Protect the basket first.

Defending against a One-on-One Fast Break

Occasionally, every player will end up as the only defender protecting the basket against a good ball handler or scorer. The best response is to turn the dribbler toward his or her weak dribbling hand by overplaying the ball toward one side, and then preparing to move in the same direction that the offensive player is dribbling the ball. Nine out of ten times, a ball handler moving at full speed will make a dribbling move while keeping the ball on the same side of their body. Good examples of this are the jab step, the stop and go, and the change of pace. Force the dribbler to one side of the floor, be prepared to move in the same direction, and keep at least two arm's lengths away from the ball. This may also force the dribbler into settling for a jump shot or a retreat. In either case, help defense will be trailing the play and should arrive quickly.

ONE-ON-ONE FAST-BREAK SITUATIONS AND MOVES

Any one-on-one situation in the open court *is* a fast-break opportunity, but players seldom take advantage of this chance. Because the defender is backpedaling over a long distance at full speed, this person will have a much tougher time reacting to a quick move or attack by an offensive player. Three very simple drills can encourage players to become sound open-court offensive players on the fast break.

All the dribbling moves prescribed here have been demonstrated in Chapter 8 and should be reviewed before practicing. The difference in practicing the drills in this context is that you are trying to score in the frontcourt, rather than in the open court or backcourt.

Move 1: The Jab Step

This straight-ahead quick move freezes the defender or gets a defender to commit to one side of the court, while you go to the opposite side. To execute the move, begin at half court and move at full speed toward the basket. When you get to the three-point line, if you are dribbling with your right hand, simply take a short lateral step, or jab step, with your left foot to the left side while maintaining the dribble with your right hand. As you plant your left foot, use it to push you forward with a quick thrust around the defender moving to your right. You can also work on dipping your left shoulder forward as you make your jab step, but do not use a head fake as you make a jab step. A defender will be watching your lateral body movement, not your head. Complete five repetitions of this move. Also practice it using a left-handed dribble and a jab step with your right foot while making a move to your left side.

███ **TRAINING TIP** _____

If a player initially is not comfortable with coordinating both dribbling and foot-fake movements at the same time, try practicing the jab step while pretending to dribble a ball. The player can rehearse the jab-step footwork and add dribbling with a ball later.

Move 2: The Stop and Go

The second move in the open court is a stop and go. Typically, this move functions in the open court but never lower than the three-point arc. Begin the drill at half court and dribble at full speed toward the rim. After advancing a few dribbles, come to a quick stop while maintaining the dribble, then immediately explode ahead past the defender. The stop-and-go movement will freeze the defender. This timing move makes the defender stop at the same time that you start to move again.

Move 3: The Between-the-Legs Dribble

Another excellent move in the open court is the between-the-legs dribble. Every player should have some type of change-of-direction move. A crossover move is useful and effective in the open court when a defender is not within two arm's lengths of the you and the ball. However, in tighter quarters, a between-the-legs dribble is preferable to a crossover dribble for several reasons:

1. When you dribble the ball between your legs, it is protected from a defender's reach.
2. When performed correctly, the between-the-legs dribble allows an explosive forward step after a change of direction.
3. Unlike the crossover dribble, the move can be executed without a retreat or half-step back.

To execute the drill, begin at half court, dribbling ahead at full speed toward the basket. After advancing two to three dribbles, come to a quick jump stop, immediately dribble through your legs, and explode forward. Complete five to ten repetitions, working both right to left and left to right.

███ **TRAINING TIP** _____

For players ages twelve and under, develop and use the crossover move first. For players participating at the youth league level, a crossover dribble is easier to learn and will be effective at the lower levels of competition.

COACHES' CHALK TALK: FAST-BREAK DRILLS

There's a great deal you can do to work on fast-break skills and maneuvers with your team. The following concepts and drills will help you set goals for practice and play.

Teach Players How to *Create* a Fast Break

Help players understand the difference between running a fast break and creating one. Players need to practice moving at full speed while dribbling the ball. Most players can run a fast break and dribble the ball up the floor, but very few players have the ability, while dribbling, to sprint with the ball faster than the defense will retreat, and thereby create a fast break.

The ability to dribble at this speed with the ball is an advanced skill which requires repetition and practice. To sprint-dribble with the ball requires a combination of excellent ball-handling skills, speed, and conditioning. Players who have excelled in this area earned considerable playing time. Muggsy Bogues and Magic Johnson both played successfully in the NBA. Muggsy Bogues was only 5 feet, 3 inches; Magic Johnson was 6 feet, 9 inches. They were a stark contrast in size, but both understood the value of explosive dribbling speed.

Encourage players to dribble the ball hard so that it returns to the hand quickly. This technique also enhances ball control. Players should work at pushing the ball ahead and catching up to it. Incorporate this concept into team drills or dribbling drills.

Improve Fast-Break Skills in Pregame Warm-Ups

Another way to improve fast-break skills is to practice them during game warm-ups. Fast-break skills include dribbling, speed, court vision, focusing on the basket, making good decisions, and more. Make every second of practice time count: never let players waste a repetition by working at half speed or doing a drill incorrectly. These four rules will help them improve their skills during pregame warm-up drills:

1. *Eyes up:* When beginning a layup drill from half court, players should dribble with eyes up, focused on the square above the rim on the backboard.
2. *Go through the Gate:* Have players move at full speed to the basket, taking a layup by going through the Gate.
3. *Five dribbles:* Challenge players to get to the basket in no more than five dribbles from the half-court line. This will build a speedier approach to the basket.
4. *See the ball through the basket:* Once a shot is taken, a player should focus on the target and see the ball through the basket. This builds concentration and prevents being distracted by defenders.

As a coach, be sure to run four to ten minutes of fast-break drills during normal team practices. They provide good conditioning, opportunities to teach correct principles, and enjoyment for the players. Do a little research on fast-break early offenses as well—sometimes they are just the thing a team needs to kick-start energy when they are playing somewhat sluggishly in a game. Finally, remember that (1) fast breaks create the easiest scoring opportunities, (2) fast breaks always start with good defense and rebounding, and (3) fast breaks are more fun for your players and entertaining for the crowd.

Scott Layup Drill (Team Layup Drill).   This simple drill is a variation of the two-line layup drill most teams use in pregame warm-ups. Instead of having all the balls in one line, use three balls in both lines. There is no rebounding line. This drill allows movement, ball handling, and passing for every player. It also simulates game situations because one player rebounds as a teammate drives for a layup. Each player therefore has to focus more.

SCOTT LAYUP DRILL (TEAM LAYUP DRILL)

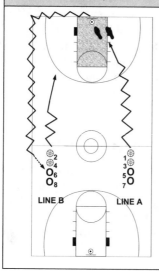

1. As player 1 in line A gets to the foul line, player 2 in line B starts to drive.
2. When player 2 gets to the foul line, player 3 in line A starts to drive.
3. Each player rebounds his or her own shot and dribbles back to half court of opposite sideline, makes a jump stop, then passes the ball to a player toward the end of the line.

▌ TRAINING TIP

Ten-in-a-Row Drill

Test individual and team skills and concentration by challenging players to make ten layups in a row. This is a great drill to use at the end of practice for individual or team competition. Junior high school and youth league players should try to make five to seven in a row. Always make sure they practice shooting layups with both left and right hands.

CHAPTER QUESTIONS

1. List two basketball situations that typically initiate a fast break.

2. Explain the difference between getting fast breaks and converting fast breaks into scored baskets. How can a team or player convert more fast-break baskets?

3. What key physical element is involved for both individuals and teams when running fast breaks in basketball?

4. Name the three most common fast-break situations.

5. Explain the "in-the-lane/out-of-the-lane" fast-break rule.

6. What does it mean to go through "the Gate" when completing a fast break? List three benefits of doing this.

7. What is the most important thing to do first when defending against a fast break?

8. What four rules for taking layups in pre-game warm-ups will help improve players' fast-break skills and scoring?

9. As a coach, how do you think that fast-break basketball can benefit a team's overall success?

How Should I Practice?

IN THIS CHAPTER YOU WILL LEARN:

- What to practice on your own
- How to master the fundamentals of basketball and conditioning
- Personal training—the key to success
- How to build your own training program

Success can only come to you as an individual from self-satisfaction in knowing that you gave everything to become the best that you are capable of becoming. Perfection is hard, but it must be the goal. Others may have more ability than you, they may be larger, faster, quicker, better jumpers, better shooters, but no one should be your superior in respect to team spirit, loyalty, enthusiasm, cooperation, determination, fight, effort, and character. Make this your motto, your goal.

—Coach John Wooden
  NCAA All-American player
  Former UCLA head coach
  Winner of ten NCAA national basketball championships

HOW AND WHAT DO I PRACTICE?

This important question needs to be broken into different categories: how often, how much, how hard, and what to practice. Considering each element will assist you in making personal practice more powerful and beneficial.

Practice Daily

If you are serious about becoming a good basketball player, practice daily. You do not need four or five hours of practice every day, but you do need a solid block of time and a well-defined practice plan. In fact, one purpose of this book is to show what to practice and how to practice more efficiently and effectively.

Practice Hard

When you do practice, work hard on each drill. Use all your effort, and practice each one with a goal in mind: how many repetitions or shots you will make for each and every drill. Daily personal practices should include a series of mini goals and drills that, once completed, will have provided a solid all-around workout. Work in short amounts of repetitions when you practice. Always work as hard as you can, exerting full intensity and effort, but stay under control. An out-of-control basketball player is not an asset to a team. By practicing as hard as you can, using short bursts of energy during short periods of time, you will also be simulating game situations.

Practice Perfectly

For every drill, practice perfectly. This will require patience because you may have to practice new skills at half speed until you can perfect each action, technique, and move. In the long run, it is much better to learn a skill correctly from the start than to go back and break old habits.

Practice with Goals in Mind

Develop a game plan. What position will you most likely play? Work on skills for that position. Once you have designed a schedule of drills, set an individual goal each day for each drill. Try to better your time or your score each time you practice a drill. Be creative, and challenge yourself. Every few months, or after you develop sound fundamentals with one skill, change the drills you are practicing to focus on skill areas that still show some weakness. Shooting should be practiced daily.

Do you need more motivation to use goals? Consider these points:

1. Setting goals for each drill will allow you to experience multiple successes each day. This builds a habit of creating success, goal by goal.
2. Goals provide a game plan and help you focus.
3. Writing down goals and tracking progress makes improvement visible and obvious. That, in turn, builds confidence.

The difference between being an average player and a good player is whether you practice during the off-season. The difference between being a good player and a great player is HOW you practice during the off-season.
—Scotism

It is not difficult to practice when you play with a team every day. But what about showing dedication as you practice on your own? Anybody can spend two or three hours a day playing in a gym, but this will develop only confidence and experience in playing. It will not improve specific basketball skills. On the other hand, if you spend all your time practicing skills and never play the game, you will be extremely proficient at drills but will lack the confidence, experience, and knowledge to use skills in game situations. The most effective wheel is well rounded.

HOW TO BECOME A COMPLETE PLAYER

FIGURE 13.1   Three Areas of Training for the Complete Player

To be a complete, well-rounded player, divide your training into three specific areas (see Figure 13.1):

1. Develop skills
2. Play basketball
3. Physical conditioning
   (Improve Individual Athleticism)

Develop Skills

It takes discipline and effort to practice alone each day. Here is some inspiration to keep you going:

Heights by great men reached and kept,
were not obtained by sudden flight,
But they while their companions slept,
toiled on and upward in the night.

—Henry Wadsworth Longfellow

Character: The ability to carry out a decision after the emotion of making that decision has passed.

—Hyrum Smith

What you practice will depend on your needs and desires. Work on your weaknesses, and try to improve on your strengths. Work hard for two or three months on one or two of the habit skills. Then work on different skills. Do not overwork yourself. Too much training can be as bad as not enough. You can quickly get tired, discouraged, or bored if you overdo it. Spend only one or two hours in individual daily practice to develop your skills.

*Maintaining consistency in the pursuit of one's goals is
more important than going after a goal full out.*

—Curt Brinkman
Winner of the Boston Marathon

Finally, use perfect technique, and you will improve faster and play much better. Practice does not make perfect. Perfect practice makes perfect.

Play Basketball

Obviously, you need to spend time playing basketball in order to develop skills and gain experience. But be careful not to develop bad habits by overplaying. First, do not play against those far below your level of ability and competitiveness. This will only make you lazy; you will not play hard or seriously. Second, play hard until you get tired. But if you continue to play after you are tired, you will walk a lot, give up playing defense, and get lazy. All these bad habits will be carried over into games.

Play against the best competition you can find, preferably players with skills stronger than yours. This will help you develop more rapidly and give you more confidence when you compete against players at your own level. Play one-on-one against the best players you can find. Challenge them, but follow the rules for one-on-one play given in Chapter 5. Don't worry about whether the other players use the rules. *You* use them. You will not always win, but do not get discouraged—the important thing is to improve. Learn, practice, try harder, and improve more; then you will begin winning in one-on-one and team basketball. Competition will bring improvement, and improvement will bring success.

Improve Your Physical Conditioning

If you are practicing each day individually as well as playing, you automatically will be conditioning yourself. But if you are thin, weak, overweight, below average in jumping ability, or a bit slow, you may wonder how to improve. Make physical conditioning part of your daily off-season training program. Conditioning is an important facet of becoming an all-around player. Diagnose your strengths and weaknesses, and then work to make your weaknesses into strengths.

Make a Daily Checklist

The final step in preparing a personal training program is making a daily checklist (see Figure 13.2). Choose drills that will develop the skills you need to improve on. Drill particular habit skills for at least one month before changing them. Make sure

MONTH-YEAR	1	2	3	4	5	6	7	8	9	10	11	12	13	14	15	16	17	18	19	20	21	22	23	24	25	26	27	28	29	30	31
Shooting drills																															
Dribbling drills																															
Cutting drills																															
Physical Conditioning —Lift Weights																															
Play ball																															

FIGURE 13.2 Daily Practice Checklist

you always practice shooting drills. This checklist will keep you on target and chart your improvement. Hang it on the door, above your bed, on the refrigerator, or at any convenient place where you will see it each day. Remember, a goal not written is only a wish.

Developing Your Own Training Program.   Now that you know the three major areas to develop in practice, design a specific training schedule by selecting drills from this book. Choose them based on the position you will play and areas that need improvement.

If you are a guard, work on shooting (three-point shots, jump shots, and so on), passing, dribbling, ball handling, and defense. Pick some drills from each chapter. Rotate the drills every two or three months, so you learn new things and get some variety. If you play a center position, work on shooting (low-post and high-post shots), passing, rebounding, pivoting, and defense. Get professional assistance from a coach or former college player who can help you to analyze areas that need improvement. All players need to play basketball.

If you need to lose weight, go running or use a stair climber for thirty minutes each day. If you need to gain weight, start a strength-training program. In fact, all players over the age of fourteen should be on a strength-training program. Consult a professional strength trainer and doctor before beginning any weight-training program.

Plan Your Work, Then Work Your Plan.

TEN SECRETS TO SUCCESS IN BASKETBALL

The quickest way to success in basketball is practice. In order to master the fundamentals, you will have to practice a lot. The two most important skills to master are shooting and passing. Begin slowly, and learn new drills and skills perfectly before practicing them at full speed. You will also want to work on scoring moves to develop the ability to attack a defender and the basket. The great neutralizer between good athletes and good players is a burning desire to play the game. You can be an average athlete and still become an excellent basketball player if you have desire. You can be a great athlete and end up being only an average player because of limited basketball skills and poor motivation.

Here are ten helpful ways to accelerate your development as a player:

1. *Use goals when you practice.* Set small incremental goals for each drill, so that you feel success and can track your progress. Keeping track will show you your improvement.
2. *Ask for help.* Talk to your coach or a top-level player for help in designing and learning a good fundamental workout program.

3. *Seek professional instruction.* Find a basketball tutor, but trust your instincts. Instruction should make sense and have a purpose. If you don't feel comfortable with what you are learning, try someone else.

4. *Study.* Hundreds of books, videos, and instructional materials are available in the marketplace. The best way to build sound knowledge about basketball is to study various techniques and trust your own judgment about what will work for you.

5. *Attend instructional classes.* Clinics, camps, seminars, and classes are available in great number for basketball players and coaches alike. Local professional stars, colleges, universities, and even high schools run their own camps for a moderate fee. Most are similar in their teaching and approach.

6. *Watch the game.* Watch games on TV, and go to games whenever possible. You will be amazed at how much you learn from watching and listening to sports announcers. You can also listen to sports talk radio stations.

7. *Play and compete.* Play as much basketball as you possibly can. Don't worry about failures and setbacks—they will help you learn to play better.

8. *Watch what you eat.* Whatever you take in will help build up or break down your body; choose wisely.

9. *Keep a balance.* Do your schoolwork. Without good grades, how will you be eligible to play basketball? Spend time with your friends and family—who else is going to cheer for you?

10. *Project your progress.* Where are you now? Where do you want to be? Evaluate your progress at set intervals of time—monthly, quarterly, yearly. This will serve as a great road map to success.

THREE STAGES OF SKILL DEVELOPMENT

A playing skill or move will never become second nature to you until you have practiced it correctly ten thousand times. There are a thousand wrong ways to perform a basketball skill; there is only one right way. In this book, I have demonstrated how to execute moves correctly. Learn to perform all basketball skills correctly if you wish to be effective during play.

There are three basic stages in the development of basketball skills:

1. *Learning stage:* During this stage, you first understand and learn the correct form, footwork, or movement of a specific skill. You cannot do it by yourself and must be correctly instructed in it. At this stage you are trying to develop new habits.

2. *Mechanical stage:* At this stage, you no longer need to be corrected in performing a skill. However, you still need to think about it to do it right. You must "think" yourself through it. Movements appear mechanical and unpolished, not smooth and fluid. You cannot perform the skill at full speed yet.

3. *Fluid stage:* When you no longer have to think about performing the skill correctly, it has become second nature to you. You execute it quickly with fluid motions and body movement. You can perform the skill at full speed in game situations.

DEFINITION OF A PLAYER:

FIRST ON THE FLOOR, *LAST* OUT THE DOOR.

SCOTISM

Alway begin practicing a newly learned skill at half speed. If you practice at full speed but lack control, you will not play well or perform a skill correctly or effectively. Skills only develop progressively over time, not instantly. And they will develop only if you work at improving them daily with dedication and consistency. The first and best way to improve in basketball always has been and always will be to practice. Learning is not a spectator sport.

Desire *can rewrite all of your scouting reports.*

Habit

I am your constant companion. I am your greatest helper or your heaviest burden. I will push you onward or drag you down to failure. I am completely at your command. Half the tasks you do you might just as well turn over to me, and I will be able to do them quickly and correctly.

I am easily managed. You must merely be firm with me. Show me exactly how you want something done, and after a few lessons, I will do it automatically.

I am the servant of all great men—and, alas, of all failures as well. Those who are great, I have made great. Those who are failures, I have made failures.

I am not a machine, but I work with all the precision of a machine, plus the intelligence of a man. You may run me for profit or run me for ruin. It makes no difference to me. Take me, train me, be firm with me, and I will put the world at your feet. Be easy with me and I will destroy you.

Who am I? I am HABIT.

—Author unknown

COACHES' CHALK TALK: PLANNING PRACTICE FOR AN ENTIRE TEAM

Coaches naturally spend a lot of time thinking about and planning practice. Here are some ideas to consider as you develop a practice program.

There are many different philosophies and schools of thought concerning this topic. Most coaches agree that certain fundamentals are essential:

1. *Team warm-up:* This does not mean stretching only.
2. *Skill and conditioning drills:* Incorporating skill drills and practice drills into the conditioning process saves time, is more game related, and is less boring for

players. Fast-break drills, defensive drills, and full-court passing drills can be utilized in this way. Make every drill competitive in some way. It will increase the intensity of practice and speed up your team's and players' development.

3. *Plays and game situations:* Develop and practice offensive and defensive plays and patterns, as well as various game situations and out-of-bounds plays. Do not forget to use shot-clock (or game-clock) situations with time winding down. Five seconds left on the clock is actually a lot of time. Players need to know what that period of time feels like.

4. *Free-throw shooting practice:* Refer to Chapter 3 for more ideas.

Spending Time on Skill Development

Deciding on how much time to allot for skill development really depends on the skill level of your team, even at the college level. The less experienced your players, the more skill work they will need. Running all kinds of plays and zone defenses will achieve little if your players cannot hit an open shot or box out and move their feet on defense. A basic guideline is 25 percent of practice time dedicated to improving skills. At the youth league and junior high school levels, up to 50 percent of practice time might well be set aside for skill drills and teaching.

Do Your Homework

Locking into one single coaching philosophy or style may not be sound. In college, coaches can get away with this—they can recruit certain types of athletes and players to fit the playing style they prefer. Coaches at the high school level or lower will encounter seasons in which the talent pool is dry or full. These situations require flexibility. A great coach can get average players to win and be competitive. A good coach will not get in the way of a great team. But an average coach can impede the success of any type of team. Be willing to study, learn, and try new things in all areas of the game. Don't ever give up on working to improve a team.

CHAPTER QUESTIONS

1. Give three reasons why goals are important to practice.

2. What three areas of training are needed in order to become a complete player?

3. List five of the ten secrets to success in basketball that you will use when training. Why did you choose them?

4. Explain the three stages of basketball skill development.

5. What is the definition of a player?

The Mental Game
of Basketball

IN THIS CHAPTER YOU WILL LEARN:
- To cultivate confidence through how you practice
- To develop mental toughness
- To process thoughts during performance
- Visualization—gaining a picture of your success
- To make your team better through your mental mind-set

Basketball is a mental game.
—Coach John Wooden

We did not walk in expecting to lose.
—University of Utah coach Rick Majerus, commenting on his team's upset of Western Regional #1 seed Arizona and nationally ranked #1 North Carolina in the same week of the NCAA tournament. Utah advanced to the 1998 championship game before losing a close game to Kentucky.

IT'S ALL IN YOUR MIND . . .

The quotations that open this chapter perfectly describe the power of attitude and mind-set. What you believe you are is often what you will achieve. Your mental game or mind-set can be your best friend or your worst enemy.

We all want to look good and to play well while competing in basketball. That's how we picture the game's star players. Have you ever seen Larry Bird miss a game-winning shot? Have you ever seen Lisa Leslie have one of her shots blocked? How about seeing Michael Jordan miss a dunk? I have, and more than once. Players at every level fail sometimes. All players fail, and all players succeed. The trick is to become consistent in how frequently you succeed. A great deal of this consistency comes from your state of mind, or mental game. Most players are their own worst enemy during the game. This problem can be overcome, however. The simplest solution is to recognize the problem, fix the problem, then go on to the next challenge. Let's address some common problems with the mental game as well as their solutions.

CULTIVATING CONFIDENCE THROUGH HOW YOU PRACTICE

To master the game, you must master your mind. As we have discussed in earlier chapters, "where the mind goes, the body will follow." The habits you develop physically and *mentally,* in and through practice, will follow you wherever you go, into games and into life. This all begins with how you practice and what you think about.

You must learn to talk to yourself positively. Your mind is like an enormous computer; it remembers everything you tell it. And what you tell yourself carries over into your actions and your body language. During practice sessions, get into the habit of talking to yourself in a positive way. Never use the four-letter words *can't, won't,* or *quit.* Anyone can be a better basketball player by learning the fundamentals correctly and practicing them consistently. Reinforce these facts with positive self-talk: "I can do this," "I always complete my workout," and so on. Positive thoughts will help you meet challenges during games too.

This book contains many motivational sayings. Underline those that are especially helpful to you. Hang them on the wall to remind you of your goals. If you have quotes of your own that you like, use them too. Take in positive thoughts, ideas, and quotations. You probably can think of fifty negative ones that you say to yourself every day. The following examples show the difference between negative and positive self-talk:

THE POWER OF SELF-TALK

Negative Self-Talk	Positive Self-Talk
I'm not good enough.	*I am good enough.*
I'm too tired to practice.	*I need to get in better shape.*
I can't do it.	*I will do it.*
I don't feel like doing it right now.	*My competition isn't resting; neither will I.*
It's too hot or cold to practice.	*I must learn to play under all conditions.*
I can do it later.	*I will do it now.*
I need one more hour of sleep.	*I can get an extra hour of practice in.*
It won't hurt to miss one day.	*I will learn something new today.*
I hope I play well today.	*I know I will play great today.*
I am having an off night.	*There is no such thing as an off night.*
I can't make this shot.	*I can make this shot and will practice until I do.*

Another way to cultivate confidence during practice is to practice success. Complete a specific number of repetitions successfully, or make a certain number of shots or moves successfully. Accomplishing a number of small goals each day will build confidence. Do not quit when the going gets tough. Drills will get easier each day, and the workout will take less time also. Both positive self-talk and success during practice will develop mental habits of concentration that will carry over into game situations. Learn to talk to yourself positively through adversity and setbacks. Your mental habits are game skills too.

FIVE WAYS TO DEVELOP MENTAL TOUGHNESS

If you want to be a player, practice. When you lose, if it hurts enough to make you practice more, then you will become a player. Becoming mentally tough as a player means choosing to do difficult things, not just easy things. When real adversity hits, most players quit, give in, give out, or give up. Instead, they should get up. Responding positively to adversity is the first step in building mental toughness. Study other athletes who have this trait. Find out what they do, and try out their techniques. Here are five steps for becoming a mentally tough athlete:

1. *Set practice goals.* Set daily, weekly, monthly, and yearly practice goals, and meet them. A weekly goal might be to do your complete workout five or six days. A monthly goal might be to make 2,500 three-point shots. An annual goal may be to complete practicing two thousand repetitions of a specific move (only seven repetitions daily for a year—they add up!).
2. *Put in extra practice time.* Arrive fifteen minutes early to practice, and stay fifteen minutes after the team leaves. That's thirty minutes extra a day, which will equal forty extra hours of practice in a four-month season or twenty extra days of practice! Not only that, your teammates will respect you because they know you are working hard and your coaches will respect you for your efforts.
3. *Be consistent.* Practice every day. Develop the habit of doing something to work toward your goal each and every day. Practice at the same time and place as often as you can. Your body and your mind will respond, and you will gain greater confidence as you finish each practice on a regular schedule.
4. *Be persistent.* Mentally tough players stay with something until they get it right. Never quit. If you don't allow yourself to quit in practice, you will not quit in games. Practice it right until you get it right. Every trial and obstacle you are willing to fight through and overcome will make you tougher.
5. *Be tough.* When the Going Gets Tough, Get Tough. Don't get down when things are not going well—instead, get mad. Anger brings energy; sadness drains energy. Learn to channel your feelings properly. If you develop a minor pain (not a real injury), use it to develop toughness, not a "loser's limp." Get mad and tell yourself you can do it, then go out and do it. That will definitely help to make you tougher. You will also become more steadfast, resilient, reliable, and focused. You must learn to compete against yourself before you can successfully compete against others. Push yourself to succeed. The great poet Goethe once said, "Talent is nurtured in solitude"—so is toughness.

▌ TRAINING TIP _____

If you learn to keep trying during mentally tough times, you will become mentally tough at all times.

▌ PROCESSING THOUGHTS DURING PERFORMANCE

When competing in games, you will make mistakes—accept that fact. The chapter on foul shooting discusses talking to yourself as you execute the movements of the free throw. This fosters mental focus on the correct things at the correct time. Other features of the game are similar. Focusing on the right thing at the right time will greatly enhance your performance. What do you say to yourself when you make a turnover or miss an easy shot? Do you say "I am terrible" or "I can do this"? Only one of these two powerful thoughts can take center court in your mind. If you think the negative thought, start changing it. Every time something goes wrong, start telling yourself "I can do this." Soon you will notice a big difference in how you feel and how you play.

Every player makes mistakes. Babe Ruth of the Yankees had more strikeouts than home runs. Mia Hamm missed more shots on goal then she made, but she helped the U.S. women's soccer team to win both an Olympic gold medal and the World Cup Championship. Terry Bradshaw, the former quarterback of the Pittsburgh Steelers, had more career interceptions than touchdowns but went on to win three Super Bowls. Michael Jordan missed more field goals in his career than he made. Wayne Gretzky, the greatest hockey player of all time, said, *"You miss 100 percent of the shots you never take."* Do you think that these athletes would have become successful if they had quit after their first few misses and setbacks?

Reggie Miller, a future Hall of Fame player for the Indiana Pacers, was interviewed after another great performance against the New York Knicks (whom he always buried) during the NBA playoffs. Reggie had a terrible first-half performance, shooting only three for fifteen shots. He came back to hit a three at the end of the game to send it into overtime and then scored another six points in overtime to lead his team to victory. When asked about the turnaround in his shooting performance, he said, "My gun [shooting gun] still had bullets in it, so I kept shooting. I knew I would start hitting shots at some point." And he did. Reggie Miller finished the game with 38 points, and led his team to victory. He "knew" he would start making shots at some point. How could he possibly know that? He had developed physical and mental habits that taught him that he could. So can you. An intelligent player recognizes that mistakes are part of the game. Recognize your mistake, but give yourself some mental first aid by saying "I can do this."

A large part of your ability to filter out negative input during game situations will come from mental practice habits and positive self-talk. Having a greater understanding of the game and how it works is also important. Figure 14.1 shows a set of typical box scores. Look closely at the shooting percentages. If you have

Starzz 78, Lynx 65

MINNESOTA	Min	FG M-A	FT M-A	Reb O-T	A	PF	Pts
Lennox	14	4-9	1-1	3-5	0	6	11
Smith	27	3-10	4-4	2-2	2	5	11
Folk	28	2-9	1-2	0-8	4	4	5
Daley	33	5-7	1-3	2-3	2	1	11
Brumfield	27	3-6	3-3	2-3	2	2	9
Lloyd-Curry	20	1-3	2-2	0-2	1	2	5
Dickerson	16	0-3	1-2	0-3	0	4	1
Martin	12	1-3	4-4	1-2	0	5	6
Paye	18	2-5	0-0	0-1	2	2	6
Stires	5	0-0	0-0	1-1	0	0	0
Totals	200	21-55	17-21	11-30	13	32	65

Percentages: FG .382, FT .810. 3-Point Goals: 6-16, .375 (Lennox 2-4, Smith 1-5, Daley 0-1, Lloyd-Curry 1-2, Paye 2-4). Team Rebounds: 7. Blocked Shots: 3 (Folk, Brumfield, Dickerson). Turnovers: 22 (Lennox, Smith 5, Daley 4, Brumfield 2, Dickerson 3, Martin 3, Paye, Stires 3). Steals: 11 (Lennox, Smith, Folk 2, Daley 3, Lloyd-Curry, Martin 2, Paye). Technical Fouls: None. Illegal Defense: None.

UTAH	Min	FG M-A	FT M-A	Reb O-T	A	PF	Pts
Goodson	26	5-9	2-3	2-3	0	1	14
Williams	31	5-9	6-12	5-14	2	5	16
Mulitapele	6	0-0	0-0	1-1	1	1	0
Hiede	11	0-1	0-0	0-0	2	2	5
Johnson	22	1-3	3-6	0-2	2	2	5
Rasmussen	13	2-3	1-1	1-3	0	3	5
Ivanyi	10	0-3	0-0	0-0	3	2	0
Starbird	21	3-10	1-1	0-0	3	2	7
Dydek	14	4-5	3-3	0-0	1	1	11
Herrig	7	1-1	0-0	2-3	1	0	2
Bills	10	1-4	0-0	0-1	0	0	3
Kromhoek	10	0-4	0-0	0-1	1	0	0
Frose	10	3-5	3-4	0-1	1	1	11
Gaither	9	1-1	2-2	2-4	0	2	4
Totals	200	26-58	21-32	13-33	19	22	78

Percentages: FG .448, FT .656. 3-Point Goals: 5-18, .278 (Goodson 2-3, Johnson 0-1, Ivanyi 0-2, Starbird 0-3, Bills 1-2, Krommenhoek 0-4, Frose 2-3). Team Rebounds: 11. Blocked Shots: 6 (Williams 3, Starbird, Gaither). Turnovers: 18 (Goodson, Williams, Mulitauaopele, Hiede 3, Johnson, Rasmussen 3, Ivanyi, Starbird 2, Dydek, Herrig 2, Bills, Frose). Steals: 9 (Goodson 2, Williams, Hiede, Rasmussen 2, Starbird 2, Dydek). Technical Fouls: None. Illegal Defense: None.

Lynx	35	30	—65
Starzz	32	46	—78

FIGURE 14.1   A Set of Typical Box Scores

studied box scores as long as I have, you realize that even the best players make an average of only 45 to 50 percent of their shots. This means they fail more often than they succeed. Yet they are still considered to be successful, good players. Don't let a narrow idea of perfectionism ruin the game for you. The best players work hard but know they have to take a certain amount of failure in stride.

If you feel nervous during competition, focus on one specific area or goal. Dennis Rodman did this in rebounding. That is all he ever wanted to do to help his team—and could he rebound! If you are nervous about scoring or shooting, focus on a different area, such as defense, rebounding, or creating shots for your teammates. Find one thing to focus on, and the game will come easier to you.

That which we can conceive and believe, we can achieve.

Box-Score Mentality

What you should realize first is that all players miss shots. Work on developing what I call a "box-score mentality." This simply means that your scoring total per game will be determined on the average by the number of shots you take, not the number of shots you make. If you are a good player and shoot 50 percent from the field, you will miss half your shots, but you will make half of them. Since most field goals are worth two points, you can average out that by taking fifteen shots in a game, you will score fifteen or more points. (Keep in mind that an attempted field goal statistically does not show up on the box score when a player is fouled in the act of shooting unless it goes in.) Once you add your free-throw totals to the equation, everything balances out. This understanding should help you focus on the number of attempts you take and less on the number you make.

Therefore, if you want to score ten or more points a game, how many shots do you need to take? Ten. If you want to score twenty or more points a game, you need to take twenty shots. It's that simple. Recognize that you must have good shooting skills to score more than ten points a game on the average and good scoring skills to average over fifteen points a game. That is where the practice will come in.

Visualization: Picture Your Success

Visualization has become a standard practice in enhancing sports performance. To use visualization, you must try to mentally picture yourself performing skills

WHEN LOSING HURTS ENOUGH TO MAKE YOU PRACTICE,

THEN YOU KNOW YOU ARE A PLAYER.

SCOTISM

perfectly in game situations over and over, just like replaying a movie. See yourself making a shot, boxing out and getting rebounds, playing perfect defense, dribbling the ball well, making scoring moves correctly, and so on. Just as in physical practice, you will want to rehearse the process over in your mind five or ten times before going on to the next thing. Visualization is a very powerful tool because it allows for perfect mental practice—you never make a mistake when you visualize. Your mind cannot tell the difference between imaginary and real physical practice. It will accept both kinds of input.

What you see in your own mind is what you get. In his book *Imagery: A Tool for Success,* Brian L. Kennedy states, "Visualization allows a larger number of neural patterns to be printed on the brain, which sends additional messages to the muscles and allows a higher level of performance." Ken Griffey Jr., the future Hall of Fame major league baseball player, said, "Most of my off-season work involves visualization."

It is important to focus on specific techniques, movements, and skills as you visualize, as well as picturing yourself being successful. Even practice seeing yourself being a good sport—not worrying about a mistake or a missed shot—and making an important free throw. A good time to practice visualization is before going to bed at night or in preparation for competition while in the locker room. You can even try it out during TV commercials. Do not, however, replace practice time with visualization. Use visualization to augment, not replace, your basketball practice time. It will help you to paint a mental portrait of the player you want to be.

MAKING YOUR TEAM BETTER THROUGH YOUR MIND-SET

How do you make your teammates better? There are several ways to accomplish this, all of which are important. First, be positive with them and toward them. They will know that you accept them and will appreciate your encouragement when they make a mistake and enjoy your recognition when they do well.

Second, push them in practice. Try to be first in each drill. Get on them when they are not hustling. Set the pace and example for the group. An old saying notes that "If you cannot win, make sure the one ahead of you breaks the records!" Be willing to put more pressure on yourself and your teammates than you will ever see in a game situation. Outwork and outhustle your teammates, or at least try to. Slap hands with them throughout practice, and help to keep up their confidence and enthusiasm. Everybody likes to be recognized and encouraged; everyone likes to slap hands. Bring out the best in your teammates.

Third, set an example of dedication and hard work. Be the one who goes the extra mile by getting other players around you to commit to practicing extra free throws each day or spending fifteen extra minutes each day practicing a weak area of the game or even lifting weights before school. If you are the team's best player, it will be a tremendous boost to your teammates to realize that the best player on the team is also the hardest worker.

Fourth, respect and back up your coaches 100 percent. Do not talk back or find faults. Coaches are imperfect, and they know that they can make mistakes too. If

DEFINITION OF A TEAM:
PLAY TOGETHER,
STAY TOGETHER,

NO MATTER WHAT.

SCOTISM

you have an honest and legitimate concern, address it with the coach before or after a practice (never a game) when you can talk quietly alone without interruption or concern for being embarrassed in front of others. Your coach will appreciate and respect this mature approach. Remember, if you are not part of the solution, then you are part of the problem.

Do not let your teammates complain or condemn your coach in public either. Tell your teammates to knock it off or to get the captains to air the complaints by meeting with the coach in private. It will make your entire team better. Finally, root for your team if you are not in the game. Mentally, this will make you feel better and look better too. When coaches need a substitute and look down the bench, the last player they will choose is the one pouting or slouching back with arms folded. They will put in the player who is into the game, encouraging teammates and watching what is happening. You can count on that.

PLAYER PERFORMANCE SCORING SYSTEM

You have probably watched enough games to know the meaning of a "double double." It means getting a total of ten or more points, rebounds, steals, assists, blocks, and so on, in any two statistical categories in a single game. A "triple double" is to obtain ten or more in any three statistical categories in a single game, and a "quadruple double" is to obtain ten or more in any four statistical categories in a single game. A double double is an achievable feat for most good players, even at the high school and college levels. However, professional players have a much better chance of accomplishing triple and quadruple doubles than do players at lower levels of competition, for three reasons. First, the games last longer, up to forty-eight minutes compared to thirty-two or forty minutes. Second, pro players are allowed six fouls, compared to five for all other levels of play. Third, pro games use a twenty-four-second clock, so the game is played at a much faster pace.

This makes the task of surpassing a double double, at the lower levels of competition, a more difficult goal on a regular basis. But all young players want to imitate what they see on TV and in pro basketball. For this reason I have developed a player performance scoring system that allows teams and players at levels below the professional ranks to still have a trackable, measurable, accurate, and fun system to challenge them and make the game more enjoyable.

Where performance is measured, performance is improved.

The purpose of this scoring system is to motivate athletes to develop into well-rounded players and become more focused on all aspects of the game—not just scoring, but also passing, rebounding, defense, turnovers, and so on. Players will start to buy into this system and look forward to checking it the day after each game.

The system designates a specific point value for each skill area of the game, giving equal consideration to both perimeter players and post players. For example, it is usually much easier for a taller player to get a lot of rebounds, so one point is given for a defensive rebound, but two points for an offensive rebound and also for an assist, which encourages unselfish passing and balances the scoring system for shorter players. The following table shows how it works:

PLAYER PERFORMANCE SCORING SYSTEM

Statistical Category	Statistical Point(s)
Points scored from baskets	2-point basket = 2 points 3-point basket = 3 points
Assist	+2 points per assist
Defensive rebound	+1 point
Offensive rebound	+2 points
Steal	+1 point
Blocked shot	+1 point
Taking a charge	+2 points
Turnover	−1 point

Example of Game Totals

Center: Scores 18 points, 9 defensive rebounds, 2 offensive rebounds, 1 steal, 2 blocks, 2 turnovers
   Total = 32 points

Guard: Scores 15 points, 3 defensive rebounds, 1 offensive rebound, 6 assists, 2 steals, 2 turnovers
   Total = 32 points

This system brings a real balance to all player positions and helps players recognize what their real contributions are. Also, each player's earned points can be categorized to show the overall performance in a game. For example, a player who scores between ten and nineteen performance points is called a "single." Look at the following table:

LEVELS OF PLAY
PLAYER PERFORMANCE SCORING SYSTEM

Total Game Points	Level of Play
10–19 points	Single
20–29 points	Double
30–39 points	Triple
40–49 points	Quadruple
50–59 points	All-American
60–69 points	All-Pro
70+ points	Hall-of-Famer

Tracking performance this way is a lot of fun. It puts less emphasis on just scoring points and more emphasis on being a complete player. Two points are given for an offensive rebound, taking a charge, and an assist. It takes a lot of hard work to get an offensive rebound, and the benefits to the individual and team are the equivalent of one additional stop on defense and one more possession on offense. Also, an offensive rebound usually leads to a layup or drawing of a foul for free throws. An assist must be rewarded with two points to be fair to players on the perimeter who have fewer chances at rebounding opportunities. It also rewards a player who is willing to sacrifice personal gain to benefit the team. These point allotments reward hustle, team play and hard work and balance out the scoring system.

By using the player performance scoring system to evaluate your game performance, you will become more aware of all areas of the game and take your play to the next level.

One thing that you can count on in this life is that if you are not fired with enthusiasm, you will be <u>fired</u> with enthusiasm.

—Vince Lombardi

COACHES' CHALK TALK: HOW TO PLAY TOP-RANKED TEAMS AND WIN

Have you ever seen a team lose early in the season by twenty or more points only to come back later in the season and win? Have you watched a top-rank team be upset by a lesser opponent? How does this happen? The following suggestions may improve the mind-set of your team and players when they face a really big game:

1. If your team has previously lost to the particular opponents, statistically dissect how many offensive rebounds, layups and open three-point shots were made by the winning team. Subtract that from the total score, and positively emphasize to your players that if they will better manage the errors that led to these shots, they can win. You can also add the number of layups your team missed and the number of free throws missed that would have put your team at 70 percent from the line (if they shot below 70 percent). You will be amazed at how your players' mind-sets improve. Review the statistics and game film each day the week before the game.

2. If your team had played the first half or the first quarter of a game (or any quarter) close in score to the opposing team, show your team only that segment of the game film. Show it over and over again before the next game (no more than once a day). Several things will happen. They will get sick of watching it, they will start to believe more and more they can beat that team, and they will be mad because they had to watch the game so many times.

3. Have your team track all of the statistics from the game. Make them scout each opposing player whom they will play against and list those players' strengths and weaknesses. List their habits and moves, and preferred places to score from. This familiarity with the opponent will add to your team's confidence. They will start to see the chinks in the armor.

4. Condition your team so they will not be fatigued for the game. Before every hard sprint and in every team huddle in practices, have the players yell out the opposing team's name. They will become more focused on that team and how to beat them.

5. Find sources of motivation—quotations from the papers, news, or statements made by the opposing coach. Type these up, enlarge them, and hang them in the gym, locker rooms, and other facilities. This will remind your players that there is a score to settle. Positive emotion is a good medicine.

Preparation is 90 percent of the battle.

CHAPTER QUESTIONS

1. How can players cultivate confidence in themselves through how they practice?

2. List five ways to develop mental toughness during practice.

3. Explain how a box-score mentality works and why it can be effective.

4. How does visualization work, and how is it beneficial in sports?

5. List four ways in which players can make a team better based on mind-set.

6. Define a double double and a triple double in basketball.

7. What benefits can be gained by using the player performance scoring system?

8. How can a coach develop confidence and positive mind-set when the team faces a top-rank opponent?

Sportsmanship and Attitude

IN THIS CHAPTER YOU WILL LEARN:

- About sportsmanship and attitude
- How sportsmanship is an important part of athletics and why it is important
- Why good attitudes toward officials create a better sports environment and competition
- How positive attitudes and efforts toward academics will help to elevate your game and life
- The effect of your attitudes toward teammates and other people
- The value of positive attitudes toward life
- How to handle when the competition is over and your sports days are finished
- How to be an example and a leader

Promise Yourself
- *To be strong so nothing can disturb your peace of mind.*
- *To make all your friends feel that there is something great within them.*
- *To look for good in everything and make your optimism come true.*
- *To think only of the best, to work only for the best, to expect only the best, and never to settle for anything short of the best within yourself.*
- *To be just as enthusiastic about the success of others as you are about your own.*
- *To forget the mistakes of the past and press on to the greater achievements of the future.*
- *To give so much time to the improvement of yourself that you have no time to criticize others.*
- *To wear a cheerful countenance at all times and give every living creature you meet a smile.*
- *To be too large for worry, too noble for anger, too strong for fear, and too happy to permit the presence of trouble.*

—Author unknown

ATTITUDE IN ACTION

Sportsmanship is an important part of basketball. Ask yourself, Why am I playing the game? Is it for fun, for competition, for prestige, for popularity, for money? No matter what your answer, good sportsmanship will help you to have greater success in each one of these areas. No coach enjoys dealing with someone who represents the team or the school badly, a player who puts self and ego above the rest of the team, the program, and the fans. Nobody wants to see, hear, or watch someone with a bad attitude.

When players try out for teams, it's amazing how often a coaching staff must decide between two or three players of equal ability for the last spot. More often than not, sportsmanship and attitude become the determining factor. This occurs at every level, especially in the college and pro ranks. A coach would rather have a twelfth or fifteenth player with a little less talent who is a good sport, works hard, and has a positive attitude; such a player is far preferable to someone who pouts over every decision or call by coaches and officials, who wears outlandish or provocative clothing, or who has a wild streak. More players get cut from poor sportsmanship, selfishness, and bad attitude than from lack of talent.

A dangerous trend that has emerged in the past decade is "trash talking." This is the ritual of belittling an opponent's game or the opponent as an individual, which takes place during, before, or after competition. Young players do it to emulate professional players or even college players they see on TV. Trash talking is a terrible habit and only brings negative response and attention toward any player. The fans hate it, coaches loathe it, and opponents get mad at it. If you are smart, you will not incite your opponent's anger. Let your playing do your talking. Let your opponent talk trash, and you take out the garbage. Learn to control opponents mentally by breaking them down physically. Keep quiet and play. If you open your mouth at all, do it to compliment your opponent. This sounds funny, but it will work in your favor. Think of it this way:

IMPROVEMENT IS POSITIVE LEARNING FROM A NEGATIVE EXPERIENCE.

SCOTISM

If you have played as hard and as well as you can on defense but your opponent hits a tough shot anyway, how would you react to these actions of your opponent:

1. Your opponent runs by you, saying, "I told you you can't cover me!" Now that should get you mad, which would make you play harder and with more intensity. This is not the stimulus you want to give to an opponent.
2. Your opponent runs by and says sincerely, "Good box out" because after the shot you screened your opponent from an offensive rebound.

Thus, it's wiser to pacify the enemy. Taunting a player with his or her faults will just make the player work harder. Instead, give a compliment. Do it sincerely; be genuine. Why not? This does not mean you won't play hard or go after your opponents. When you get inside the lines of the court, go to war. Just keep your mouth shut unless you have something nice to say. Talking trash is just that—trashy.

Keep this professional attitude during any mishaps that occur in a game. If you knock someone down, help the person up and say "Sorry" *without* a smirk on your face. Then pat the player on the back. If you get an abusive response, say "I didn't mean to—it's just a game." Do not add fuel to a fire that is burning, or you will get burned yourself at some point. Remember that what comes around, goes around (and usually with added momentum). Being positive toward opponents can help you play hard and play smarter. You will also enjoy the game more, and so will your opponent. Sportsmanship is not an act; it is an attitude. If you want to enjoy the game, don't talk the game. Play the game, and play it with class.

Never celebrate an accomplishment simply for your own glory. Another element of sportsmanship is to be a team player. Celebrating by yourself can also incite your opponents to get angry and fired up. Nobody likes a showboat or hot dog. If you make a great play, act as if you've done it before. Don't taunt opponents, dance around, make gestures, or draw attention to yourself. Celebrate with your teammates. Basketball is a team game. If you score a big basket, act like it is no big deal for you. Do not draw attention to yourself. Your level of play should do that for you.

In today's game, some players make themselves stand out with funny haircuts and hair color, tattoos, earrings, and so on. Although how you dress and groom yourself may make a fashion statement off the court, it will do nothing to help you on the court. The only thing that will make you stand out as a player is preparation through practice. Also, when representing a school or program, most coaches care little about the latest fashion trends but do care about the impact of players' appearances. Dress accordingly. There is no place in sports for clowns, nor do people like to cheer for one on the court. The less attention you bring to yourself in dress and appearance, the more people will take you seriously—this includes opponents, coaches, and fans. When coaches vote on two players equal in ability and statistics for an all-star ballot, they'll choose the one with the better attitude and more acceptable appearance. Such considerations are indeed important.

As you begin playing basketball and developing your skills, you will develop attitudes at the same time. Perhaps you have been playing for a few years and have already adopted attitudes about the game, your conduct, and life. These attitudes will be a direct reflection of you and your actions both on and off the court. Try to develop good attitudes. If you already have formed bad attitudes, realize that attitude is a mental habit. It can be changed, so change it. It will help your performance as a player and also as a human being. Your attitude on the basketball court will be the same attitude you carry out of the gym and into life.

Attitude Determines Results.
Good Attitude = Good Results
Fair Attitude = Fair Results
Poor Attitude = Poor Results

ATTITUDES TOWARD OFFICIALS

As a coach or player, try to seldom, if ever, say anything to basketball officials. They speak a different language. Whenever I see a player or coach with an attitude try to talk with a referee and the referee cannot understand them, the official will make a funny-looking T-sign with their hands!

Among the many times you have seen players complain to referees, have you ever once seen a foul or violation call changed? The only thing accomplished by complaining is to aggravate an official. A player who does this is labeled a complainer, a poor sport, and a crybaby by the fans and other officials. Basketball is one of the only sports in the world in which players constantly complain to the referees. This makes players look silly. They embarrass their team, friends, and family.

Have you ever known a player who could concentrate and play well while complaining to the officials? It's doubtful. But you probably have seen hundreds of players stop to complain about a call or walk down the court, leaving their teammates to play defense because they believe they are the only ones ever to get fouled or never to have made a mistake. Most officials are honest, and they try to be fair. If you don't believe it, watch what happens the next time a player complains about a missed foul or bad call by an official. The referee will be so conscious of the mistake, he or she will try to do better the next time. The next time is usually at the other end of the court and to the benefit of the other team!

Referees do not do this intentionally or with malice. Their concentration has been shaken because of a complaining player who embarrassed them, so they try to immediately make up for it with a "good call." They may even become concerned about missing a call and may start calling nonexistent fouls and violations just to make sure they do not miss anything. Complaining only causes more problems for the referee and for players. The official will not be concentrating properly on the game, and neither will the player.

PEOPLE MAY NOTICE HOW YOU LOOK, BUT THEY WILL ONLY REMEMBER HOW YOU PLAY.

SCOTISM

No player ever plays a perfect game, and no referee can officiate a game perfectly either. However, many players and officials can perform exceptionally well when they concentrate on what they need to do and try to do their best. Realize that referees are not supposed to talk directly to players. (That's why they have a whistle in their mouth.) So do not talk to them. Hand officials the ball politely after a call. It will help you to have a good attitude toward them and help them to do their job better. The result will be a better officiated and better played game. Good attitudes toward officials create good official attitudes.

ATTITUDES TOWARD ACADEMICS

Better grades mean better opportunities. There is nothing wrong with wanting to pursue basketball as far as you can, but continue your other interests and ideas for careers as well. Do not put all your eggs in one basket. Give yourself other options, other hobbies, and future plans to rely on. Even a car has a spare tire in case one of the original ones does not make it to its destination.

The investment of time and effort you make in studying will pay off. It may give you the opportunity to receive more offers for basketball scholarships and opportunities to play in college. If nothing else, you will have greater academic and career opportunities for the future.

Do not let your peers or friends make you think studies are not important. If you invest two hours a day in schoolwork, you will still have a lot of time for your friends and basketball. Most people waste four to six hours a day doing nothing (sitting around, watching TV, goofing off, riding in a bus or car, and so on). Do not let laziness in school rob you of opportunities to play basketball or to have a good career. Employers will look at your records to judge your attitude, maturity, and effort in the past.

Basketball requires at least as much intelligence as any other active sport. Be smart on and off the court; study hard. Success in school will help you feel good about yourself and exert a positive influence on friends and teammates. It will open up important options in the future. If you do not strive to become what you want to be, by default you will become what you do not want to be.

ATTITUDES TOWARD TEAMMATES AND OTHER PEOPLE

The best thought ever heard for promoting good sportsmanship comes from the Bible: "Do unto others as you would have them do unto you." Tensions and pressures can get extremely high in competitive sports, and if you want to play the percentages and win in the game of basketball or life, you must develop the ability to be understanding and encouraging.

Have you ever known a player to intentionally make a dumb mistake, foul, or turnover in a game? As a friend and teammate, you can do one of two things when people make mistakes: you can tell them how stupid they are and make them feel worse, or you can encourage them. Help them concentrate on the game or current situation; the past cannot be changed.

"It's okay. We'll get it back."
"Don't worry about it. Let's play defense."
"It's all right. Get the next one."
"It's okay. Good try."

These are all ways of encouraging the other person. They will help you both feel better as you work together to concentrate on the present. This approach will make you a better player and your teammates better players as well.

The only way you can look down on others is by stepping on them. You will never be able to climb to the top of the hill by stepping on someone else. Not all players on your team will be stars. Not all people will be attractive, funny, or appealing to you. (You may not appeal to them!) But people do have some good qualities. All want to be respected and treated as human beings. The belief and encouragement of another person can have a remarkably positive effect on people.

If you do not like being laughed at, do not laugh at another.
If you do not like being yelled at, do not yell at another.
If you like to be encouraged, encourage others.

If you like people whom you admire and respect to acknowledge you, take time to acknowledge others—all others, no matter how unimportant or insignificant some feel they may be. Follow the simple rule: "Do unto others as you would have them do unto you." By being friendly, encouraging, and polite to all people no matter who they are, you will win respect and friendship. If you play basketball for your school or community, many people will know who you are, and younger kids will watch you. Whether you know it or not, some young child will want to be exactly like you. Be your best. Be an example of kindness, encouragement, and honesty. You will have a better attitude and gain more happiness out of life. You cannot build and tear down a building at the same time, so build. No matter what your "lot" in life, build something on it.

ATTITUDES TOWARD LIFE

If you are reading this book, you have eyes to see, a mind to think, an education, and the ability to learn. This should give you a good attitude about yourself and the opportunities you have. Millions lack the freedom or opportunity to read and learn.

I believe that you have the tools you need to get anything out of life you want, if it is for a good purpose. You need simply to seek knowledge so that you can learn and grow. Nobody was born a success, a natural athlete, or a great personality. These characteristics are learned and developed. Instead of spending time thinking you are not good enough, learn, train, practice, and improve.

Every action, thought, effort, and attitude will have a positive or negative effect on your life. You cannot build negative thoughts and attitudes and expect positive results. Positive in, positive out; negative in, negative out. This is one of life's simple rules.

Not all things in basketball or in life will be fair or just. But we can learn something from whatever happens, whether learning not to mistreat other people because of how we were treated or gaining experiences that strengthen and test us. Every basketball player has played horribly at one time or another and felt like quitting. But mentally reviewing a bad game usually yields lessons for improving performance. You have to experience some incorrect plays to learn how to do them correctly. Learn from mistakes, but do not make them an excuse not to succeed. Experience is a lesson to be learned not taught. Focus on positive learning from a negative experience. Always try your best and be your best. That is real success.

WHEN IT'S OVER

There will come a time in every player's career to hang up the shoes, put away the ball, and find other things of interest in life to pursue. These might include furthering an education or starting a job, a career, a family, a hobby, or involvement in an organization.

No matter what level you have competed at—junior high, high school, college, or pro—walk away feeling good about basketball and the opportunities it has given you. James Naismith invented the game of basketball to give young people a constructive physical activity and to keep them out of trouble. More than likely, basketball has helped you in these ways already. When the time comes to stop playing, or if you don't progress to the next level of competition, remember that the important thing is not what you have lost, but rather all that you have gained. You have been a part of a team. You have gained friendships, good health, and positive experiences. You have learned the importance of sacrifice, discipline, good sportsmanship, citizenship, and proper mental and physical habits. Most important, you have learned that hard work at whatever you do in life will bring you success. You can walk away with the positive experiences and the maturity with which to find success in other areas of your life.

Life will offer many challenges. Basketball is simply one step on the stairway of life. Many new and exciting experiences and opportunities await you. Hold your head up to see them.

What lies behind us and what lies before us are tiny matters compared to what lies within us.

—Ralph Waldo Emerson

LEADERS SET THE PACE FOR OTHERS; THEY DO NOT PACE THEMSELVES.

SCOTISM

▌ COACHES' CHALK TALK: BEING A LEADER

As a coach, have you ever convinced an official to change a call? You probably never will, especially in calls involving a referee's judgment. Try to focus on the game and pretend the referees do not exist. If an official's performance is below average, the accuracy of calls is probably below average for both teams. If you pay attention to the officials in games, your players will too. They will blame the officials for how the game is going instead of playing hard or finding ways to change the tempo, pace, and outcome of the game itself. The coach's attitude and respect for officials will carry over to players. If you show respect toward others, your players will follow the standard. Bad attitude often stems from poor self-esteem. Work on both. Take up jogging or start lifting weights. It will relieve stress and improve self-esteem and attitude at the same time.

Expect excellence from your players in citizenship, academics, basketball development, and effort. A coach's level of expectation is the wind in the players' sails. Very little wind will generate very little progress. A coach is the force that moves the team forward. Hot air is not the same as a guiding wind. In every aspect of coaching, your attitude determines everyone else's attitude.

CHAPTER QUESTIONS

1. How can you counter "trash talking" during a game in a positive way? Why is it important to do so?

2. How is it possible to celebrate during competition while still being a good sport?

3. How can good academic performance benefit a basketball player or future coach?

4. How important is the example of a coach to the team, and why?

5. What does it mean to be a mentor for players? What, if any, responsibility is involved?

Motivation

IN THIS CHAPTER YOU WILL LEARN:

- To create a positive environment to enhance performance
- How to increase focus and develop self-discipline
- That real motivation comes from within
- The value of using goals to keep you motivated and moving forward
- Ways to improve and motivate an entire team

CREATING A POSITIVE ENVIRONMENT FOR POSITIVE PERFORMANCE

> *Do not modify your goals according to what you think you can achieve or what other people think is achievable. Decide what you want to achieve, and modify your life.*

Napoleon Bonaparte, one of the greatest generals in history, said, "I see only my goal; the obstacles must give way." You have to respect this philosophy. If you are serious about becoming a better basketball player, the only motivation you should need is the goal itself. Practicing your drills each day should become a habit like brushing your teeth or eating. Things of great value are seldom free. They take hard work, daily consistency, and persistence. Obstacles are simply stepping-stones on the stairway to your goal. You encounter obstacles only when you take your mind off your goal. Do not get sidetracked or discouraged. Every successful person has had to overcome obstacles. Remember your goal; put on blinders and let nothing distract you.

Try compiling several positive sayings and quotations to help motivate you. Write them down, then put them up on bedroom walls, the bathroom mirror, the refrigerator, and your locker to remind you of your goals and how to meet them. Here are a few to help you get started.

To every person comes in their lifetime a special moment when they are tapped on the shoulder and offered a very special job, fitting and unique only to their talents. What a shame and a tragedy if that moment finds them unprepared or unqualified for the work.

—Winston Churchill

You go up or you go down, but you never stay the same. In life there is no neutral.

—Scotism

There are three kinds of people:
*   those who want to make things happen,*
*   those who don't know what happened,*
*   and those who make things happen.*

—Author unknown

There is no chance, no fate, no destiny that can circumvent, hinder, or control the firm resolve of a determined soul.

—Author unknown

If you perceive a goal, and reach it, you live a dream.

—Lou Brock

Make no small plans, for they have no magic to stir people's souls.

—Author unknown

Basketball and academics are first and everything else comes after.

—Julius Erving ("Dr. J")

Each day is like a stitch in your own little pattern. The more time and effort you put into your goals, the stronger your design will be.

—Scotism

The only way to coast is by going downhill!

—Zig Zigglar

Success is found underneath the alarm clock.

—Author unknown

Too many people itch for what they want, but won't scratch for it.

—Author unknown

The weak let their thoughts control their actions; the strong make their actions control their thoughts.

—Author unknown

NEVER GIVE UP, ALWAYS GET UP.

SCOTISM

That which we persist in doing becomes easier for us to do; not that the nature of the thing itself has changed, but that our power to do it has increased.

—Ralph Waldo Emerson

With ordinary talent and extraordinary perseverance, all things are attainable.

—Thomas Buxton

The biggest room in the world is the room for improvement.

—Zig Zigglar

Success is to be measured not so much by the position that one has reached in life as by the obstacles he has overcome while trying to succeed.

—Booker T. Washington

It is not enough to know, it is not enough to want. You have to know what you want and know how to get it.

—Author unknown

Work is the only fuel the vehicle of success will run on.

—Scotism

God doesn't ask about our ability or inability, but about our availability. When we prove our dependability, he will help us with our capability.

—Neal A. Maxwell

The smallest action is better than the greatest intention.

—Author unknown

The greatest oak tree was once a little nut that stood its ground.

—Author unknown

Winners contemplate their desires, not their limitations.

—Author unknown

Repetition is the best teacher.

—John Wooden

If you want different results, you must either do different things or do things differently.

—Author unknown

COACHES' CHALK TALK: BUILDING A BASKETBALL PROGRAM

Any coach can have one successful season, but building a successful program is far more challenging. This means developing a system and style that enables you and your team to compete for a championship every year. The following ideas can help you build a program that achieves excellence year after year.

Goals and Records

Have your managers or captain(s) set up a board that lists all team and individual records for your school, conference, and state. It should be a large, attractive board that can be displayed in your gymnasium or locker room (a board for each category is preferable). Have additional boards made up listing all players from your school who received all-conference, all-state, or all-American honors or other special achievements. The boards will constantly remind all players that it is possible to achieve, which will motivate them to work harder during the season and, more important, during the off-season.

Also assemble a brief team notebook and give copies to each player. Enclose a team history, team plays and philosophies, and daily workout charts. Have pages listing your school's records—team, individual, conference, and state records, as well as records of individual games and seasons. Make a top ten list for each category, so that even those players who cannot break a team or school record will work very hard to get into the top ten list. Include all former all-conference, all-state, and all-American players. Set up a board that lists all players who went on to play in college. Initiate a school basketball hall of fame. Dig up all the information and records you can find. Put in a one-page biography about you—the head coach—and brief sections about each of your assistants. You would be surprised how little your players know about you and your staff. They need to know, and they will find the whole notebook interesting and inspirational. It will help them feel they are part of a very special program. Pride increases a player's intensity and desire to improve.

Conferences with Players

At the beginning and end of each season, have a personal conference with each player in your program. Go over the player's season statistics, effort, areas of improvement, and areas needing improvement. Be constructive. Let them know exactly where they are at and what they need to do to get to the level they want to achieve. At the end of the year, outline an off-season training program based on a player's strengths and weaknesses. Many players have the desire to do this—they just need to be shown how to improve and to know it matters to you if they practice or not. Use the drills in this book as a guide in organizing players' programs. When they come back for the preseason, sit down with them again and hold them accountable. See what they have done. These meetings will help players to take responsibility for their own development as basketball players and as human beings.

Remember, too, that as a coach you may help to develop a few all-star players, but you can help to develop a lot of all-star people. Take a sincere interest in each player, not just in your top players. Be aware of their home situations and personal problems. Whether you realize it or not, you will be an important influence in their lives. Encourage them to visit with you when they have problems. They won't expect you to have all the answers, but just the ears to listen and a heart to show concern and interest. Share your own experiences with them. Your winning and caring attitude as a coach, a mentor, and a good human being will help to determine their attitudes and the course of many of their lives.

Tryouts

Perhaps the most difficult thing you will have to do as a coach is cut players from the program. Here are a few suggestions that might make things easier and fairer for the players. First, keep a record of "vital statistics" from your scrimmages, such as shooting percentage, shot selection, rebounds, assists, turnovers, fouls, steals, and, of course, a rating of a player's defensive abilities. All players trying out should be given equal playing time so that the vital statistics will give a true indication of their abilities. The statistics will help you make better decisions and give you evidence to show players who want to discuss why they were cut. You may even find a few diamonds in the rough whom you did not pay enough attention to. No coach is perfect, but be as fair as possible. Your players will know the difference and respect you for it.

Second, weigh the intangibles. Does a player hustle? Does a player encourage teammates or criticize them? Is a player a hard worker or lazy? How will the player react to being on the second or third team? Will a player enhance team spirit? Will a player be a good practice player? Does a player share in someone else's success on the team? Remember two important things. First, hustle and team unity are worth ten points a game to your club. Second, a strong desire from a player with average talent can beat a player with strong talent but average desire. They are called underdogs, and they cause many upsets in athletics. In a short time and with a little work, a player with desire will surpass a talented player who doesn't work hard—especially if you coach the less talented athlete in a positive way.

Third, if you have a particularly difficult time deciding whether or not to keep a certain player, ask the player to consider being a manager for the team. The athlete might blossom as a player during the year, or you may have several players go down with injuries and need an extra body to practice. If so, the player can suit up for practices and games. If not, the person will at least gain familiarity with your program, which will affect trying out the following season.

As a final note, did you know that former University of Nebraska football coach Tom Osborne used to save a few spots on his team each year for "walk-on" players? The word soon got out, and tryouts at Nebraska became a real event. From all around the country, players came to Nebraska to go to school and try out just to have a chance to play football. Over the years these forgotten walk-ons comprised more than a dozen all-American and all-conference players and the heart and soul of two national championship teams. If a coach is fair and honest, the word will spread. Players want a fair chance to play.

ANY COACH CAN DEVELOP A FEW ALL-STAR PLAYERS, BUT A GOOD COACH WILL ALSO DEVELOP A LOT OF ALL-STAR PEOPLE.

SCOTISM

The Importance of Teaching Correctly

This book has explained in each chapter ways to implement skills in a team practice and defined their importance. It has stressed the importance and value to coaches of teaching these skills correctly. Consider using the first two weeks of your basketball season as a preseason preparation period in which correct skills are taught to new players and the old players relearn important skills. After this two-week period, you should practice a different habit skill each day. During the regular season allow ten to fifteen minutes in your daily practice schedule to refresh your players fundamentals. This will allow your players to stay sharp in the skills they have learned during the first two weeks.

Use your wisdom and experience and apply it the right way by teaching your players correctly. Very few games are ever won because a coach used the perfect strategy in the last seconds of the game. Ninety percent of coaching is done in practice and in dealing with your players, not in games. When there is nothing to lose by trying, but a great deal to gain if successful, by all means try.

CHAPTER QUESTIONS

1. Give two sources of motivation that coaches can provide. How can these be beneficial?

2. List three ways in which coaches can motivate players to practice during the off-season.

3. How can coaches use team tryouts as a vehicle for motivation?

4. Explain the benefits of establishing team and school records in a basketball program.

5. Describe two additional ways that you might use to motivate players or teams.

Strength Training and Stretching

IN THIS CHAPTER YOU WILL LEARN:

- Methods to increase your athletic performance
- How to reduce and prevent potential injuries
- Ways to increase your body's range of motion and athleticism
- How to relieve muscle soreness, tightness, and aches
- Why, how, when, and where to practice strength training
- Strength-training tips for becoming a better athlete

In eight years of National Basketball Association training there have been noticeable changes. Years one through five offered our professional basketball players no sustained or organized stretching program, resulting in numerous hamstring and groin injuries. . . . our players lost valuable practice and playing time. Over the last few years, a strong, daily, structured stretching program has resulted in the virtual elimination of those injuries and an overall decreased susceptibility to injury.
—Ronald E. Culp,
    Trainer, NBA Portland Trail Blazers

This chapter provides general information and guidance on the benefits and value of stretching and strength-training programs. Needless to say, hundreds of professional texts and videos in the marketplace can assist you in learning the most advanced techniques available. The information revolution in both of these areas is advancing every year. This chapter is not intended to teach all the available techniques and drills. Each topic could take up an entire book. The focus here is on the benefits of adopting both a sound stretching program and a strength-training program and integrating them into basketball preparation and workout programs.

THE BENEFITS OF STRETCHING

Before any physical activity, stretching provides a way to warm up the body. It is also one of the most neglected areas in basketball training. Players will work on developing their skills, on playing, or even on getting in better physical condition. Yet players seldom take the time to warm up properly before practicing. Most athletes do not realize or have not been taught the benefits of a good flexibility and stretching program.

Perhaps the greatest benefit of supplementing your training program with a stretching program is that it can help improve your athletic performance. Stretching helps loosen up and lengthen the body's muscles, ligaments, joints, and tendons, while also increasing their movement and range of motion. A body limited in its range of motion will also be limited in bending, reaching, jumping, and striding to its full potential. The natural tendency of unused body muscles is to tighten up and contract. Stretching counters this muscle contraction while increasing range of motion and decreasing potential injuries. Muscles need to be stretched in order to perform at full potential and efficiency. Research has confirmed that the players with the greatest physical flexibility and range of motion are also better performers.

No one should start a car in cold weather and immediately drive off without letting it warm up properly. The cold car will not run efficiently, and the engine will suffer wear and tear. The body is no different. Before every practice, game, or workout, stretch and warm up properly.

Daily stretching helps protect against injuries. Numerous reports from thousands of coaches and trainers about stretching programs have produced three general conclusions. First, the number of injuries was greatly reduced compared with when the athletes were not on stretching programs. Second, the injuries that did occur were usually less severe. Third, injured athletes recovered more quickly if they had been on a stretching program before the injury.

When should you stretch? Too many players, coaches, and trainers believe it is important to stretch only before a workout or competition. Actually, you can benefit as much from stretching *after* a workout as you can before. And the benefits are numerous. Stretching can also be extremely helpful in dealing with muscle soreness. If your muscles become sore or stiff, do stretching drills for the area involved. This should alleviate much of the ache and pain.

When should you not stretch? First, do not stretch an area of your body in which an injury has just occurred. You will be adding trauma to an area that has just been pulled, torn, or sprained. Wait at least forty-eight hours, and consult an expert in sports medicine or training before resuming stretching. The body registers pain to say that there is something wrong. Listen to it. Second, do not stretch to get rid of cramps. If you regularly experience soreness or stiffness after working out, you may want to stretch each day immediately after your workout. If such pain and stiffness persist, consult a trainer or physician. For most players, though, this will not be necessary.

A final benefit of stretching exercises is that they require very little exertion, leaving you with energy and strength for practices, workouts, and games. Stretching properly will help you to perform better and assist in preventing injuries and muscle soreness. Remember, "an ounce of prevention beats a pound of cure."

Spend a few minutes each day in stretching before and *after* working out to improve your athletic performance.

Be sure to study the various types of stretching to understand what stretches are best for your particular needs. Stretching exercises range from static stretching to stationary with movement to innervation stretching and more. As a player or coach in today's competitive game, it is vital to understand and use the benefits of a complete stretching program.

◼◼ TRAINING TIP

Understand the difference between pain and injury. All athletes experience pain—shortness of breath, fatigue, bruises, and bumps. Great competitors will play with pain that is not detrimental to further injury. Injuries are badly sprained ankles, torn ligaments, strained knees, torn rotator cuffs, and so on. Mental toughness involves playing past the point of pain and fatigue, but never injury.

◼ THE BENEFITS OF STRENGTH TRAINING

Until the 1980s most people considered weight training to be unbeneficial for basketball players. This attitude stemmed from a lack of knowledge and inexperience about weight-training programs for basketball. Also, little equipment was available for weight training in sports. For decades it had been limited to barbells and free weights. The typical athletes in weight rooms were bodybuilders and power lifters. Little or no equipment had been designed for sport-specific movement to meet the needs of athletes in team sports.

Now things are completely different. Not only is strength training an important element in the game of basketball, but also it is almost mandatory now in order to keep up with the competition. Dozens of books, videos, and programs are specifically devoted to strength training for basketball. Dozens of companies make sport-specific equipment and design strength-training programs. Off-season, preseason, and in-season strength-training programs abound. Almost all NBA players use strength-training coaches. Karl "The Mailman" Malone, one of the NBA's greatest power forwards of all time, gives credit for his long career and lack of serious injuries to the "strong" benefits associated with a sound strength-training program.

Today, every NCAA school has a strength-training facility and coaches. Iowa State University did research on the benefits of strength training with its basketball program. The strength of the Iowa State players improved by an average of 15 to 25 percent in the first six weeks of using the program. Vertical jump increased by an average of 3 inches. Both are significant improvements in a short period of time.

Common fears and myths about strength training for basketball players, men and women alike, is that "it will affect my shot," "I will get too big," or "it will make me slower." These assumptions are incorrect. You can get stronger *without* getting bigger. Your shot will be affected positively. (Just don't lift weights right before a practice or a game—do it afterward.) Strength training will make you faster, quicker, more athletic in appearance and performance, and more confident. You will also develop greater endurance conditioning and jumping. Weight lifting or strength training will reduce body fat while increasing muscle tissue. Muscle tissue weighs more than fat tissue, but fat tissue takes up more space than muscle tissue. Strength training will also tone, tighten, sculpt, and strengthen the body.

Players of today are better athletes than those of twenty years ago and the integration of strength training in sports is a major reason for this development. Becoming a better athlete will help you become a better player. You will be able to run longer, rebound stronger, shoot better, jump higher, and play defense more quickly—all from strength training.

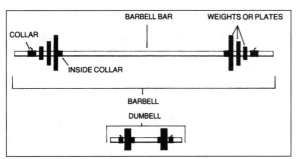

FIGURE 17.1   Barbells and Free Weights

The best place to lift weights may be in your own home if you have equipment. It is convenient, you can listen to a radio or watch TV while you work out, and the shower is close. You can buy a weight set at a local sporting goods store. You can even lift weights at home with a barbell set and free weights (see Figure 17.1). You can also try your school, a local recreation center, or a health club. Consult a professional and study available resources to develop a proper weight-lifting program.

▄▄ TRAINING TIP _____

Before you begin a strength-training program, consult a trainer, strength-training coach and/or a physician. Be sure your health allows you to participate. Gain a sound understanding of the rules, use, and benefits of strength training and how to perform the exercises correctly. For the first two weeks, expect to feel sore and tight. This is normal and typical of any new exercise or training program that requires physical exertion. The soreness and tightness will soon go away, but the benefits and results will stay with you for a long, long time.

▌ HEALTH HABITS: WORDS OF WISDOM

To get from one destination to the next, everyone must use some means of travel: a car, plane, bus, bike, the feet, and so on. If you have a destination you want to reach in basketball, you also need to use a vehicle—your body. Like any other vehicle, your body must be "tuned up" regularly, treated with care, and fed the right fuels if you are to obtain maximum use and productivity.

BECOME A BETTER PLAYER BY BECOMING A BETTER ATHLETE.

SCOTISM

You can keep your body tuned up by practicing regularly and by playing. Treat your body with care by not pushing it too hard. Do not overwork it. Do not stay out late every night. Dress properly in bad weather. Do not sleep in every day. Use proper personal hygiene daily. These will all help you to get more use out of your body.

Finally, consume the right fuels by eating healthy foods and maintaining a proper diet. Do not consume products that will impair your ability to play, function, or think clearly, now or in the future. These include cigarettes, alcohol, marijuana, or drugs of any other kind. If you believe it's okay to use any of these "fuels," you are not serious about playing basketball. The mental or physical edge you sacrifice will be the thing that beats you. As I have said, basketball is a game of seconds and inches. If you are sacrificing the care of your body by using any of the substances just listed, you are losing a split second of quickness and thinking ability, and an inch or two of speed and endurance. You may be able to get by now, but in time, as you play at higher levels and the competition gets tougher, those little inches will add up. You may miss your opportunity to make your school team, to get an important basketball scholarship, or to try out for a professional team.

I am not a health food addict. I am, though, an addict of life. I have watched many players, teammates, and friends who thought they could "steal" a few seconds or inches from their game and still come out ahead. It would take only a few years to see how they failed. One is an alcoholic, four never finished college, and two who did finish have not found good, well-paying jobs. Many players have been and may be better athletes and more talented than you, but you can go further in basketball if you take care of your body at all times and keep trying. Do not sacrifice your chances and opportunities for a few minutes of useless pleasures that add nothing positive to your life. William Shakespeare put it best:

What win I, if I gain the thing I seek.
A dream, a breath, a froth of fleeting joy?
Who buys a minute's mirth to wail a week,
or sells eternity to get a toy?
For one sweet grape who would the vine destroy . . .

Before you decide what to do, look ahead by looking back. To predict the future, learn from the past by observing the experiences of others. Look at players, friends, classmates, peers, and others who have followed both good and bad roads regarding health and happiness. Weigh the results, and then choose what you want, not what your peers say is okay to do "one time." No intelligent person steps into a two-way street without first looking both ways for possible problems. Your health is no different: look at both sides closely. You must plan ahead if you want to get ahead.

◼◼◼◼ COACHES' CHALK TALK: IMPROVING ATHLETICISM IN YOUR PLAYERS

The techniques, biomechanics, and knowledge in the areas of stretching and strength training are constantly improving and changing. As a coach it is vitally important to stay up-to-date and current in both of these areas. Get the latest materials and information every year. Follow a simple rule before adopting anyone else's teachings or philosophies: be sure it makes perfect sense and is logical. There are leading experts in the field, but also some runner-ups. Be sure the data you decide to use is the best.

Remember that stretching and strength training for basketball enhance performance and prevent injury. You owe it to yourself and your team to provide every competitive edge available.

CHAPTER QUESTIONS

1. List three benefits of a sound stretching program.

2. Explain how a strength-training program can help a player improve in basketball.

3. Why is it important to maintain good nutrition and health when participating in sports?

4. What should be a coach's objective when teaching stretching and strength-training activities?

5. What other types of exercises or activities would be beneficial in developing athletic skills for players?

Increasing Your Jumping Ability

Basketball is one of the few sports in which an athlete's ability to jump can win instant recognition from peers and coaches. Many players will make a team because they can really jump, or "sky." Being able to jump not just higher but also *quicker* can make the game more fun for players because of the attention it brings, the opportunity to slam-dunk, or even the opportunity to improve rebounding.

Still, the desire to be a great leaper should not cause a basketball player to forget to practice fundamental skills. Drills for shooting, working with the triple-threat position, dribbling, individual defense, and other skills should have first priority every day because players spend less time jumping in a game than they do in performing other skills.

As a realistic goal, players can add daily jumping exercises to an in-season and off-season conditioning program. The drills, exercises, and tips in this chapter appear in order of the benefits they can offer: the best first, and so on. Organize your own program accordingly.

JUMPING DRILLS AND EXERCISES

TRAINING TIP

The exercises and drills in this chapter have been thoroughly researched and found to be effective for athletes who want to increase their vertical jump. Consult a physician and/or professional trainer or strength coach to determine a personal program and any training limits that might be important for you. Your safety and health are your responsibility.

Stretching

Whatever program of exercise you decide on, supplement it with a sound stretching program. For maximum benefits, stretch before and after working out. Stretching will help you reach your full jumping potential. In fact, proper stretching can by itself help increase your vertical jump by 4 inches or more!

Weight Training

Weight training is probably the quickest and least painful way to improve jumping ability and to do it in a hurry. It is also one of the best ways to strengthen jumping muscles and gain total athletic body development. Before beginning any strength training, do your homework or consult a trained professional for help in developing a fundamental program. Remember, improvement will be demonstrated over weeks and months, not days and hours. Be committed, and stay with it. It is strongly recommended that you adopt a total weight-training program for the entire body, not just exercises for making legs stronger for jumping. A complete program will give you total body balance and will assist in overcompensation of one muscle group in your body over another. This will translate into greater athleticism and fewer injuries. Besides, it will take only a few minutes longer each day and will give you greater overall strength in your upper, middle, and lower body. You will also look and feel better and play with more confidence.

Plyometrics

Plyometrics is a training technique that uses the principle of overload training. Jumping off and onto boxes in quick explosive movements, adding body-weight vests, and using medicine ball resistance are all forms of Plyometric training. Scott Phelps, president of Speed Quest and the premier speed and quickness coach in the world, explains: "The objective of Plyometrics is to increase muscle recruitment while maintaining the same speed time. There has to be a moderate overload of resistance with a *fast* response time. Explosive steps and movements. Do not add too much of an overload; light to moderate resistance is the key."

For example, it's better to begin with a 12-inch box rather than a 40-inch box. An athlete will respond much more quickly on a 12-inch box and therefore gain greater explosiveness. As an athlete's ability to respond increases, the overload can then increase. Progress to taller boxes *only* if the same quick response time can be maintained. Always use quick, explosive movements. Consult a resource guide or product to learn more about exercises. A good resource library can be found at www.sportamerica.com. Taking the time to research the benefits of and products for Plyometrics will be time well spent.

Running Hills

Running up steep hills is an exceptionally good way to increase jumping ability. You can do it separately or together with weight training. If you do weight training, run only on your nonlifting days.

There are two ways to run on hills to receive the greatest benefits. First, find a steep hill that is one to two miles from bottom to top. Run it daily, all the way up and back down again. If the hill is steep for only half a mile, then run it two or three times in a row without stopping. Pace yourself the first two weeks, and give yourself time to build up to running the full distance. This will be an extremely difficult exercise at first, but it will improve your jumping dramatically within six to eight weeks.

The other option is to find a steep hill 30 to 40 yards long. Sprint up the hill six to ten times at full speed, jogging down each time. Then run six to ten sprints at full speed up the hill, backward! Stretch properly before running. *Check with a physician or trainer before doing either of these exercises. You are responsible for your health.*

Using a "Leaper" Machine

Your school or college weight room may have this machine. Many health clubs and fitness centers with a weight room have it as well. When using the machine, do three or four sets of twenty to thirty repetitions each. Break for one to two minutes between each set. Do the repetitions as quickly as possible. This will help you jump higher and more quickly.

Touching the Rim, Backboard, or Net

One of the best ways to improve jumping is to practice jumping. Try this drill. Stand underneath the target (the rim, backboard, or net, depending on which you can touch at the high point of your jump). Jump and touch it with both hands, twenty-five times. Without stopping, jump off your right leg twenty-five times as high as you can, touching the target with only one hand. Next, jump off your left leg twenty-five times. Finish by jumping off both legs and touching the target with both hands another twenty-five times.

Jumping in Place

Stand at attention, hands at your sides. Without bending your knees, jump quickly as high as you can off both feet, fifty times. Next, hold your right leg behind you with your right hand, and jump off your left foot fifty times. Then hold your left leg with your left hand, and jump off your right foot fifty times. Finish by quickly jumping off both feet fifty times without bending the knees. Do two sets of the drill if you can, resting five minutes between sets. You can do this drill while watching TV.

Jumping Rope

Daily, jump rope for fifteen to thirty minutes, or complete a specific number of repetitions. One revolution of the rope equals one repetition. Do a different jump-rope exercise every five minutes or for two hundred repetitions: jump off both legs, the left leg alone, the right leg alone, while running in place, off both legs again, and so on.

JUMPING STANDARDS

People are always fascinated by how high their favorite star players can jump. The following table will give you an idea of how good a jumper you are. Do not, however, begin to measure your jump before at least age fourteen. These figures won't mean much until you've grown in height and strength as an adolescent.

STANDARDS FOR VERTICAL JUMP

	Males (inches)	Females (inches)
Superior	32+	24+
Excellent	28	20
Very Good	24	18
Above Average	20	16
Average	15	12
Below Average	10	8
Poor (Take Up Badminton)	5	4

How to Measure Your Vertical Jump

If you are old enough to begin measuring your vertical jump, mark 1-inch intervals on a wall (see Figure 18.1). Then stand with your toes and chest against the wall. Now raise one hand up as far as you can while leaving the other hand at your side and your feet flat on the floor. The inch mark that your fingers reach is your point "0."

Now stand sideways to the wall and no more than 1 foot away from it. Jump up and touch the highest mark you can. Repeat the jump in the same manner two more times, for a total of three jumps. The highest mark you touched is your measurement point. Count the number of inches or marks between point 0 and the measurement point. If there are 24 inch marks, for example, your vertical jump is 24 inches.

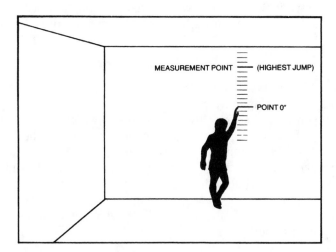

FIGURE 18.1   Measuring a Vertical Jump

> ### ▆▎ TRAINING TIP
>
> To get a true estimate of your vertical jump, make sure to warm up properly before measuring it. Do not measure your jump more than every two to three weeks as you train. This will keep you from getting discouraged. It is extremely difficult to improve in only a few days.

▆▆▆▆▎ TRAINING FOR VERTICAL HEIGHT AND QUICKNESS

The general belief in basketball is that 90 percent of all rebounds are grabbed below the rim. If this is so, then the quickest player to the ball will win. As you work on improving how high you can get your vertical jump, also train to improve your vertical quickness, an ability that is often overlooked. The two skills make good companions. The longer you take to reach the height of your jump, the greater chance gravity has to slow you down and keep you down.

Vertical Conditioning

Vertical conditioning means building the body's endurance capability in vertical movements, not just in linear movements up and down the court or lateral movements. A good way to improve vertical conditioning is to take a ball in both hands above your head while standing in front of a backboard (or a wall if you cannot reach a backboard). Jump as quickly and as high as you can, and as you reach the top of your jump, tap the ball hard against the board. Upon landing, automatically recoil and explode quickly back up to tap the ball again. Complete twenty to twenty-five repetitions. Practice two sets daily, resting at least one full minute between sets. Shooting free throws is a great intermission drill.

More Tips for Jumping and Slam-Dunking

1. Ride a bike everywhere you go. Bike riding is great for conditioning and will help build jumping muscles.
2. When you walk up stairs, always take them two or three at a time.
3. Lose weight if you are overweight. The less weight your body has to carry, the easier it will be to jump. If you are on the thin side, don't lose weight. It will only make your body weaker. Try building up your weight and strength, which should help both your endurance and your jumping.
4. Fingertip push-ups are great for strengthening the fingers and increasing the ability to palm or hold the basketball. Do as many as you can every night before you go to bed.

5. Hand grips can be purchased at most sporting goods stores for only a few dollars, and they will last for years. They are great tools for increasing hand strength. These too will increase hand and finger strength and make it easier to palm the ball.

6. When you are trying to go to sleep, picture yourself going up to dunk. The human mind does not know the difference between mental and physical practice. It only records what it is fed.

CHAPTER QUESTIONS

1. List four exercises or drills that can be used to increase the height of vertical jumping.

2. Explain the proper way to measure a player's maximum vertical jump.

3. Give two reasons why vertical quickness in jumping is important.

4. Write four tips that can improve jumping and dunking skills.

5. Describe how Plyometrics training works and why it is beneficial.

Where Can I Go to Play and Coach the Game?

Whatever your age, ability, or level of commitment, you can find an organization that will give you a chance to compete and grow as a basketball player or coach.

PLAYING YOUTH LEAGUE BASKETBALL.

Once you or your child starts to play basketball for fun, you will want to get involved in team competitions and activities. If you live in the United States, contact any youth league organization (there are thousands) or junior high school in your area. If you need help, contact the following national offices to locate local branches in your area:

American Amateur Union
P.O. Box 10000
Lake Buena Vista, FL 32830-1000
(407) 934-7200
Website: www.aausports.org

Boys and Girls Clubs of America
1230 West Peachtree Street N.W.
Atlanta, GA 30309
(404) 815-5700
Website: www.bgca.org

YMCA National Offices
101 North Wacker Drive Suite 1400
Chicago, IL 60606
(800) 872-9622
Website: www.ymca.com

NRPA (National Recreation and Parks Association)
22377 Belmount Ridge Road
Ashburn, VA 20148
(703) 858-0784
Website: www.nrpa.org

PLAYING RECREATIONAL BASKETBALL

For playing in organized adult leagues, consult local park and recreation departments. Also call health clubs, local public gyms, and college intramural programs. All may have open gym times during which you can play, usually for a small fee. For all other countries outside of the United States, contact the Federation of International Basketball Associations (FIBA):

FIBA
P.O. Box 700607 D-81306
Munich, Germany
Phone: 49-89-748-1580
Website: www.fiba.com

PLAYING HIGH SCHOOL BASKETBALL

High school basketball can provide numerous opportunities for competition. As players get older, the tougher the competition will be. Many high schools have freshmen teams, sophomore teams, junior varsity teams, and varsity teams. Smaller high schools may only have one or two teams because of the size of the student body. Most states have several classifications. This makes it possible for more than one state champion to be crowned in each sport every year. This change from one classification per state to multiple classifications, along with population growth, are the main reasons for the greater number of participants in sports today. The classifications match schools of similar size for competition.

High school teams typically practice daily for two to three hours and require a serious commitment of time and energy. Players must also maintain a good grade point average to remain eligible to participate in sports. Talk to school coaches for details.

PLAYING COLLEGE BASKETBALL

There are various levels of college basketball. The most familiar is NCAA Division I, which is on television and radio regularly and is featured in newspaper and magazine headlines. However, many other levels of competition in college involve players of different abilities and interests. Here is a breakdown of various levels of college basketball competition:

National Collegiate Athletic Association (NCAA)
P.O. Box 6222
Indianapolis, IN 46206–6222
(317) 917-6222
Website: www.ncaa.org

Currently more than 1,041 colleges and universities participate in NCAA Divisions I, II, and III.

These programs range from full scholarships for some athletes to Division III nonscholarship programs.

National Association of Intercollegiate Athletics (NAIA)
6120 South Yale Avenue Suite 1450
Tulsa, OK 74136
(918) 494-8828
Website: www.naia.org

Currently more than 300 colleges and universities participate in the NAIA. It has both Division I and II levels of competition. Many participating colleges do offer athletic scholarships, but availability varies among the institutions. Population size of the school usually determines which division a school participates in. The NAIA is a different governing body from the NCAA for college athletics and has similar but different academic requirements.

National Junior College Athletic Association (NJCAA)
P.O. Box 7305
Colorado Springs, CO 80933-7305
(719) 590-9788
Website: www.njcaa.org

Currently more than 500 junior colleges throughout the United States participate in this organization. These are two-year colleges that offer associate's degrees as well as general education credits for four-year institutions. Many players use junior college basketball as a stepping-stone to play at four-year colleges.

California Community College Commission On Athletics
2017 "O" Street
Sacramento, CA 95814
(914) 444-1600
Website: www.coasports.org

Currently more than 100 junior colleges in the state of California participate in this organization.

Northwest Athletic Association of Community Colleges (NWAACC)
1800 East McLoughlin Boulevard
Vancouver, WA 98663
(360) 922-2833

Currently more than thirty junior colleges in the states of Oregon and Washington participate in the NWAACC athletic championships. All of these schools are junior colleges.

National Christian College Athletic Association (NCCAA)
302 West Washington Street
Greenville, SC 29601
(864) 250-1199
Website: www.thenccaa.org

Currently more than 120 colleges and universities are involved in the NCCAA. Typically these schools belong to the NCAA, NAIA, or NJCAA fields of competition as well.

More about College Basketball.   Playing college basketball can be a realistic goal for most players who are willing to do the work. Keep in mind that around two thousand colleges in the United States have basketball programs.

Three Things to Consider

1. *Practice is repetition.* Every year in high school, more than 600,000 players participate in varsity basketball. In college, more than 20,000 players are involved in college basketball each season. Therefore, if you want to play college basketball, during your high school years you will have to complete 580,000 more repetitions of skill work than your competition. It is that simple. Oh, by the way, of the 20,000 college players each year, fewer than 1,000 will go on to play at some level of professional basketball after college. You guessed it—the work cycle starts again when you get to college. You will have to practice 76,000 repetitions more than everyone else. That is 19,000 repetitions each year throughout your college career more than your competition. This is just to have a chance at playing pro basketball in the United States or overseas. Go to work.

2. *Go where you are wanted, not where you want to go.* Are you getting recruited by a junior college, but you have dreams of playing at NCAA Division I? Go to the junior college. It's better to be a big fish in a little pond than a little fish in a big pond. Go where you can get playing time, not get cut from a team. That would be an expensive education. Here is a hint: if a college does not recruit you, they do not want you. Be smart. That's what school is for.

3. *Attend a college development camp.* These can be hard to find. The premier college development camp run with college coaches as instructors is the Converse College Camp. It is open to players ages sixteen and over and is run once a year. For more information, contact: www.sportamerica.com.

PLAYING PROFESSIONAL BASKETBALL

This is an elite class of players and athletes. Every year fewer than one thousand players worldwide get to play at some level of professional basketball. Fewer than four hundred play in the NBA (National Basketball Association). How do you go after the opportunity? You don't. If a pro team or scout thinks you are good enough to play, they will find you. The chances of playing professional basketball without having played in college are one in ten million. Professional teams pay good money for players to represent them. They want results. The more exposure a league gets, the higher the stakes and the better the competition.

Some minor league pro teams offer tryouts and charge you a fee to try out. Typically, hundreds of players will pay to try out, and they all will get cut after the first practice or day. It is a moneymaker for a pro team or vacation money for the coaches. Here is a helpful hint: if you are not invited to try out by a pro team and they do not pay your way there, plan on getting a tour of the city after practice because it will be your last time on the court. Beware of what you pay for. If you are still determined to follow the shooting star of pro basketball, here are a few tips:

1. *Search the Internet for opportunities.* Look for tryout opportunities that involve no fees. If the situation guarantees a player a specific number of games over two or more days, then players may get a legitimate chance.

2. *Find an agent.* Honest agents take a commission percentage of a player's future earnings. They will let you know if they think you are worth representing or not. Since they make a living from this, they will be brutally honest—they have to be. By the way, your chances of acceptance increase tenfold if you are 6 feet, 8 inches or taller in height. Beware of agents who want to charge you up-front signing and legal fees, or fees of any kind. They will probably take the money and run after making a few half-hearted attempts to place you through form letters or a computer listing. Unless you have unbelievable statistics from high school, college, or international competition, take two aspirin and be prepared to lose your money. You are officially a legend in your own mind.

3. *Play in summer pro leagues.* Typically, you will not be accepted by such leagues unless you have the goods to market (which means that you are a player). If you can really play, they will let you. Your level of consistency is equal to your level of performance. Scoring only two to four points in a summer pro game means that you are a long way from the Hall of Fame or a pro contract. If you have been at least an all-conference player at the college or international level of basketball, the door may be unlocked, but it is not yet open.

4. *Age matters.* If you are thirty years of age or older and have not played professional basketball yet, you officially qualify for basketball retirement. You took your best shot, even though it was an air ball. Now it's time to grow up and get a new occupation that will pay the bills.

COACHING BASKETBALL

There are numerous opportunities available to those who want to coach the game of basketball. Although a lot of people are good armchair coaches while watching games on TV or from the stands, it is much different once you put a whistle in your hand and have dozens of eyes waiting for instruction, teaching, and motivation. A beginner coach should start at the youth-league level. Begin by trying to teach skills, then basic Xs and Os. Here are ten rules to use as simple guidelines:

1. Keep it simple. Don't try to do too many fancy or detailed things.
2. Teach the fundamentals well. No matter how great a play you run for your team, if they do not have sound fundamental skills, they still won't be successful.
3. Be positive at all times. Participation in competition for players and coaches is voluntary.

4. Use constructive criticism. Never criticize physical mistakes such as a missed shot or turnover. No player ever plans on missing a shot or making a turnover, so do not compound the problem. If you criticize anything, it should be lack of effort or a mental mistake such as not running a play that was called. Even in these situations, be positive; criticize the action, not the actor (player). You will get better results, and everyone will have a better experience.

5. Be prepared. Your players will have more confidence in you, and you will too, if you are well prepared. Do not expect players to buy into what you are trying to do or the way you are trying to do it just because you're the coach. Players recognize preparation, whether it is for a game, an upcoming opponent, or how skills and fundamentals are taught. A coach that tries to fake it is a fake coach. Be real.

6. Be yourself. Although it is important to learn from great coaches and the things they use, draw on others' success but be who you are. It will take you a lot further.

7. Be available. Players today have fewer and fewer positive role models. Your job is not to be their best friend, but their best example. Be a good mentor and someone they can rely on when they need to. They will have enough friends.

8. Be an all-star coach. You will help develop more all-star people than all-star players. Have your priorities in the right place. If you work hard, teach good principles, and coach sound fundamentals, you will have your share of success too.

9. Keep learning. There is always something new to learn. Take advantage of resources such as books, videos, coaching clinics, camps, and so on.

10. Have goals. Develop regular goals and game plans for yourself, your players, and your teams.

Coaching experience, just like playing experience, has a lot to do with success. When you are on the bench, you'll experience the emotions of the game differently than you do in the stands. Try to go easy on coaches in the middle of a game. The game itself is enough pressure to deal with. Most coaches will actually do a better job if they know they have the parents' and fans' support. They will be able to relax more and concentrate on the game.

If you want to get involved in coaching, begin by learning to teach skills properly. Then try to get involved as an assistant coach for a local youth league team. These groups are always looking for good volunteers. These national organizations can provide additional guidance, opportunities, and information:

SPORTAMERICA INC. RESOURCE LIBRARY (world's largest sports
instructional video library)
P.O. Box 95030
Salt Lake City, UT 84095
(800) 467-7885 or (801) 253-3360
Website: www.sportamerica.com

National Association of Basketball Coaches
9300 West 110th Street Suite 640
Overland Park, KS 66210-1486
(913) 469-1001
Website: www.nabc.com

Women's Basketball Coaches Association
4646-B Lawrenceville Highway
Lilburn, GA 30247
(770) 279-8027
Website: www.wbca.org

▬▬I TRAINING TIP

Off-Season Pick-Up Games

Most coaches will conduct open gym of some kind. Pick-up games often go to eleven points if baskets are scored in one-point increments.

If you want to make it more competitive, have players play to only seven points and compete in a playoff series of four out of seven games or three out of five games. If you have a lot of players waiting to get in, play only to five points. This will pick up the energy level and intensity in a hurry. Nobody likes to be kept waiting.

20

Backyard Basketball Games

For decades, people have been playing different games of basketball in the backyard for fun and for competition. To enhance your time spent in practice, try playing some of the twenty-seven backyard games compiled in this chapter. Some you can play on your own, some with family, or some with friends. Try them all. They will provide hours of fun for everyone.

GAMES FOR ONE OR MORE PLAYERS

The first six games are timed games for one or more players. Play using two time periods, thirty seconds or sixty seconds. The shorter period will help develop quickness, speed, and coordination. The longer period will develop endurance and concentration. The best way to improve is to play each game using both time periods once daily. Try to beat your own best record each day. You can play timed games on your own for practice.

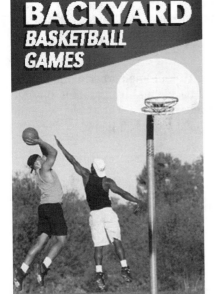

Game 1: Layups

In this game, make as many layups as possible against the thirty-second clock. Prior to making a layup, dribble to the opposite foul line corner. The player's feet must always come above the foul line. Work both corners of the foul line to develop both left- and right-handed skills and dribbling and layup skills.

Game 2: Drop Step

To begin each move, make a jump stop outside the foul lane by the block or second hash mark. Slap the ball as if you had received a pass, then take a drop step with the foot closest to the basket along with one dribble, and power up to score. Work both sides of the foul lane to develop both right- and left-handed shooting skills.

Game 3: Hook Shot

Begin by standing in front of the rim. Step with the left foot, shoot with the right hand, then step with the right foot, and shoot with the left hand. Repeat for the duration of the time period. Record daily the number of shots made within the given time.

Game 4: Hot Spots

Hot Spots is played against the sixty-second clock and is a lot of fun. The scoring is as follows: a shot outside the three-point line is worth four points. A foul-line shot is worth three points. A shot below the foul line is worth two points, and a layup is worth one point. You can take only one layup in a row. In this game, the best way to score the most points is to make several of the shots from the three- and four-point areas. A score of twenty-five points or more is considered excellent.

Game 5: Right Hand/Left Hand

Keep the ball in the lane area, and keep the eyes up at all times. The game is played by dribbling from the baseline to the foul line with the left hand and from the foul line to the baseline with the right hand. Score by getting one point each time the length of the foul-lane area is covered. Both feet must cross over each line in order to score a point.

Game 6: Between the Legs

The same rules apply as in game 5. Dribble the length of the foul-lane area with the left hand, and return using the right hand. Dribble between the legs before pivoting to change direction. Keep the ball at hip height or below for better ball control.

GAMES FOR TWO OR MORE PLAYERS

Game 7: Cradle Jump Shot

This is also a timed game. Move from foul corner to foul-line corner without dribbling. Shoot the jump shot by squaring up to the basket and using follow-through as you shoot. This game is played with two or more players. The player with the highest score wins; in the event of a tied score, have a play-off game!

Game 8: Jump Shots off the Dribble

This is a timed game (the last timed game offered here). The shots are always taken from the perimeter, and the player will always dribble to a different side of the court with each shot. Shoulders should be squared up to the basket, with follow-through as you shoot. Again, the player with the highest score wins the game.

Game 9: Around the World

Around the World is an excellent game for improving shooting concentration and skills. Look at the three perimeters in Figure 20.1. The closest to the basket is appropriate for centers and power forwards and all beginning players at the junior high level of competition and under. The outer two perimeters are correct for

FIGURE 20.1. Perimeters for Game 9: Around the World

guards and small forwards and players at the high school level of competition and above.

To play, take one shot from each position on the court then move to the next spot. Each player takes a total of twenty shots. The player who makes the most baskets wins.

Game 10: Twenty-One

To play Twenty-One, you need two players and one ball. A foul-line shot is worth two points, and a layup is worth one point. You can only take one layup in a row. Start by shooting a foul shot, getting your own rebound, and shooting a layup. Get the rebound and pass back to the other player to shoot. Then go back to the foul line, and repeat the process. The first player to get twenty-one points wins.

Game 11: Triple Twenty-One

Here is another version of Twenty-One that uses three players and two balls. Again, the first player to twenty-one points is the winner. Triple Twenty-One is a much faster-paced game. To keep track of your score, call out your score each time you make a basket.

Game 12: Team Twenty-One

A third version of Twenty-One is what I call Team Twenty-One. It is played with four or more players, divided into equal teams. Each team works from one corner of the foul lane. The first team to score twenty-one points wins.

Game 13: Thirty-Three

This is a new game. To play Thirty-Three, take three-point shots only. Rebound your own shot, and pass it to the next player in line. After you rebound, go back to the end of the line and wait for your next turn to shoot! There are no layups or two-point shots. The first player to score eleven baskets or thirty-three points wins the game.

> ### ▮▮ TRAINING TIP _____
>
> To increase the degree of difficulty, have the players move around and shoot from different spots beyond the three-point line during the course of the game. This will improve shooting accuracy from all areas of the court.

Game 14: Triple Thirty-Three

The second version of Thirty-Three is called Triple Thirty-Three. The rules are the same, except that the game is played with three players and two basketballs.

GAMES FOR FOUR OR MORE PLAYERS

Game 15: Team Thirty-Three

Divide into two or more equal teams. The first team to make eleven three-point baskets is the winner. Each team can use one basketball or, to speed up the game, two basketballs per team.

Game 16: Forty-Four

In Forty-Four, three-point shots count for three points, and layups or rebounded shots are worth one point. You must shoot the ball from where you get the rebound. You get only one rebounded shot. The first player to get forty-four points or more wins this game.

Game 17: Triple Forty-Four

In the second version of Forty-Four, the rules are the same except that the game is played with three players and two basketballs.

Game 18: Team Forty-Four

Played the same as Forty-Four but in teams. Divide into two or more teams, and the first team to score forty-four points is the winner. Each team can use one ball or, to speed up the game, two basketballs.

GAMES OF ELIMINATION

Game 19: H.O.R.S.E.

To play this game, match the shot and make the basket that the person ahead of you makes. If the person misses the shot, then you become the leader, and the player behind you must match the shot you make. If you are the leader and miss your shot, you become the follower without a letter or penalty. If you can't make (or match) the shot made by the person ahead of you (the leader), then you receive a letter such as *H, O, R,* and so on. You receive one letter for each shot you miss. When you finally spell the word *horse,* you are eliminated. Play this game with two or more players.

Game 20: P.I.G.

This game is like H.O.R.S.E., except instead of taking normal game shots, you play only with trick shots. In this game you can be really creative—use shots behind the back, shots bounced off the floor, shots from behind the backboard, or even shots off your head, knee, or foot. Invent your own shots!

Game 21: Follow the Leader (FTL)

To play FTL, each player must have a ball. The object of the game if you are the leader is to *not* wait until the follower has shot, but to shoot as often and as quickly as possible. The follower(s) must make the same shot as the leader. If the leader misses, he or she immediately goes to the end of the line, and the first follower becomes the leader. In this game, you get a letter by not matching and making the same shot that the leader makes. When a player gets all three letters, *F, T,* and *L,* the player is eliminated. This game is fast paced and fun! Play with two to five players.

Game 22: I.C.E.

Another game of elimination, called I.C.E., uses pressure-packed foul shots only. Any player who misses a foul shot gets a letter, and any player who misses three foul shots or gets all three letters (*I, C, E*) is disqualified (one letter for each foul shot missed). This game can be played with two to five players. You can also play it as a one-shot elimination and yell "ICE" when someone misses and is eliminated.

Game 23: Lightning

One of the most popular games of elimination is known as Lightning (or Bump). This game is played with only two basketballs. To play Lightning, all players shoot from behind the foul line area first and missed or rebounded shots second. If you miss your long shot, you must make your rebounded shot before the player behind you scores a basket by making a foul shot.

  If you make a foul shot or rebounded shot before the player behind you makes a shot, you are still in. Go to the end of the line. At your next turn, try to eliminate the player in front of you before the player behind you eliminates you. If the player behind you scores a basket before you do, you're out. If you are the last player to be eliminated, you win.

  Players must try the foul shot first. If they miss, they must try to make the rebounded shot second. The rebounded shot must be taken only if the player missed the foul shot.

  If you make your shot before the person behind you makes one, go to the end of the line and keep playing. But if the player behind you scores before you do, lightning strikes and you have been eliminated.

Game 24: In-a-Row Free Throw

This game is easy to play and fun to practice. You can play by yourself or with an opponent. The object is to make as many free throws in a row as you can without missing. Your opponent has to beat your score. If you play on your own, you have to beat your own best score. Now there's a real challenge!

COURT GAMES (HEAD-TO-HEAD COMPETITION)

Game 25: One-on-One

To play One-on-One using pro rules, never take more than two dribbles to attack the defender and the basket. This rule makes players quicker and more efficient in offensive game situations.

Always begin with the ball in your perimeter area. If you score, move to defense, and the first player to score seven baskets wins. If you are playing on defense and you stop your opponent from scoring and get the rebound, you get to take the ball out on offense. Check the ball in. Normal game rules apply. When you play one-on-one, be prepared to check your ego on the table!

Game 26: Triple One-on-One Championship

The One-on-One Championship is played with three or more players. Two players will play one-on-one to one point, and each time a score is made, a new player rotates in. If you score, move to defense. The first player to score seven points wins. Once you become the defensive player, you can get the ball back in only two ways:

1. Get scored on and come back through the rotation line.
2. Stop the offensive player from scoring and/or get the rebound to go to offense.

Game 27: Two-on-One Championship

Two-on-One Championship consists of two defensive players and one offensive player. If you get a rebound, you become the offensive player. If you score, you stay on offense. The first player to score seven baskets wins. Two-on-One Championship is played in the same way as One-on-One Championship except all the players remain on the court. If you score, you get the ball out again. The rebounder becomes the offensive player. Two-on-One Championship is excellent for improving and developing ball-handling skills and concentration.

▎▎I TRAINING TIP _____

To make games more competitive, you MUST WIN by two or more points. By playing in this manner, you'll improve your ability to score.

Try thinking of variations on the games listed here. You might try Two-on-Two, Team H.O.R.S.E., Three-on-Two, Team I.C.E., Three-on-Three, Team Lightning, Four-on-Four, and so on. All for fun and fun for all!

▎▎I TRAINING TIP _____

You may also use the play-off game idea, which means the player or team that wins the most out of seven rounds of competition is the champion. Any player can be a winner, but it takes the best player or team to be the play-off champion.

Basketball Dictionary

Air ball   A shot that misses both the rim and the backboard and touches nothing.

Alley-oop   A play in which a lob pass is thrown up by the rim so another teammate can jump up, catch the ball in midair, and dunk the ball or tip it in.

Alternating possession   To resolve a tie-up of the ball, the two teams alternate possessions instead of using a jump ball to decide each possession.

APG   Assists per game. The number is usually preceded by the player's assist average that season (for example, 8.6 APG).

Assist   A pass or handoff by an offensive player or a teammate that leads directly to a basket.

Assistant Coach   A secondary coach, subordinate to the head coach. The assistant coach assists in the coaching of the team, offers suggestions, provides motivation, and helps in achieving the objectives of   head coach and the team.

Athleticism   The athletic capacity or ability of a player. All players are athletes, and all players can improve their athleticism.

Backboard   The surface to which the rim or basket is affixed. It is either rectangular or fan-shaped and is usually made of fiberglass or wood.

Backcourt   (1) The half of the court that is farthest away from the offensive basket. (2) A violation in which the ball has advanced to the forecourt, then is passed or dribbled again over the backcourt line by the offensive team.

Backdoor Cut   A cut made away from the side at which a defensive player is overplaying the offensive player. This cut enables the offensive player to get free for the ball.

Backspin   A reverse rotation placed on the ball when shooting to soften the shot as it hits the rim. Backspin allows contact with the back of the rim and creates a reverse movement, spinning the ball into the net.

Ball   See *Basketball.*

Ball side   The side of the court on which the ball is located. Also known as *strong side.*

Baseball pass   A long-distance pass, usually extending over the full length of the court, that is thrown like a baseball with an overhand throw.

Baseline   Line at the end of the court that separates the in-bounds area from the out-of-bounds area.

Basket   (1) The rim and net through which the ball is shot. (2) A made free throw or field goal.

Basketball   (1) The round leather ball with which the game is played. (2) The name of the game in which teams and players attempt to shoot a ball into a basket for points.

Basket interference   See *Goaltending.*

Belly-up defense   An aggressive physical move deployed by a defender by invading the offensive player's space and almost touching belly to belly. The purpose is both to force the player with the ball into a different course of action other than shooting and to create frustration.

Block   The rejection of an offensive player's shot made by a defensive player, who blocks the shot with a hand.

Blocked shot   A shot deflected by an opponent before it reaches its downward flight toward the basket.

Blocking   A foul whereby a defensive player illegally blocks the path of an offensive player.

Blocking out   A positioning move whereby a player screens an opponent from the ball by getting between him or her and the basket after a shot is taken. The purpose is to obtain good rebounding position and to retrieve the missed shot.

Board   A rebound of a missed shot.

Bonus   A situation in one half of the game during which a team goes over the limit of allowable fouls. A bonus situation occurs, and free throws are awarded to the team that has been fouled. This happens each time a new foul is called during that particular half.

Bounce pass   A pass made by using one bounce of the ball. The bounce hits the ground usually two-thirds to three-fourths of the way to the target.

Box and one   A zone defense in which one player is free to guard an offensive player one-on-one or to strictly chase the ball, while the four other defenders play in a specific zone area.

Boxing out   See *Blocking out.*

Breakaway   A one-versus-zero fast-break situation that occurs due to a steal, a long pass, or a ball lost by the opposing team.

Brick   A bad shot that hits the backboard or the rim very hard.

Carrying the ball   A turnover caused by a player who is dribbling with the palm underneath the ball rather than the fingertips above the ball. See also *Palming.*

Center   Often, but not always, the tallest player on the team, who plays close to the basket. A player position.

Center court   See *Midcourt.*

Center jump   The method of putting the ball into play at the beginning of each period, half, or game. An official tosses the ball up at half court between two rival players.

Change of pace   A cutting move without the ball or a dribbling move with the ball made to deceive the defense by changing the pace of movement from half speed to full speed, or vice versa.

Charging   A foul whereby an offensive player with the ball runs into a defensive player who has legal position.

Chest pass   A pass made from the chest area of the body to a teammate. The ball starts close to the chest area and is pushed toward the target, snapping the wrist for power.

Clear out   An offensive strategy whereby a team empties one half of the offensive court to let a teammate go one-on-one against his or her opponent.

Coach   The head or director of a team. The coach plans game strategies, practices, and player development and organizes, delegates, and oversees all activities involving the team.

Crossover move   (1) A dribbling move in which the ball handler changes direction by crossing the ball left to right or right to left in front of them. (2) A driving move in which the offensive player crosses the body and the ball over in front of the defender to drive to the basket.

Cut (1) A move used to elude or deceive a defender by planting a foot to move from one direction to another or from one spot to another quickly. (2) Not making the team; being released from the squad.

Defender An individual player who defends against an offensive player.

Defense The team without the ball, which tries to prevent the opponent from scoring.

Delay See *Stall.*

Delay game A strategic offense in which a team holds the ball as long as possible before attempting a shot. The idea is to shorten the game time or run down the clock by using as much time as possible, thus keeping the game close. A strategy typically used by an underdog team or by a team that is ahead on the scoreboard.

Delay of game A rules violation in which a team or player delays the continuing of the game through (1) knocking the ball away after a made basket or (2) staying in a time-out or huddle for too long. An official typically is required to give one delay-of-game warning to the offending team before enforcing the violation. A technical foul is assessed to the team called for the violation.

Diamond and one A zone defense used by playing one defender on a top offensive player while the other four defenders play a zone shaped like a diamond: one player under the basket, two on the wings, and one at the top of the foul-line area.

Disqualification Removal of a player from the game for too many fouls or for misconduct.

Double double A statistical phenomenon in which a player gets a total of ten or more points, assists, rebounds, steals, or turnovers in any two of these categories.

Double dribble A turnover caused by dribbling the ball, touching it with both hands simultaneously, and dribbling again.

Double team To use two players to defend one offensive player in possession of the ball.

Dribble Continuous bouncing of the basketball with one hand at a time to advance or control the ball.

Drive An aggressive move to the basket with a dribble by an offensive player in an effort to score.

Drop step An offensive low-post move executed near the basket area, with the player's back to the basket. An offensive player will read which side a defender is playing on and drop his or her opposite leg around the defender, take a dribble, and score.

Dunk To slam the ball through the basket. A shot that is stuffed with force into the rim. Counts the same as a field goal.

End line See *Baseline.*

Fast break Style of offense in which a team tries to move the ball to its offensive end with a numerical player advantage before the other team can set up a defense.

Field goal A shot scored from the court during a live-ball situation. It counts as two or three points, depending on the distance from which it is taken.

Filling the lanes A tactic in which a player runs out on a fast break and takes a specific full-court-lane area to participate in a fast-break situation.

Five-second violation Breaking one of these rules: (1) The ball must be inbounded and touched by a player within five seconds, or (2) a player cannot hold the ball or dribble it for longer than five seconds when closely guarded by a defender.

Flagrant foul   A foul involving intentional or violent contact.

Flip pass   A one-handed shuffle pass or short, quick underhand pass to a teammate in close range.

Follow-through   A technique used to create backspin when shooting a basketball. A shooter begins with the shooting hand's palm facing up toward the ceiling. When shooting, the hand pushes forward, rolling the ball off the fingertips to create backspin. The hand finishes in a postion with the palm facing down toward the ground and the arm fully extended above the head.

Forward   A player position. Most teams have two forwards. A small forward often tends to be the most versatile player on the team, able to play well both in the post and perimeter areas of the court. A power forward plays more like a center and is usually a good rebounder.

Foul   Illegal contact by an opponent, which results in stoppage of play. Players are typically allowed five fouls before being disqualified from the game.

Foul lane   See *Lane.*

Foul line   The line 15 feet from the basket behind which a player stands to shoot a foul shot.

Foul play   (1) A play in which a foul occurs. (2) A dirty or intentional foul. (3) A player who stinks at playing. (4) A bird that plays basketball (not Larry).

Foul shot   See *Free throw.*

Four-point play   (1) A successful three-point shot by a shooter who is fouled and then also makes a foul shot. (2) A successful field goal, followed by two free throws for a technical foul or score after an inbound pass from an intentional foul after the field goal is scored.

Free throw   A free shot from the foul line, usually awarded because of a foul by the opposing team. Each successful free throw is worth one point.

Freezing the ball   Holding the ball without attempting to score, usually in order to preserve a lead.

Frontcourt   The half of the court where the ball is in play; the offensive team's half of the court.

Front the post   A defensive technique to discourage an entry pass to the offensive post area, which is done by standing in front of the offensive post player and in the passing lane. A dangerous tactic without help defense from a teammate on the back side of the post.

Game clock   A clock usually placed at both ends of the court or above center court for easy viewing, which counts down the remaining time left in the quarter, half, or game.

Give and go   See *Pass and go.*

Goaltending   Deflecting a shot that has begun its downward trajectory toward the basket or clearing a rebound that is directly above the basket or rim cylinder.

Guard   A player position usually in the perimeter areas of the court. A point guard runs the team and advances the ball up the floor. A shooting guard is typically the best perimeter shooter on the team.

Gym rat   A player who "lives" in the gym, totally dedicated to the game and spending any spare time practicing or playing basketball.

Help side   Also known as the weak side of the court, opposite the ball. It is called help side because defensive teammates on this side of the court should be in a help position in case a teammate guarding the ball gets beat.

Hook pass   See *Wrap-around pass.*

Hook shot   A shot attempt by an offensive player in which the ball is hooked toward the basket with the player's side facing the basket. This shot is used to shield the ball from a defensive player. Hook shots are usually attempted in close proximity to the basket.

Hoop (1) The basket or metal ring or rim. (2) A successful field goal. (3) A slang name for the game of basketball.

Inbounds pass A pass that occurs when the clock is stopped. The passer is out of bounds and must pass to a teammate in bounds to start the game and the clock. Five seconds are allowed for the offensive team to enter the inbounds pass. If this pass is unsuccessful, the opposing team is awarded the ball.

Intentional foul A foul that is not considered a legitimate attempt to steal the ball or guard the defender. When called, an intentional foul awards two free throws and the ball after the free throws to the team that was fouled.

Jab-and-Attack Position An offensive scoring position similar to a sprinter's starting position in track. This position enables an offensive player to make a quick, explosive first step when driving.

Jab step An offensive step toward the defensive player to make the person retreat and back away.

Jump ball A resolution to the situation in which two opposing players obtain equal possession of the ball. A referee aligns the opposing teams and tosses the ball up between the two players.

Jump shot A shot attempted while jumping in the air. A jump shot creates shooting rhythm, can create space away from a defender, and is often easy to shoot.

Jump stop A two-footed stop from a half- or full-speed run, in which both feet land on the floor simultaneously (making one sound) to stop a player's progress. A jump stop establishes a sound, strong body base for rebounding, receiving a pass, or playing defense. An excellent tool to prevent traveling calls.

Key, or keyhole The three-second-lane area. It was originally shaped like a keyhole, with the lane only 6 feet wide. It was changed to 12 feet in width in 1955.

Kicking A rules violation in which a defender tries to stop a pass or progression of the ball by kicking it.

Lane The rectangular area at both ends of the court in the middle of the baseline area. This is known also as the foul-lane, paint, or key area.

Layup An offensive shot attempt taken within 3 feet of the basket, usually while a player is moving toward the rim.

Lob pass A soft pass made with a high arc, usually toward the basket for dunks or to post players who are being fronted by a defender.

Man-to-man defense A defensive strategy in which each player is assigned a specific opponent to defend.

Match-up zone defense A zone defense with man-to-man defense principles. Each defender guards only against the opponent in one's own area of the zone. Match-up zones are very effective but also require great team help defense and communication.

Midcourt The half-court line or area.

Mismatch A term used to describe a contest in which one opponent is clearly superior to the other.

Motion offense An offensive strategy designed to move players among five positions or spots on the court. All five players move to all five spots before the cycle starts over. There are many types of motion offenses. The objective is to provide structured patterns of constant movement, making it more difficult to defend.

Offense Team that has possession of the ball.

Offensive foul (1) Same as charging. (2) Any foul committed by an offensive player.

Offensive goaltending   See *Goaltending.*

Offensive rebound   A rebound secured by the offensive team after shooting the ball, giving them another possession or shot opportunity.

Off-the-dribble pass   A pass made directly from the dribble without both hands touching the ball. A one-handed pass made while dribbling.

One-and-One   A bonus foul-shooting situation—if the player makes the first free throw, the player is awarded a second free throw. If the first foul shot is missed, the rebound is live.

One-on-one   (1) A situation in which a player tries to score against only one defensive player. (2) A competitive game or drill for pairs of players.

Outlet pass   A pass made off a defensive rebound, which starts a fast-break situation.

Overtime   The extra period played to determine a winner when the game ends in a tie. In basketball, no games can end in a tie, so the game will continue with extra overtime periods until a final winner has been decided.

Paint   See *Lane.*

Palming   An overly high dribble or a dribble in which the ball is palmed in the hand and the ball turns over. A dribbler is not allowed to dribble the ball with the palm of the hand facing up; if this occurs, a violation of "palming" is called by the official. Also known as *carrying* the ball.

Pass   Movement of the ball from one player to another by means of a toss, throw, or handing off.

Pass and go   A situation involving two offensive players. Player A passes to player B, and immediately cuts to the basket. Player B passes to the cutting player A for a shot or layup. Also known as a *give and go* or *pass and cut.*

Peripheral vision   The ability of a player to see both to the left and right sides while looking straight ahead.

Personal foul   Illegal physical contact with the opponent, in which a foul is called on the offending player. Typically, players are allowed five personal fouls per game.

Pick   A legal method of providing space for a teammate to get open for a shot or cut by using your body as a wall and screening the opponent.

Pick and roll   An offensive maneuver in which you set a pick for your teammate and then roll toward the basket, anticipating a pass. Also called a *screen and roll.*

Pivot   (1) Another name for the center position. (2) The area in and around the foul lane near the basket. (3) The act of turning on your foot to change direction.

Pivot foot   A stationary foot used when holding or possessing the ball. An offensive player with the ball is not allowed to lift the pivot foot without dribbling or passing. A player can pivot, or turn, in different directions while maintaining contact with the ground.

Play for one shot   To attempt to take the last shot of a quarter, half, or game before time runs out. Often used as a strategy to control the point spread or number of team possessions.

Point guard   The lead guard on a team who sets up and runs plays. The point guard is as much a role and position as it is a specific player.

Post   A name for the player(s) occupying the lane area down low near the basket.

Power forward   A strong forward who can usually play center as well. Typically an excellent rebounder and sometimes the enforcer or intimidator for the team.

PPG   Points per game. This figure is usually preceded by a number indicating a player's scoring average.

Press   A defense in which a team guards the opponents aggressively to try to get them to turn the ball over. There are full-court, half-court, man-to-man, and zone presses.

Rebound A missed shot retrieved by a player.

Reverse layup A layup that begins on one side of the basket or rim and is completed on the opposite side. The strategy is to use the net to protect or seal the ball from a defender.

Reverse pivot A dribbling move done to change direction. The player pivots while turning the back from the defender to protect the ball and change direction while dribbling.

RPG Rebounds per game. This figure is usually preceded by a number indicating a player's rebounding average.

Screen and roll See *Pick and roll.*

Shooting guard Typically the off guard or non–point guard. This role is usually given to the best-scoring guard.

Shot Any attempt to shoot the ball into the basket in order to score.

Shot clock The clock that allows the offensive team a specific number of seconds to get a shot off before losing possession of the ball.

Sideline The lines on the length of the court from baseline to baseline.

Sixth man Reference to a player who comes off the bench and makes important contributions to the team on the court. Often teams will have more than five good players; when this happens, the "sixth man" becomes even more important. The "sixth man" is more of a role position than a single player. The term expresses endearment and value.

Slam-dunk See *Dunk.*

Small forward Typically the best athlete on the team and often the most versatile player. Often able to play on both the perimeter or in the post. May also be a medium-size player.

Stall To hold the ball to run the clock down until it expires, done by an offensive player or team. Also known as *freezing the ball.*

Steal To take possession of the ball by intercepting an opponent's pass or dribble.

Strong side The side of the court where the ball is located.

Substitute A player who checks into the game for another; a substitute player, or "sub."

Switch A defensive technique in which players who have man-to-man assignments exchange responsibilities to combat an offensive maneuver of using screens by the opposing team.

Technical foul A foul by any player, coach, or team participant. It is usually not a physical foul, but rather a foul for acts of poor sportsmanship, conduct, behavior, profanity, vulgarity, hanging on the rim, or even for excessive rule violations.

Ten-second line The half-court line, which must be crossed by a team within ten seconds after obtaining control of the ball at its defensive end of the court.

Three-on-two A offensive fast-break situation in which three offensive players advance to the basket, opposed by two defenders.

Three-pointer A field goal from outside the three-point line. Also called the *three-point shot.*

Three-point line The arc on both sides of the half court, which extends from above the top of the key to the baseline on both sides. Also called the *three-point arc.*

Three-second lane A lane in which offensive players may not remain for more than three seconds or else it is a violation and the team loses possession. Also called the *foul lane.*

Three-second violation See *Three-second lane.*

Time line The half-court line. The name is used because a team must advance the ball over the half-court line within ten seconds of receiving the ball.

Time-out Both teams in basketball are allowed a specific number of time-outs (usually five).

Their duration ranges from twenty seconds to sixty seconds. Time-outs are used to make strategy adjustments, change momentum, give players a rest, set up a play, and even to "ice" a player (make a player think about a free throw to be taken).

Tip-in   A scored basket off an offensive rebound, tipped into the basket by a player.

Tip-off   The jump ball at the start of the game. A referee throws the ball up in the air to begin the competition. The team that obtains possession wins the tip-off.

Trailer   A player trailing the ball, usually on an offensive fast break. Trailers typically cut down the lane to rebound and receive a trailing pass or take an open jump shot.

Travel *or* **Traveling**   A turnover caused by advancing the ball without dribbling or passing, thereby running with the ball.

Trey   A slang term or expression meaning a successful three-point shot.

Triangle and two   A defensive strategy in which three defensive players play a zone area usually close to the basket, while two other defenders try to defend and keep the ball out of the hands of the opposing team's top two scorers.

Triple-threat position   An offensive stance from which three scoring options can be initiated: to shoot, to pass, or to drive to the basket.

Triple-Threat Scoring System   A scoring system by basketball clinician John Scott that involves seven scoring moves, two positions, and twenty-eight scoring options, all of which begin out of the triple-threat position.

Turnover   Any loss of the ball by the offense due to a violation or mishandling of the ball.

Two-on-one   A offensive fast-break situation in which two offensive players advance to the basket opposed by one defender.

Underdog   A team or player considered to have little or no chance of succeeding or winning against a superior opponent.

V cut   An offensive pattern of movement used to set up a defensive player by moving in one direction, then cutting sharply in the other direction to get open and receive a pass or shot opportunity.

Violation   An infraction that causes loss of possession; not considered a foul.

Visiting team   (1) The team that has to travel to the opponents' gymnasium. (2) The team typically wearing the darker-colored uniforms in a game.

V-Shot principle   A shooting principle used to simulate game situations during shooting practice.

Weak-side   The area of the court opposite to the side where the ball is located.

Wing   The perimeter area of the court ranging from the foul-line area to the three-point line. Typically the perimeter area starts around 15 feet from the basket.

Wrap-around pass   A pass executed by an offensive player pivoting around the defender and hooking or wrapping a pass around, away from the arms of a defender. The pass is usually completed with one hand on the ball. Also called a *hook pass.*

Zebras   Slang for the referees, who usually wear black-and-white-striped shirts.

Zone defense   A defensive strategy in which each player covers a specific area of the court instead of a specific opponent.

Zone, in the   A mental state in which nothing can faze a player. Everything the player does works, scores, or succeeds. This is called being "in the zone."

Index